THE KREMLIN & THE
HIGH COMMAND

THE KREMLIN & THE HIGH COMMAND

PRESIDENTIAL IMPACT
ON THE RUSSIAN MILITARY
FROM GORBACHEV TO PUTIN

Foreword by David M. Glantz

Dale R. Herspring

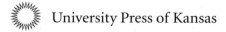 University Press of Kansas

Published by the University Press of Kansas (Lawrence, Kansas
66049), which was organized by the Kansas Board of Regents and is
operated and funded by Emporia State University, Fort Hays State
University, Kansas State University, Pittsburg State University,
the University of Kansas, and Wichita State University

Library of Congress Cataloging-in-Publication Data
Herspring, Dale R. (Dale Roy)
The Kremlin and the High Command : presidential impact on
the Russian military from Gorbachev to Putin / Dale R. Herspring;
foreword by David M. Glantz.
    p.   cm. — (Modern war studies)
Includes bibliographical references and index.
ISBN-13: 978–0-7006–1467–7 (cloth : alk. paper)
ISBN-10: 0–7006–1467–2 (cloth : alk. paper)
 1. Civil-military relations—Russia (Federation) 2. Civil-military
relations—Soviet Union. 3. Russia (Federation)—Politics and
government—1991- 4. Soviet Union—Politics and
government—1985–1991. I. Title.
JN6693.5.C58H47 2006
322'.50947—dc22   2006024232

British Library Cataloguing-in-Publication Data is available.

Printed in the United States of America
10 9 8 7 6 5 4 3 2 1

The paper used in this publication meets the
minimum requirements of the
American National Standard for Permanence of Paper
for Printed Library Materials Z39.48-1984.

TO JOSEPH AISTRUP

If a lion stands at the head of an army of lions, victory is assured.
If a lion stands at the head of an army of asses, the chances are fifty–fifty.
But if an ass stands at the head of an army of lions, you can call it quits.

General Alexander Lebed, "On Leadership"

CONTENTS

FOREWORD

Throughout the more than seventy years of its existence, but particularly after 1945 when it emerged from World War II as one of the world's two superpowers, the Soviet Union used three internal state institutions as vital pillars of power to insure the survival of the Union of Soviet Socialist Republics (USSR). These were the Communist Party of the Soviet Union (CPSU) and the Party's general secretary; the USSR's state security organs (variously termed *Cheka*, NKVD or KGB, and MVD) and their respective commissars for State Security and Internal Affairs; and the Soviet armed forces and the USSR's Commissar of Defense. The first of these pillars, the Communist Party, provided the USSR with its ideological inspiration, guidance, and foundation. Whether unitary in nature during Lenin and Stalin's time or collective in nature during other periods, the CPSU provided the country's political leadership. The second pillar, the state security organs, served, often ruthlessly, as the guarantor of the Soviet Union's internal security and the Communist Party's dominance of the state by identifying, engaging, and destroying all threats, real or potential, to continued Communist rule. The third pillar of power—and principal subject of this book—was the Soviet armed forces, which included the Red (Soviet) Army, the Navy, and later the Air Force. These forces provided both an indispensable defensive "shield" for the Socialist Homeland and the Soviet Union's vital "sword" leading the inevitable world revolution.

Externally, although neighboring states often perceived the Soviet armed forces, particularly the Red Army, as the Soviet Union's most awesome, formidable, and threatening institution, in reality, the Soviet armed forces and the Red Army were by far the weakest of these three pillars of power. Subjected to stringent Party control and, frequent, often bloody purges of their leadership, the Soviet armed forces did indeed rise to defend both Party and state successfully in periods of crisis, such as World War II and the ensuing Cold War. But thanks to these controls, the Soviet armed forces remained remarkably servile to their political masters in wartime as well as peacetime. However, despite their clear subordination to Party and state security organs, the Soviet armed forces were perceived as the "savior" of the state because of the key role they had played in the Soviet Union's victory over Hitler's Germany during the "Great Patriotic War." After the war ended, given the perceived perils of the

Cold War, the Soviet political hierarchy and the Soviet population as a whole considered the Soviet armed forces to be the essential guarantor of the Soviet Union's continued existence, if not the success of the socialist world revolution overall. As a result, during periods of collective political leadership, particularly in the wake of Stalin's death in 1953 and in the mid-1960s when Khrushchev was ousted from power, the leadership of the Soviet armed forces managed to play a significant role in shaping the state's political leadership.

The largely bloodless Russian Revolution of 1991, which resulted in the dissolution of the USSR and the creation of a new Russian Federation, also fundamentally altered the institutional basis of the new Russian state by removing the Communist Party from power and by destroying its ubiquitous control over the government and the state's two other traditional pillars of power. However, while the revolution replaced the Party and the state's Party-dominated political structure (of president, premier, and Supreme Soviet) with a new political structure (of president, prime minister, and State Duma), it left the state security service (reformed as the Federal Security Service or FBS) relatively intact, and it truncated the massive Soviet armed forces into far smaller Russian Armed Forces. In short, the Revolution of 1991 removed one pillar of power, the Communist Party, from the political equation in the new Russia. By doing so, it also eliminated the "glue" or binding force that ensured the Soviet Union remained a viable political structure, namely, the strict control by the Communist Party and, by extension, the state's Communist political leaders, over both the state's security services and its armed forces.

The removal of the Communist Party, the most dominant pillar within the Soviet Union, from power, and its replacement by a new non-party presidential structure within an ostensibly democratic Russian Federation raises several important questions. First, without the Party as a unifying third pillar of power, can this new structure provide a coherent and effective basis for the formation of a viable democratic Russian state? Second, can the president and other political organs in this new structure master the two other former pillars of power, neither of which, traditionally and in practice, is compatible with a democratic state?

Herspring's new study compares the relative power of the president and Party in the Soviet Union just prior to the Revolution of 1991 with that of presidents during the first fourteen years of the new Russian Federation's existence. More important still, it thoroughly analyzes the vital second question, the relationship between the president and the armed forces since 1991, and by extension also ponders the more important first question regarding the likely viability of a future democratic Russian Federation.

Studying these questions both chronologically and topically, Herspring examines the presidencies of Mikhail Gorbachev during the last six years of the Soviet Union and of Boris Yeltsin and Vladimir Putin during the ensuing development of the Russian Federation into the twenty-first century. In addition to these issues, he also considers how, when deprived of the arbitrary methods employed by their Soviet predecessors, present and future Russian presidents can foster the reforms necessary for the military's future effectiveness, internally as a responsible democratic institution and externally as an effective defender of the state's legitimate strategic interests, both regionally and internationally.

Herspring clearly and cogently catalogues the many problems the Russian state and its armed forces face, all the while suggesting solutions within the context of what has occurred in the past. Finally, Herspring suggests what must be done in terms of the relationship between presidential power and authority and the Russian armed forces if the Russian Federation is to evolve into a modern and democratic state—as well as the pitfalls and likely consequences if these things are not accomplished.

David M. Glantz
Carlisle, PA

PREFACE

This book is the result of many years of study and observation of the Soviet and then the Russian armed forces as a diplomat, naval officer, and scholar. I studied the Soviet military as a scholar and wrote a number of books and articles on the topic. I also interacted with it both as a diplomat from the U.S. Department of State and as an officer in the U.S. Navy. During the process I gained considerable respect for those who served in its ranks. The life of a Soviet soldier was hard, in many ways far more difficult, and certainly far more brutal than what I witnessed on the American side.

While it may sound like an oversimplification, understanding the Soviet military was simpler than understanding its successor—despite the explosion in material that is now available on the Russian armed forces. Once I understood the basic structure and procedures in the Soviet military, it was relatively simple to draw the lines linking one part to another.

That situation changed dramatically with the deterioration and subsequent collapse of the Soviet Union. By 2001 the USSR was part of the past. Now the West—and the Russians—faced a whole new world. Russia was smaller and searching for a new political system. For the military that meant a period of confusion as they looked to the political leadership for guidance, but often found the country's political leaders as confused about what should be done on a policy level as they were.

Meanwhile, I was working on a book on civil-military relations in the United States, *The Pentagon and the Presidency: Civil-Military Relations from FDR to George W. Bush*. While I recognized that there were tremendous differences between Russia and the United States, it was clear that the role of presidential leadership stood out in the United States. To a large degree, the president's leadership style played a major role in determining the level and nature of conflict between the White House and the uniformed military.

I wondered, could this be the case in the USSR and Russia? The country was first collapsing and then transitioning to a new and different type of political system and new forms of civil-military relations. Perhaps presidential leadership would provide a key to understanding civil-military relations there as well. After all, the country's institutions were malleable and the president's type of leadership would play a major role in determining the nature and shape of the Russian armed forces. So, I decided to look at presidential leadership, asking the question: to what degree did the nature of presidential leadership affect the Russian high command? The result is this book.

A number of individuals played major roles in bringing this book to fruition. David Glantz and David Stone read the manuscript from cover to cover and provided invaluable criticisms and suggestions throughout. I am deeply grateful to both individuals, who are highly respected in the field of Soviet and Russian military history, for taking the time to read and comment on this manuscript. I can honestly say that I avoided a number of historical and conceptual mistakes thanks to their critical comments. I alone am responsible for any inaccuracies.

I would also like to thank my wife of forty years for putting up with my constant comments to the effect, "I'm sorry, but I have to work in my study this weekend." I know there were many occasions when she was ready to strangle me, but instead she smiled and said "OK." President Jon Wefald of Kansas State University and his executive assistant, Dr. Charles Reagan, provided much-needed support and encouragement. Mike Briggs of the University Press of Kansas once again helped guide me through the many pitfalls involved in writing a book of this type.

Finally, this book is dedicated to my friend and colleague Joseph Aistrup. Joe knows little about militaries in any country, and that includes the USSR and Russia. However, he not only encouraged me to write this book, but whatever value it has is due in large part to his willingness to read and critique the introduction and conclusion. His conceptual insights were invaluable. His support and willingness to go out of his way to be there when it counted is valued far more than he will ever know.

Dale R. Herspring

CHAPTER ONE
INTRODUCTION

> It is entirely up to the president: whether true military reforms take place, or whether the military bureaucracy continues pretending that reforms are under way.
> *Alexei Arbatov*

If there is one thing that has become clear since Mikhail Gorbachev came to power in 1985, it is that presidential leadership plays a key role in determining the nature of civil-military relations in the Soviet and Russian armed forces. From 1985 to 1991, when the USSR collapsed, and in subsequent years as the transition from communism to a new and different kind of political system began, Russia has been characterized by instability that has sometimes bordered on chaos. The three presidents that have served since 1985 did not have the benefit of clearly defined rules, regulations, and procedures. The old order was being destroyed, but there was nothing to replace it. Experimentation and confusion became the order of the day.

Two words describe the ideal world for Russian military officers: stability and predictability. Without those conditions, the military, probably the most structured and tightly organized group in any society, faces the possibility of organizational chaos. Thus the need emerges for a strong president, an individual who is prepared to enforce order in the system.

In this sense, the nature of presidential leadership differs from what is expected in the United States, where, as Richard Neustadt has argued, it is often defined as the "art of persuasion."[1] The basic structures and processes by which a president exerts leadership are established or regularized. There are differences between presidents and how they deal with the armed forces, but the basic outlines of the system do not change. Processes change only gradually.[2] Before the collapse of the USSR, the Soviet president could rely upon organizations such as the Communist Party or the KGB to keep order and ensure that the high command did as it was told. The country's collapse—from one country with fifteen republics to fifteen countries with fifteen different and independent armed forces—meant that new procedures and routines had to be established. Thus the president was forced to go beyond persuasion, although that skill remained important. It was up him—working with others—to create new rules for the functioning of the country's political system: executive, legislative, and judicial. That is equally true of the military. Everything from its relationship to civilian authorities to the budget (which is more transparent now than under the Soviets) and the country's military doctrine had to be decided anew. And dealing with the military was only one of the many questions that consumed the president's time.

Understanding presidential leadership in such a collapsing and transitional regime is critical for understanding how the military responds to sudden change. The Russian (and Soviet) political system has long had a centralized governmental structure. Whether it was the czar, the general secretary, or the president, it was the chief executive who played the critical role in what political scientists call a "subject culture." People waited to be told what to do, especially in the armed forces. The generals and admirals took their orders and guidance from the political leader.

During the past eighty-nine years, the Russian military—and the Soviet military before it—did not present a problem for civilian authorities. There is not a single case of the military acting against the Kremlin's orders, much less of carrying out a coup. Both militaries have a history of accepting civilian authority, even when it creates problems for them. There have been instances when individual officers made their opposition to policies known—for example, Marshal Nikolai Ogarkov reportedly told Defense Minister Dmitri Ustinov privately that he opposed the 1979 invasion of Afghanistan, and Marshal Georgii Zhukov stood up to Stalin on a number of occasions—but the military has always been a compliant tool in the hands of the Kremlin's rulers.

A key question for the Soviet and Russian military leadership has been how to relate to three very different types of presidents with their very different leadership styles at a time when the polity was undergoing systemic changes. What if the leader ignored the military? How should the armed forces relate to him if he failed to provide guidance or leadership? What if he lied to the military? What if he provided confusing and even contradictory statements on an issue as critical as military reform? What if the military was assigned tasks it was not able to carry out? Should the generals resist such orders? What if a president provided leadership, but only incrementally, which meant that the problem persisted, even if it was gradually dealt with?

It is the thesis of this book that the key to military reform in a collapsing or transitional country like the USSR or Russia is presidential leadership. Political structures are weakened and changing. It is up to the country's president to step into this vacuum and provide the leadership necessary to ensure that the high command transitions to the new polity successfully. If he does not, the situation in the military will deteriorate, combat readiness will drop, and there is the danger that the generals and admirals could become politicized. On some occasions this means he must interject himself into internal military matters, while in others it means he should remain in the background, nudging the process in this or that direction. Finally, I will argue that too little attention has been paid to presidential leadership from the perspective of the generals and admirals. I am not trying to explain presidential leadership, why a president does this or that. Instead, I am focusing on how the high command reacts to the president's leadership style.[3]

In this book I will provide an overview of the impact that the actions (or non-actions) of Soviet and Russian presidents have had on the Soviet and Russian militaries since 1985 by focusing on the military's reaction to the president's actions (or non-actions). In particular, how has the president's attention or inattention affected the military's ability to maintain stability and predictability in terms of structure, doctrine, strategy, tactics, weapons procurement, and personnel policies in the armed forces?

It is important to keep in mind that as all three political leaders were dealing with the military, they were plunging into *terra incognito*. While a number of political systems moved from non-communism to communism, no political system as large and complex as Russia has traveled in the opposite direction. As a result, the most that could be said about the tasks that faced Gorbachev, Boris Yeltsin, and Vladimir Putin was that there was no road map, and this went far beyond reforming their militaries to meet the new and changing world they faced. This uniqueness helps explain not only the confusion of their policies toward the military, but it also sheds light on some of the reasons for the chaos that the USSR and Russia have been through during the past twenty-six years. It is also important to stress that the military was only one factor among the many, if not thousands of, problems that each of the leaders had to face. Indeed, in no case was rebuilding or restructuring the military their most important concern.

Conceptually, a key problem was that the high command's education, training, and military culture conditioned them to look to the past, not to the future. I do not mean to suggest that some officers did not try to find a new way to fight wars; certainly Marshal Nikolai Ogarkov was one of those. But he left his position as chief of the General Staff in 1984, shortly before Gorbachev came to office. And while he was a strong advocate of modern technology,— "weapons based on new principles," as he called them, he was probably too wedded to the mass army of the Cold War to have been able to make the kind of conceptual and intellectual changes needed to meet the challenges of the post–Cold War period. That is probably one of the main reasons he was removed from his post as chief of the General Staff and sent to command the Western Theater of Military Operations.[4]

Prior to 1985 civilian political control of the modern Soviet military more closely approximated what Samuel Huntington called "objective" control measures.[5] There was no question that the military was politicized; the Communist Party's Main Political Administration was present at most levels of the armed forces. The problem, however, was that Huntington and many others missed a critical point in their analysis of Soviet civil-military relations: *Change occurred*. Huntington was right in arguing that "control" structures were originally "subjective" control measures, because there was a disconnection between the values and loyalties of the czarist officer corps and the new Bolshevik leadership. The Bolsheviks were forced to rely on the czarist officers during the Russian Civil War (1919–1922). However, they did not trust them. As a consequence, the Bolsheviks created a number of subjective control devices, such as the much-vaunted "political commissar," to make sure that the line officers were loyal. However, over time the political commissars became superfluous.

Loyalty and a congruence of values between the Soviet officer corps and the Bolshevik leadership meant that subjective control devices became less and less important. In time commissars became an obstacle in the way of military efficiency. Splitting authority between line and political officers created confusion: Who was in charge? What if the two differed? Which one should the soldier obey? Why have political commissars split authority when line officers had proven their mettle in battle against the Whites? The Civil War showed they were reliable. As a consequence, the function of these control devices changed between 1925 and 1930.[6] The political commissar, for example, became the deputy for political work, an officer who worked *for* the commanding officer (the so-called *edinonachalie* or unity of command) although he was also part of the Communist Party apparatus in the military. His primary task became less one of control (there were other officers, the so-called Section 00, to worry about security and disloyalty), and more one of responsibility for motivation, performance, and training. In short, the subjective control measures became objective measures as the political officer's role changed and he primarily focused not on control, but on unit performance, whether in combat or in training exercises.

By the time Gorbachev came to power, it was a well-established fact that the Soviet military was autonomous when it came to civilian involvement in areas such as tactics, strategy, or almost any other part of military matters. For example, in 1989 I spoke with the late Colonel General Dmitri Volkogonov. During our conversation, Volkogonov commented that the decision by Gorbachev (at that time) to permit civilians to comment on military matters would never have happened in the past. "There were two reasons," he noted. "On the one hand, they would not have had access to the relevant material on military matters, and second, no one would have published anything they wrote without permission from the General Staff—and it would have been very unlikely that it would have been given."[7] The Soviet military ran its own affairs. The message to civilians, except those at the very top, was "leave military matters to military experts."

THE MILITARY AND SYSTEM COLLAPSE

Few things are more difficult for a military, especially a conservative, tightly knit one like the Soviet armed forces, than to sit by and watch while the system its officers swore to defend deteriorates and eventually collapses. After all, unlike other segments of the polity, the military is distinguished by the fact that it works solely for the state (or in this case the party-state). To a certain degree, the loss of state structure means that the military loses its *raison d'etre*. Furthermore, the web of structures and procedures within which it is accustomed to operating ceases to exist.

Faced with such a situation, the military can follow a number of courses of action. It can seize power; something that has never happened in a post-communist state to date. Second, it can stand aside and do nothing while the system falls apart or, as in the case of the East German military, facilitate the country's transition to a democratic state, even though it meant the end of a career for thousands of officers and non-commissioned officers.[8] Third, it can "muddle" through, having an important impact by refusing to become involved in the political machinations of the time. Finally, it can support one political faction against another.

The key problem for the military's high command during system collapse is that it is trying to hold the military together at a time when institutions are collapsing and traditional relationships are falling apart. The generals cannot count on precedent to guide their actions because precedent is collapsing along with the rest of the polity. In this situation, the generals and admirals look to the country's leader—in this case, the president—for guidance. They look for him to take charge of the increasingly chaotic situation, give clear orders, show that he understands what needs to be done, and do it. They are put off by leaders who equivocate, who do not seem to understand what to do, or who give contradictory orders. From their perspective, weak leaders are not leaders. Soldiers live in a world where orders are given and carried out, where the leader is supposed to take charge, be responsible for his actions, and give clear orders to his subordinates. In their minds a person of this type is especially important in a time when institutions, procedures, and precedent are collapsing and the country is entering a world of the unknown.

THE MILITARY AND TRANSITION

Once the system has collapsed, the issue becomes "what next?" What kind of a political system will succeed the old one, and, most important from the military's standpoint, what kind of a role will it play in the new polity? How will its new role differ from how it functioned under the old system? This is especially important if the country is making major changes in its political structure and processes. Assuming the military remains more or less cohesive after the collapse of the old system, the generals want to know how they will fit into the new system. What is expected of them and their organization? Are major changes in store for the way the military is organized and how it operates? What impact will the creation of a new polity have on such fundamentals as strategy, tactics, funding, personnel, equipment, weapons, deployments, etc.? This is particularly true in a country like the USSR or Russia where the military has not tried to seize power. What it wants is direction, stability, and predictability during a transitional period.

Adapting to a new political system is a two-way street. While the president's role is critical, the high command must also adapt to the new situation. For the Russian military this meant that it must learn how to play the game of politics. Under communism the military was excluded from the political process. The generals and admirals sat in the Supreme Soviet, but that was an honorific reward and the legislature had very little power. Now, however, the high command is no longer isolated from politics. The generals and admirals are thrown into the political process, which is a whole new experience for them.

For example, in the past the generals believed what they were told by the politicians. Now, however, they might be told one thing on a particular day, only to be told the opposite four days later. Furthermore, just because they were promised or allocated a certain amount of money, that did not mean that they would actually receive it. They might get only 40 percent of what they were promised. They have to convince the politicians, whether it be the president or members of parliament, that their need for resources is greater and more pressing than is the case with another claimant.

In the new conditions, the armed forces must lobby for funds and fight off attempts by civilians to become involved in their internal affairs, including not only strategy and tactics, but in seemingly sacrosanct areas such as discipline and service regulations as well. This is a very difficult adjustment for military officers who long enjoyed a monopoly over military affairs. The idea of civilians interfering in "their affairs" or having to explain military behavior to "outsiders" opened up a whole new role for them. Some would learn to play this game better than others.

Most important, the generals and admirals will have to work out new institutional and procedural arrangements for dealing with almost all aspects of military affairs. This includes not only their relationship with the president, but with the legislature and judiciary as well as the many pressure groups that will inevitably arise. For example, how will they deal with the military-industrial complex, civilian energy organizations, local authorities, draft boards, etc.? All these arrangements will have to be created anew, because the old relationships will no longer hold.

During a transitional period, one of the generals' first concerns will be the maintenance of their organization. After all, if the generals and admirals are overseeing a organization of up to 5 million soldiers and sailors, they need to know the size of their budget as well as what kind of threats they are to prepare the country for. In many countries, and especially the Soviet Union under Leonid Brezhnev, the high command always knew what was expected of them and what they would receive to carry out these missions. It is no surprise that they would continue to look for these characteristics from the country's new political leadership.

Meanwhile for the politician, and especially the president, the transitional stage opens a whole new era in civil-military relations. The president is now in a position to make major changes or modifications in how the military operates as well as how it relates to the civilian world. Institutions are weak and procedures are not yet established, routinized, and bureaucratized. Consequently, the president has a tremendous opportunity to reshape the military as he sees fit. He can cut its size, change its missions and force structure (e.g., less emphasis on a mass army in favor of a smaller, high-tech military), increase or decrease its budget, change its leadership, or redesign its educational system. He can end or modify the draft, even force the military to become professional and get rid of conscription. What is most significant is that in a transitional state the military is more open to change than it would be under normal circumstances.

To be effective, however, the president must pay attention to the military. He must establish his credibility among the generals and admirals. When he says something, it is important that the generals and admirals know that he means what he says. If he lies to the military or makes promises he does not intend to keep, he runs the risk of alienating the high command. It is also important that he gives the military clear and concise instructions on what he wants done and how he wants it to occur. Failure to provide the military with what it needs to carry out its job or to provide it with clear guidance will lead to stagnation and even deterioration within the organization. The Russian military has traditionally been very conservative. As a consequence, it is unlikely to change on its own. It will tend to keep the same size, force structure, personnel policies, strategy, and tactics it had prior to the transitional stage, unless the president forces it to modify its behavior. In practice this means that unless the president provides clear guidance (and resources), internal problems such as a lack of training, discipline, crime, corruption, and, most important, a decline in combat readiness, are inevitable.

Lest the reader get the wrong impression, I am not suggesting that the Soviet/Russian president needed to merely lift a finger and changes *would* take place inside the military. The point is that the Soviet/Russian military had been *isolated* from politics for the past fifty-odd years. Russian generals and admirals had their own "military culture." They were not accustomed to having "outsiders," including the president, interfere in their internal affairs. This meant that the president had to be both tough and willing to persevere. The problem was that if the president did not provide leadership to a high command that was seeking direction, the result would be even more chaos and confusion in the armed forces. As noted above, the USSR and Russia's generals have not sought political power. Rather, they preferred to work inside the political system under the direction of political officials while enjoying internal autonomy.

AN APOLITICAL MILITARY?

How do the changes affect the Soviet and Russian military officers who became involved in politics during both stages? To many, the presence of generals in politics and the comments of outspoken officers like Major Vladimir Lopatin and General Alexandr Lebed suggest that the military tried to take over policy direction in the government. While Lebed's action showed that he had political ambitions, the military was too divided to act as a cohesive political force. The political actions of a few officers were not the same as an effort by the military to take over and run the country. One of the major surprises to many Western analysts over the past two decades has been the overwhelming desire of the Russian high command to stay out of politics.

Consequently, this study proceeds from two assumptions: that the generals and admirals cringe at the thought of becoming directly involved in politics and that they will do so only in an extreme situation after considerable soul-searching and pressure from political leaders. After all, for years the political leadership had pounded into their heads that their primary task was to defend the country from external—not internal—enemies.[9] The coup attempt of 1991 and Yeltsin's use of the military against parliament in 1993 were cases in point. The military reluctantly involved itself in a political action but returned to the barracks as soon as the conflict was over.

In short, the Soviet and Russian General Staff simply wanted to be left alone; it did not want to get involved in the use of force against civilians as occurred in Tbilisi, Baku, Vilnius, and the First Chechen War. It also wanted to handle military matters without civilian interference. The military's primary concern has been with issues like military strategy, tactics, force structure, training, and other "internal" military matters.

While the jury is still out on many aspects of the evolution of presidential leadership in the USSR and Russia and its impact on the armed forces, enough has been written in Russia to enable us to outline the type of political leadership the three presidents provided and its impact on the armed forces.

RUSSIAN MILITARY CULTURE

When dealing with the Soviet/Russian military, it is important to understand the cultural environment in which it operates. I have constructed an ideal type that illustrates the main factors that have characterized the Army from 1985 to the present. Not every officer will be characterized by all of these factors in every instance. Some elements will be more evident in one officer than in another. However, the one thing that is predictable is that they will create problems for the interaction between political leaders during system collapse or system transformation. Like it or not, political leaders like Gorbachev, Yeltsin, and Putin had to deal with officers from this cultural milieu.

This different mind-set and the collapsing or transitional nature of the policy make it necessary for the president to be assertive. I am not referring to the reimposition of a neo-Stalinist-type purge of the 1930s. Rather, I have in mind the kind of insistence on change that is indispensable when it comes to getting any bureaucracy to modify how it thinks and acts. Creating a smaller, more flexible, and mobile military means cutting back its size, and it also means changing its strategic, tactical, and operational thought processes. As noted above, the generals need to think in a new and different fashion because they are planning to fight a different kind of war, and since fighting wars remains as much an art as it is a science, the way a general approaches fighting a war is critical.

At this point it would be useful to take a careful look at the kind of military culture that existed in the Soviet armed forces when Gorbachev came to power. Many of these cultural factors remain operational to this day, and they are the factors that the Soviet/Russian political leadership must deal with if it hopes to create a new military.

The Soviet military in 1985 was characterized by a military culture with many unique aspects, at least when compared with Western, and especially the American, armed forces. In short, some parts were shared and some were unique to Russia. First, let us look at the shared components of Russian military culture.

CHARACTERISTICS SHARED WITH OTHER MILITARIES

Chain of Command

All militaries are based on a chain of command, and the Russian military is no exception. [10] It is a hierarchical organization that works on the basis of orders given and received. For military officers, it is therefore important that orders pass through a clear chain of command, ideally from the president to the minister of defense to the chief of the General Staff. Carrying out instructions is very difficult when the recipient is unsure who sent them. Orders that bypass the chain of command are likely to create confusion. This is especially true of a transitional polity, where standardized procedures may be lacking. Rather than being able to fall back on routine, senior officers may have to make critical decisions concerning whose order to follow.

All military officers expect clear and unambiguous orders. However, clarity is critical when a system is collapsing or transitioning, especially if there is instability in the country. In a stable political system, where procedures have been routinized and there is a tradition of clarifying orders when necessary, there is always the possibility of that happening. However, in a polity in flux, where there is confusion over who is in power or what is expected of the military, a confused or unclear order can be dangerous.

Strategic Decision Making and Respect for Military Expertise

Senior military officers usually accept the idea of the civilian authority playing the key role in strategic planning and decision making. However, they expect to be consulted. Traditionally, the Russian high command has been more apolitical than the U.S. military in this area. Generals and admirals are not deeply concerned about being involved in the policy process, although senior officers are prepared to offer their opinions if requested. What Russian officers desired—indeed, demanded—was clear guidance concerning state policy. Like other military officers, the Russian high command wants to know what is expected of it. A lack of clarity leads to confusion and could result in organizational chaos.

Virtually all military officers share a common belief that they are experts and they expect civilian leaders to value their expertise. Service in the Soviet military was highly respected. Competition to get into an officers school was keen, and the views of Soviet military officers on issues involving the use of military force were highly regarded as far back as the Khrushchev era. If political authorities planned to use force, the high command expected to have their views on how and when such an operation should be carried out given careful consideration.

Operational and Tactical Autonomy

No military professional likes the idea of civilians interfering in operational or tactical matters. This is true of the U.S. military as well. However, in Russia the military has enjoyed an almost total monopoly over the application of the more complex forms of military force. It was an area where by the mid-1960s civilians were forbidden to become involved. Only military experts understood how to use military force.

Personal Responsibility

One of the key canons of leadership in all military organizations is the willingness to accept responsibility for what happens. For example, the captain of a ship is responsible for what happens to his ship—regardless of the circumstances. If the captain is asleep and his ship runs aground because of the action of a junior officer on the bridge, he is responsible; he should have done a better job training the subordinate. The same is true of officers in other services—do well and there will probably be a medal. If the unit does poorly, however, "command responsibility" comes into play, and the officer in charge will pay the price.

Consequently, it is not surprising that military officers expect those in charge—especially the president—to accept responsibility for actions he orders the military to perform. After all, they are only carrying out his orders. Failure to do so results in a lack of respect for that individual.

Personnel Appointments

All military officers recognize that civilian authorities have the final word when it comes to personnel appointments. While the Soviet military always accepted civilian supremacy in the appointment of senior military officers, they expected to be consulted.

Internal Military Policies

No military officer in any country likes the prospect of having outsiders tell him or her how to run the armed forces. The military is a closed organization. This was true of the Soviet military as well, even with the Communist Party's presence. The Kremlin left internal military matters such as discipline, promotion, and allocation of resources to the generals. Rightly or wrongly, the high command believes it knows best how to run the military.

In addition to these commonalities, there are several military cultural factors unique to Russia.

UNIQUE SOVIET/RUSSIAN CHARACTERISTICS

Conservative High Command

All militaries are conservative, but the pre-Gorbachev Soviet armed forces were more conservative than most others.[11] In contrast to the U.S. military, the Russian and Soviet military looked to the past as a way of understanding the present and the future. Officers might be asked to explain the relevance of the Soviet theoretician Alexander Svechen's work from the 1920s on defensive strategy for the present. Or what does World War II tell the military about how to fight the Afghan War? Similarly, what did World War II say about how the Russian Army should fight a war with NATO, should that ever happen? These topics are carefully studied by students at the General Staff Academy as well as at other senior military educational establishments.

Foresight and Stability

Similarly, in fighting wars, the Soviet and Russian militaries have traditionally placed strong emphasis on working within established conceptual frameworks—what they call their military doctrine. This approach relies heavily on stability and predictability, which tends to reinforce their conservative nature. Where most U.S. military thought tends to be tactical, occasionally operational, but always highly flexible, Soviet and Russian thought has emphasized strategic models or war plans. They want a president who provides them with a stable and predictable world in terms of budget, support, resources, and threats. This is also why doctrine is so important. It serves as the basis for strategy, operations, tactics, and even training as well as the kinds of weapons that are to be purchased and employed. Without a doctrine, most Soviet military officers would be at a loss.

Mass Army

Heavily influenced by the World War II experience, the pre-Gorbachev military placed tremendous emphasis on the importance of mass armies. The regular Soviet Army of around 5 million was backed up by millions of reservists who would support regular forces in a crisis. This was part and parcel of the idea of placing heavy reliance on tanks, artillery, and masses of soldiers.

Human life was not as valuable as in the West. Furthermore, Soviet technology was never as advanced as that possessed by the Kremlin's opponents and one way of dealing with technological inferiority was to use overwhelming force and masses of troops.

Initiative Discouraged

Soviet opposition to initiative on the part of soldiers or even junior officers was legendary. In accordance with the idea that military operations should be carefully planned, senior Soviet officers expected junior officers to carry out the plan exactly as stipulated. There was little room for deviation.[12] Consequently, flexibility was discouraged, and the Soviet military casualty rate was often very high.

Opposition to initiative was one of the major reasons why the Soviets traditionally refused to rely on a corps of non-commissioned officers (NCOs). The idea of an NCO—or even a junior officer—showing initiative has been anathema to the high command. Brutality was also a common fact of life in the Soviet military. Why create NCOs when it is easier to allow other conscripts to use violence to enforce discipline? Beatings of enlisted personnel by officers or enlisted soldiers and sailors were commonplace.[13]

Nowhere was the combination of brutality and the lack of NCOs more evident than in the *dedovshchina* process—the bullying of junior conscripts by more senior ones. To officers, it was a way of maintaining discipline and control. When Gorbachev came to power NCOs were new conscripts who had attended a short course and then sent back to their units. They were ignored by more senior recruits when it came to the beatings and other crimes they inflicted on more junior recruits—on some occasions on the NCOs themselves. As a result they had little or no influence in the barracks. Meanwhile, junior officers were overworked and went home to their own quarters at night. As a result, conscripts who refused to do what senior conscripts told them to do were beaten. While fully aware of the existence of this process, senior Soviet officers relied upon the secrecy that surrounded the military to hide it from the public. The idea of permitting senior enlisted personnel to act on their own, whether overseeing soldiers in a barracks or leading them in battle, went against the Soviet idea of how to run the military. The same was true of junior officers. During World War II, the Soviet military had NCOs (*starshina*), but they either left or retired from the Soviet military in the late 1940s and early 1950s. This led the high command to take conscripts (in some cases, individuals who had military training in high school) and make them non-commissioned officers, but, as noted above, they hardly had the same authority of a Western NCO.[14]

One answer would have been to rely more heavily on junior officers. While good in theory, in practice it did not work for a number of reasons. First, increasingly the military was forced to rely on young men who had just graduated from civilian universities, which meant that they had very little military experience. Second, they were not active in the barracks as was the case with NCOs in the West. Third, economic conditions deteriorated to such a degree that junior officers often held second jobs, leaving them little time to worry about life inside the barracks.

Extreme Secrecy

The Soviet military lived in a world of extreme secrecy. Indeed, secrecy went all the way to the refusal of Soviet military officers to wear name tags. While they would provide their names if asked, the idea of permitting outsiders to know "who was who" was foreign. Military matters were secret. Take the example of General Mikhail Milshteyn, who was a member of the Institute for the Study of the USA and Canada during the late 1980s and one of the Kremlin's top spokesmen on military issues. During the period of glasnost Milshteyn told me that he regularly cleared everything he wrote with the General Staff, even though he no longer had to.[15] When I asked why, he responded, "Because that is the way it has always been done." Milshteyn's comment serves to underline the fact that the vast majority of articles on military issues prior to Gorbachev's rise to power were published in military journals or in military newspapers. Other Soviet military officers made similar comments to me. Drafts of articles were routinely sent to the Ministry of Defense or General Staff for prior clearance.

While there were some exceptions, by the mid-1960s the military had *carte blanche* when it came to the budget. The idea of a transparent budget as it exists in the West was nonsense, and there was no such thing as fiscal accountability. Senior Russian officers generally never had to defend what they spent as long as the weapons system could be justified for military reasons. Indeed, what was especially unique about this system was that senior Soviet military officers themselves did not know the size of the budget. For example, when Admiral William Crowe asked Marshal Sergey Akhromeyev how big the Russian military budget was, he reportedly responded, "I don't know. That is not something that we have worried about in the past."[16] The generals considered such matters to be in the military's purview, not a concern for civilians. Telling them that they would have their budget cut by 5 or 10 percent meant nothing. Five or 10 percent of what? It was not until 1989 when Gorbachev announced that a stunning 15 percent of Soviet GNP was being spent on defense—a statement that shocked both Western analysts and Soviet civilians[17]—that the high command and the rest of Soviet society began to realize just how big a bite the military was taking out of the country's economy.

When it came to political matters, senior military officers were not familiar with how policy was made, even in the Soviet system, because they were so isolated from the political process. Indeed, the idea that a Soviet military officer would become actively involved in politics or in the battle for resources was not something that they understood. It was only under Gorbachev that military officers began to play a political role. This stood in contrast to the U.S. high command, which learned at the end of World War II the critical importance of lobbying and how to carry it out successfully.[18] The Russian military's task was not to formulate policy, but to implement it.

THE FOCUS OF THE STUDY

This book focuses on how presidential leadership has affected the Soviet/Russian military. In other words, what kind of leadership does the president exhibit and how is it perceived by the military? It is also important to keep in mind the role that the leader's personality played in the Soviet and Russian militaries. Gorbachev was a surprise to almost everyone—both in the USSR and the outside world. Everyone knew that there was a struggle going on between Yeltsin and Gorbachev, but many wrote Yeltsin off when the August 1991 coup attempt failed. As far as Putin is concerned, I have yet to encounter anyone who predicted his rise to power five or six months before he became president. The idea of a former KGB lieutenant colonel becoming president seemed absurd!

The phrase "the military," as used here, refers primarily to the key decision makers, the high command, those senior officers of general or flag rank who are the key players both inside the military and for interacting with the president and his key civilian advisers. In particular, I have in mind the defense minister (when he is a serving officer), the chief of the General Staff, the heads of the key branches (e.g., Strategic Rocket Forces, Ground Forces, Navy, Air Force), and other officers who may play an important role, even if only at a single point in time.

The critical point is that despite the continued importance of the military's bureaucratic structure, personality factors on the part of the president, leading politicians, or leading military officers played a more important role in recent years than they did, for example, during the Brezhnev period. This is because political procedures, as well as institutions, both military and civilian, were in flux during both the system collapse and system transition stages. For example, no one can question the important role that Ogarkov played in the evolution of the Soviet armed forces when he was chief of the General Staff (1977–1984). But even he worked within a much more structured, disciplined, and constrained environment than his successors had during either the period of system collapse or system transition. Ogarkov worked for the defense minister and was limited almost entirely to dealing with military matters. The idea of Ogarkov *openly* disagreeing with his defense minister or the general secretary of the Communist Party is difficult to imagine. Similarly, while Brezhnev or Ustinov were clearly in charge of the armed forces, their ability to make major institutional and procedural changes was more restricted than was the case with Gorbachev and especially Yeltsin and Putin.

EVALUATING THE IMPACT OF PRESIDENTIAL LEADERSHIP

This raises the question of how to evaluate the impact of presidential leadership on the military. Investigations of factors such as presidential leadership in the USSR/Russia cannot meet the methodological requirements of a similar study conducted in the United States or Europe. While Russian presidential and military materials are far more informative and accessible now than they were thirty years ago, they do not provide the depth or breadth of data needed to satisfy the rules of evidence expected in Western studies. Instead, the analyst is dependent on primary and secondary material, conversations with Western experts and serving Russian officers, as well as informal encounters with former Russian soldiers, either as students or faculty members. Furthermore, for this reason data is not available for all periods on all of the characteristics.

As a result, the purpose of this study is *not* to provide an arbitrarily objective or statistical analysis of the impact of presidential leadership on military leadership in the USSR/Russia. Instead, the most that an analyst can hope to do is to provide the reader with a feeling or *Fingerspitzungsgefühl* for the impact. This means that the analyst's evaluation of the impact will be subjective, but closely tied to developments during each of the five time periods covered in this study. Toward this end, each chapter and the conclusion of this book will contain a discussion of the status of presidential leadership and the military during the period in question. Specifically, how successful (or unsuccessful) was the president in exhibiting presidential leadership, as viewed by the country's military leadership? The goal is to come up with a *rough* approximation of the impact. Which president was more effective in helping create the stability and predictability that is so vital to senior Soviet and Russian military officers? Why was one president more successful than another? Was it his style of leadership, his attention to the armed forces, his ability to deliver resources, or his willingness to permit the generals to run things as they wished?

STRUCTURE OF THE STUDY

This book is divided into seven chapters, beginning with this introduction. The second is on the Gorbachev period, focusing on his efforts to gain control over the military and its budget so he could use the money for other purposes, while presenting a less threatening USSR to the rest of the world. It also looks at how the generals and admirals reacted to the process of system collapse as well as the condition of the Soviet Army when he stepped down on December 25, 1991. The third deals with the coup attempt, the emergence of Boris Yeltsin, and the beginning of the transformation period. The focus is on Yeltsin's relationship with the high command during the coup attempt, and the generals' support for him during the 1993 confrontation with parliament. Chapter four deals with the Yeltsin administration and, in particular, the First Chechen War. It also looks closely at Yeltsin's impact on the high command as it looked for stability and predictability from the president. Chapter five focuses on Yeltsin's relations with the high command, including General Igor Rodionov and Marshal Igor Sergeyev, problems resulting from the 1998 economic crisis, Kosovo, and the beginning of the Second Chechen War, as well as the remainder of Yeltsin's time in office. Chapter six looks at the transition process under Putin. While it would be wrong to suggest that the Russian military is back on its feet (it has a very long way to go and faces extremely serious problems), Putin and his defense ministry have at least begun to try to introduce a degree of stability and predictability into the armed forces. Finally, chapter seven concludes with an attempt to determine how big an impact presidential leadership has had on the Soviet and Russian militaries and how well the Russian military has adapted to the introduction of a new, theoretically more democratic polity. Likewise, are there some lessons to be learned from the Soviet/Russian experience that might be useful in other political systems?

Not all of the characteristics cited above will be discussed in each chapter. The focus will be on events and only those that were important for understanding the impact of presidential leadership on the military during that period. For the most part, each chapter will follow a chronological approach with emphasis on the impact of actions by the country's president on the military on a variety of levels. For example, if the president called for a new military doctrine emphasizing mobility, to what degree did the high command comply? How successful was the president in getting the high command to think differently? Or did they ignore him and continue in their own ways?

Sources

While this study makes extensive use of a variety of primary sources, it also makes broad use of a variety of secondary sources. Indeed, without the pioneering work undertaken by these scholars, this study could not have been completed. All of them have been useful to one degree or another, and all of them were consulted in carrying out the research for this book.

By far the most important book both for the Gorbachev period and understanding the internal situation in the Soviet and Russian armed forces was General William Odom's now classic *The Collapse of the Soviet Military*.[19] My own *The Soviet High Command, 1967–1989,* and *Russian Civil-Military Relations,* as well as Mark Galeotti, *Gorbachev and His Revolution* were also useful.[20] When it came to the Yeltsin period, and to some degree the early parts of the Putin period, the more important were Pavel Baev, *The Russian Army in a Time of Troubles,* Robert Barylski, *The Soldier in Russian Politics,* John P. Moran, *From Garrison State to Nation-State,* Brian Taylor, *Politics and the Russian Army, 1689–2000,* and David J. Betz, *Civil-Military Relations in Russia and Eastern Europe*.[21] In addition, three recent edited works are worth mentioning. They include Yuri Fedorov and Bertil Nygren, eds., *Russian Military Reform and Russia's New Security Environment;* Anne C. Aldis, and Roger N. McDermott, eds., *Russian Military Reform, 1992–2002;* and Steven E. Miller and Dmitri Trenin, eds., *The Russian Military: Power and Policy.*[22] In addition, literally hundreds of articles from the Soviet and Russian press were utilized, as were a wide variety of journal articles published in the West. In the latter context, I should single out the outstanding work conducted by the Conflict Studies Research Centre located at the Royal Military Academy at Sandhurst.

In some cases, I disagreed with some of these authors; in other cases, I could only second their findings. However, the important fact is that all of the authors to one degree or another helped me understand the situation in the USSR and Russia better, both when it came to the issue of presidential leadership and the military's response.

Conceptual Relevance

While all of the studies mentioned above dealt to one degree or another with the situation inside the Soviet and Russian Armies, most of them were focused primarily on the nature and content of Moscow's security policy. Furthermore, none of these covered all three time periods. Some dealt primarily with the Gorbachev period while others covered the Yeltsin administration. There were also some that dealt with or focused on Yeltsin and the beginning of Putin's period in office. But none of them dealt with the three presidents' policies in a comparative fashion. This study will attempt to fill that gap by using the characteristics noted above as a device to compare the impact of presidential leadership style on the military over time.

Thus, this study represents the first attempt to compare the impact of political leadership by Mikhail Gorbachev, Boris Yeltsin, and Vladimir Putin on the Russian military. It is also the first to test the proposition that it has been presidential leadership (or lack thereof) that has been the key variable affecting the kind of military that Russia puts in the field.

This book is also unique in that it represents the first attempt to systematically look at the military's perception of the political leadership from its own perspective, as well as its efforts to adapt to a collapsing and then transitioning polity, an approach I applied to American civil-military relations in a separate work.[23] The Russian military has a military culture that in many ways is different from that in the West, although it shares a number of commonalities with other armies. This is a fact of life that the president must deal with if he hopes to get it to carry out his orders.

Furthermore, while all of the books and articles have looked at problems inside the Soviet and then the Russian military, this is the first one to compare these problems, their ebb and flow from 1985 to the present. It represents the most complete analysis to date of the impact of presidential neglect or attention on the life of the average soldier or on the military's combat readiness.

CHAPTER TWO
GORBACHEV, THE COUP, AND THE MILITARY: MARCH 1985–DECEMBER 1991

> In retrospect . . . Gorbachev had no vision of where he was heading.
> *Marshal Sergei Akhromeyev*

The generals considered Mikhail Gorbachev an enigma. On the one hand, they appreciated his efforts to come to grips with the crisis in the Soviet Union. They understood better than most citizens just how far the country was falling behind the West in general and the United States in particular. Washington was producing new high-tech weapons that the USSR had little if any chance of matching. These new weapons "could conceivably render their tanks and nuclear missiles obsolete."[1] They agreed with Gorbachev's complaints about the stagnation (*zastoi*) that had characterized the Soviet Union under Leonid Brezhnev and his successors. The USSR had little chance of catching up with the United States unless some radical changes were made in the way the country operated. As a result, the generals and admirals considered Gorbachev's coming to power to be a good sign—at least in the beginning.

However, in time the high command would become both frustrated and upset with the changes Gorbachev made in order to rejuvenate Soviet society and with the negative impact these changes had on the Army.[2] Indeed, from their perspective, he showed little or no leadership and seemed not to care about maintaining the combat capability of the Soviet armed forces. At times it appeared to them that he was uninterested in what was happening to the military, which in 1985 had been considered one of the world's most formidable. The fact that the Soviet military was slowly becoming more fractured and less capable, and was being used mostly for internal purposes, which the vast majority of Soviet officers opposed, did not appear to concern him.

By the time Gorbachev left office the generals and admirals would consider him one of the main reasons for the very difficult situation they found themselves in. There were a number of reasons why they felt this way, some of which were their own fault, while others were the result of Gorbachev's actions.

GORBACHEV COMES TO POWER

From the high command's standpoint, Gorbachev's election as general secretary was "business as usual." He was the commander-in-chief, but to the country's admirals and generals, little had changed. They would continue to run the military, and he would continue to give them what they needed to keep the Soviet Union a superpower. They saw Gorbachev as an outsider. He was the first post–World War II Soviet leader who had not served in the armed forces (he was too young to fight in World War II, and when he reached military age the armed forces were demobilizing). He also had not worked in the military-industrial complex. He had, of course, been involved with the agricultural community, but that, in their minds, hardly gave him the experience necessary to deal with them on an equal footing. He did not understand them, how they thought, or what they expected from the country's political leadership. And he acted in ways that directly conflicted with Soviet military culture. They simply did not understand him. In the long run, conflict between the two different worlds was inevitable.

In the meantime, it was obvious to Gorbachev that the country was in deep trouble. He made it clear from the beginning that he believed that something had to be done. The economy needed—at minimum—a shot in the arm; otherwise, the country would sink further and further into the morass of economic chaos or stagnation, as he called it.

Gorbachev's initial approach to the country's problems was to attack alcoholism, which was considered to be a serious drag on the economy. He then turned to his policy of *uskoreniye* (acceleration), which was intended to increase the availability of consumer goods in an effort to encourage Soviet citizens to work harder. Still the economic situation did not improve. Then he tried greater reliance on technology, but that did not help either. More radical steps were needed.

Gorbachev's answer was to introduce a policy of perestroika (restructuring) aimed at carrying out major surgery on the system. The power of the ossified bureaucracy of the Stalinist period to resist change was a major problem. It had to be removed and the economy rejuvenated. The country had to go back to the more mixed economy of the early 1920s. People had to be both encouraged and rewarded for their efforts, and those who stood in the way of progress had to be removed. Gorbachev called for a more effective use of both human and material resources, a more creative approach to management, and the revitalization of the party apparatus. He also argued that ideological-political education should emphasize "acceleration of the country's socio-economic development." With regard to the human factor, Gorbachev spoke of the need to reinforce order and discipline, to hold workers responsible for their actions, and to develop a more creative leadership style. As he put it:

> It is now no longer sufficient merely to be able to take executive action . . .
> the significance of such business-like qualities as competence, a sense of
> what is new, initiative, boldness, a readiness to take on responsibility for
> oneself, the ability to set a task and to see it through to the end, and the
> ability not to lose sight of the political meaning of management is grow-
> ing greater and greater.[3]

Implicit in this speech was his view that the existing Soviet system—with the help of science and technology, improved discipline and work habits, and other measures—was fully capable of putting the country's economy back together. However, he was aware that getting the public to accept such ideas would not be easy, as such behavior was discouraged and penalized under Stalin.[4]

The high command was not sure how to deal with Gorbachev's "call to action." Over the years the generals and admirals had heard hundreds of such calls, and the vast majority either fizzled out or had little or no relevance for those in uniform. Even when it came to those programs that were supposed to be important for the armed forces, the military had been able to either ignore them or pay lip service while it carried on the business of training soldiers and sailors to fight wars. As a consequence, the response in the military press was ambivalent at best.

As it had in the past, the military acted as if improvement in the economic sphere was primarily a civilian problem.[5] Yet the military understood the importance of greater efficiency and military preparedness, even if it did not like the signals suggesting that Gorbachev expected the high command to do more with less.[6] Consider the following from *Krasnaya zvezda:* "In accordance with the decision of the April Plenum of the CPSU CC [Communist Party of the Soviet Union Central Committee], Soviet soldiers are responsible to strive even more persistently to master combat skills, to raise vigilance and combat readiness, to strengthen discipline and regulatory order, to organize and with a high degree of expertise conclude the winter period of training."[7]

While the military press acknowledged the importance of Gorbachev's new policy of perestroika, it soon became obvious that military compliance was perfunctory. The military press said the right things, but the Army continued on pretty much as before. For example, the military press carefully reiterated Gorbachev's statements in an editorial in *Krasnaya zvezda* on June 11, 1985. "The importance of occupational characteristics such as competence, a sense for the new, initiative, boldness and readiness to take personal responsibility, the ability to follow the task to its final resolution is constantly increasing."[8]

In accordance with normal practice, the military assigned primary responsibility for implementing Gorbachev's new policy in the military to the political-military apparatus. In June 1985, for example, Admiral Alexei Sorokin, first deputy chief of the Main Political Directorate of the Soviet Army and Navy, complained that the political apparatus was failing to implement perestroika. In particular, he stated that Party members were neither doing enough to ensure that plans for training exercises were carried out nor were they setting good examples by improving their own personal qualifications and maintaining appropriate disciplinary standards.[9] A week later, addressing a meeting of officers of the Southern Group of Forces, Sorokin was again critical of the work of party organs, especially their failure to eliminate "formalism" in political-educational work.[10]

It was clear from Sorokin's comments that the party apparatus in the military was encountering resistance—or, more likely, passivity—as it tried to implement what many military leaders considered to be a civilian policy. This perfunctory treatment of Gorbachev's new effort was also evident in comments by the military's senior line officers.[11] For example, even the defense minister, who customarily led the way in introducing important party policies in the military, gave the impression that he was not especially concerned. There was no sense of urgency in his comments.[12]

Gorbachev was not pleased with the military's response. In July 1985 he met with senior military officers in Minsk and told them, "We now need energetic leaders who can command and communicate, people with initiative who are competent in their work."[13] Still, the military paid little attention to Gorbachev's new policy. To its credit, the military increased press coverage of the issue; however, it continued to be seen as a problem for the political apparatus, not for line officers. For example, Marshal Sergey Akhromeyev, the chief of the General Staff, failed to even mention the term "perestroika" in his 1986 Armed Forces Day speech, which was published only two days prior to the opening of the 27th Party Congress, while Defense Minister Sergei Sokolov limited himself to the following observation: "In line with the demands of restructuring, the following are of paramount significance: in-depth knowledge and precise execution of direct official duties by every serviceman, absolute truthfulness, the faculty of self-criticism in the assessment of the state of affairs, and the ability to organize and unite subordinates in an uncompromising struggle against shortcomings and deficiencies." [14] The implication was that the military leadership had more important things to do, such as worrying about tanks, planes, and ships. They should let the political apparatus focus on personnel and morale issues.

For his part, Gorbachev took advantage of the 27th Party Congress (February–March, 1986) to prod the military, especially when it came to the human aspect of perestroika. He believed that perestroika would not work in the USSR unless it was also adopted by the military. He could hardly exempt one of the most important and influential parts of the Soviet polity if he expected the rest of the country to take him seriously. He was determined to shake up the country and that included creating a new Soviet meritocracy so that the country, including the military, would be run by the best and the brightest, not by those who had obtained their positions primarily as a result of family connections. As he put it, "The criteria for all advancements and transfers are the same—the political and business-like qualities, abilities, and real achievements of a worker and his attitude toward people." [15]

The 27th Party Congress reinvigorated the party-political apparatus. In the latter part of March, for example, *Krasnaya zvezda* reported a high-level meeting of officials from the Ministry of Defense and the Main Political Directorate that endorsed Gorbachev's call for "accelerating the country's socio-economic development." The report stated that the Congress documents would form the basis of political-military activity in coming months and that professional competence (including efficient personnel management), the quality of officer education, and personal responsibility would be emphasized. In calling on military officers to "think and work in a new manner," the report complained, "some officers speak of perestroika, but in practice nothing changes."

Complacency remained a problem among the officer corps, however. For example, the chief of the Main Personnel Directorate of the USSR Ministry of Defense, General Ivan Shkadov, mentioned perestroika only once at a party meeting. His comment that "in recent years, a series of steps have been taken to modernize the system of training officer cadre, to improve the complex of military-training establishments of officers and cadre" suggested that he believed he had the situation well in hand. Even the party organization within the military appeared to be lukewarm toward perestroika, if one is to believe General A. D. Lizichev. At a November 1986 meeting he complained: "Even the election-and-report meetings are far from taking a demanding look at peres-troika, from fully collective work in the search for new forms and methods on the way to effectively resolving tasks. In places, criticism carries a formal, superficial character. At many meetings, criteria characteristic of bygone days, an insufficiently fresh form of analysis, a lack of sharp conclusions and self-criticism predominate."[16]

By the beginning of 1987 it was becoming clear that if the military was not openly resisting perestroika, neither was it openly embracing it.

GORBACHEV CRACKS DOWN ON
THE MILITARY

At the 1987 plenum of the CPSU Central Committee Gorbachev openly ex-pressed his irritation with the slow pace of implementing perestroika. He fo-cused directly on the personnel issue, arguing, "It . . . happens that certain execu-tives find themselves in the wrong position and in no way up to the mark . . . It seems essential to admit such errors, to rectify them, and without dramatizing them, to assign the person concerned to a job that corresponds to his abilities."[17]

It was soon clear that the military "got the message." First, General Shkadov was relieved of his position as personnel chief and replaced by the hitherto little-known General Dmitry Yazov. In addition, in recognition of his efforts to push perestroika in the military, General Lizichev was given the honor of authoring the annual article devoted to military affairs in the party journal *Kommunist*.[18] Soon, other senior officers began to jump on the perestroika bandwagon. For ex-ample, Defense Minister Sokolov devoted an unusually large part of his Armed Forces Day article in *Sovietskaya Rossiya* to restructuring, while Marshal Akhro-meyev, who tended to avoid personnel issues, singled out the importance of re-structuring for developing efficiency, initiative, precision, sober assessments, and personal responsibility.[19] Then First Deputy Minister of Defense Army General Peter Lushev wrote several articles devoted to cadres and psychological restruc-turing. Similarly, chief of the Strategic Rocket Forces General Yuri Maximov; the head of the Navy, Admiral Vladimir Chernavin; and the head of the Air Defense Forces, Marshal Alexander Koldunov, all published articles citing perestroika as a key factor in maintaining a high level of combat readiness.[20]

Marshal Sokolov then noted that some senior officers had already been re-lieved of their commands because of their failure to embrace Gorbachev's policy of perestroika, and he implied that others who did not change their approaches would suffer the same fate.[21] At the same time, General Lizichev called on party activists to bear "direct responsibility for work and the practical implementation of the most important measures connected with resolving defense tasks, the development and training of the armed forces," and he complained that party organs showed "rudeness, inaction, and contempt for relations with people, for their needs and questions."[22]

Despite the positive comments in the media, very little was changing. The Soviet military was a giant amoeba. Outsiders could pound and pound on it, and it would seem to respond. Senior officers would say the right things, and a few personnel and structural changes would take place. But nothing really changed; the military culture marched to its own drummer. In essence, "The more things changed, the more they remained the same." Gorbachev had to do something if he hoped to bring about change in the military; but the task was made more difficult because of Gorbachev's lack of familiarity with the Army and its lack of respect for him.

It should reiterated, however, that many officers believed Gorbachev was correct when he pointed out the need for a shake-up, especially in the economy. During his time as chief of the General Staff, for example, Marshal Ogarkov had argued that the economy was critical to the army, noting, "Nothing depends on economic conditions like a country's army and navy."[23] He complained numerous times about the danger that the Soviet economy's failure to keep up with the West technologically had for its armed forces. He was well aware that the country was falling further and further behind the West. However, Brezhnev and his immediate successors ignored him, and the gap between the Soviet Union and the West continued to widen.

Ogarkov's successor, Marshal Akhromeyev also believed in the importance of high technology, and he also warned of the consequences if the country failed to pay attention to developments in that area. "History knows a number of examples when the armies of states, in preparing for future war, operated on the basis of the past," he wrote in *Kommunist*, "not paying attention to the changes that had occurred in military affairs."[24] From the high command's standpoint, change was necessary, and it appeared that Gorbachev's changes would be positive. However, there was a condition attached to Ogarkov and Akhromeyev's support for Gorbachev's new policy. As Galeotti put it, "They were in favor of modernization and a revitalization of the Party as long as this meant a more dynamic economy, more advanced weapons, and healthier and more committed recruits."[25] The problem was that what the high command wanted would cost considerable amounts of money, which Gorbachev was not about to give them.

The generals and admirals first realized that they might have problems with Gorbachev's leadership when he addressed the budget in the private meeting he held with them in Minsk on July 10, 1985. He informed the generals and admirals that he expected them to learn how to "do more with less." Gorbachev also shocked the military by making it clear that he intended to change the way the USSR dealt with security policy. Only a month after he took office he announced a unilateral suspension of nuclear weapons tests as well as a freeze on deploying intermediate-range ballistic missiles (IRBMs). Gorbachev expanded on his new vision of the USSR's security policy at the 27th Party Congress, arguing about the "impossibility" of winning a nuclear war, the need to hold military forces "to a reasonable sufficiency," and the destructiveness of nuclear weapons; problems that could create "new forms of relations between different social systems, states, and regions."[26] While Soviet military officers might argue among themselves that a nuclear war would be so destructive that it would be ludicrous to think that it could be "won," they did not understand why should Gorbachev was saying so publicly.

The 27th Party Congress in 1986 represented a fundamental turning point in Soviet security policy. First, if the generals had questioned Gorbachev's seriousness in cutting the budget, he made clear his intention to reduce spending. Compare, for example, Brezhnev's pledge to "ensure" that the military had everything it needed,"[27] with the party program that was approved by this Congress. The new one merely stated that the Party "will make every effort to ensure that the USSR Armed Forces are at a level excluding strategic superiority on the part of imperialism's forces."[28] The 1986 wording carried with it the clear implication that the Party leadership might *not* be able to provide the high command with everything it believed necessary.

Two years later Gorbachev announced that he would be cutting the military budget by 14.2 percent and the production of arms and military technology by 19.5 percent.[29] He claimed that the military had "swallowed colossal material and intellectual resources, the best that there were."[30] In addition, Gorbachev "launched a highly visible program to convert defense industries to civilian production; and beginning in 1989, defense procurement orders were cut back by 30 percent per year.[31] Indeed, in 1989 Nikolai Ryzhkov, who was head of the Council of Ministers, announced plans to halve the defense budget by 1995.[32] In fact, the budget presented by Finance Minister Valentin Pavlov reduced defense spending by 8.3 percent—"with spending down from R77.3 billion to R70.9 [billion] in 1990."[33] The days of an unlimited military budget were gone.

The military appears to have been especially surprised by Gorbachev's decision to change Soviet military doctrine. In an article published only two days prior to the opening of the 27th Party Congress, Akhromeyev used the old Brezhnev formulation, "The Communist Party is doing everything to ensure that the Soviet armed forces have at their disposal all of the necessary means to perform their constitutional duty of reliably defending the Socialist Fatherland."[34] The same was true of Defense Minister Sokolov. He "relied almost exclusively on the vocabulary developed during the first ten years of the Brezhnev regime."[35] The idea that the defense minister would use language that differed from the general secretary can only mean that this new approach to military affairs was "sprung" on the military.

Gorbachev's logic was simple. He "knew that if he was to make cuts in the military's budget, he would need to convert the military's offensive doctrine to one based on purely defensive measures."[36] Accordingly, Gorbachev advocated the idea of a major change in Soviet strategy at the 27th Party Congress, from one emphasizing offense to one sufficient only for defensive operations. As he put it, "The world today has become too small and fragile for wars and a policy of force. It cannot be saved and preserved unless there is a break—a decisive and irrevocable break with the way of thinking and acting that for centuries has been built on the acceptability, the permissibility of wars, and armed conflict."[37]

Needless to say, such language sounded strange to the generals. What was this civilian, who had never served in the military, doing halting nuclear weapons tests and stopping the deployment of IRBMs? Then there was this push toward a new strategy, one sufficient only for defense. To many officers this also sounded silly. For years Soviet military strategy had always been offensive, relying on the use of massive numbers of troops and weapons to crush any opponent that chose to threaten the Kremlin's vital interests. How was the military supposed to defend the USSR by relying only on defense? What impact would it have on the balance between motorized infantry and armored forces? How many and what kind of forces should be reduced? To many generals it seemed like a recipe for disaster.

Gorbachev's new idea of a defensive doctrine not only shocked the military, it ran counter to the way the generals calculated the military balance. Prior to Gorbachev, the military had relied upon a numerical calculation: how many troops, tanks, planes, etc. did each side have, how effective would they be? Everything would then be totaled and the two sides compared. The problem, in Gorbachev's opinion, was that during the 1970s this kind of thinking had led to an arms race, one that the West was winning because the Soviet economy could not keep up. Now, however, Gorbachev maintained that it was time to move beyond the world of numbers. The Kremlin argued that in the future the key to Soviet military doctrine was for Moscow to create a force *only* sufficient to deter the other side by ensuring Moscow's ability to mount a robust defense.

Despite considerable misgivings, the high command accepted Gorbachev's contention that nuclear war was an absurdity. The new view was highlighted in the official communiqué issued by the Political Consultative Committee of the Soviet-led Warsaw Pact on May 29, 1987. It stated: "The military doctrine of the Warsaw Pact member states is strictly defensive and proceeds from the application of military means to resolve any dispute is inadmissible under current conditions."[38] In October, Yazov put his imprimatur on the new approach when he declared, "Our military doctrine today consists of a system of views on the prevention of war, on military organizational development preparation of the country and its armed forces for repelling aggression, and methods of conducting warfare in defense of socialism."[39] The military was now on board. As Akhromeyev noted, "Nuclear war can only lead to mankind's destruction," or, as he put at the end of 1987, "Today it is impossible to achieve any political goals in a nuclear war."[40] Yazov even went one step further when he stated that any kind of war would threaten humanity's very existence.[41] The high command also accepted the importance of creating a strictly defensive military doctrine. Akhromeyev commented that the military doctrine is "based on maintaining the country's defense capability at a strictly necessary level, precluding strategic military superiority on the part of imperialism."[42] Three years later he added: "In theory, and in our exercises in the field, we are planning for long defensive operations to repel a possible aggression, if it proves impossible to end this aggression by political means. Then, and only then after around three or four weeks, we might launch a counterattack."[43]

In short, Raymond Garthoff had it right when he noted, "On the whole . . . the military leadership moved beginning in 1987 to work on the problem rather than trying to fight it."[44] The problem, however, was that by 1989 the military's efforts to rationally reshape Soviet military doctrine collapsed as the anticommunist revolution in Eastern Europe turned the military balance upside down. Beginning in 1989, the Communist East European governments began to fall one after the other, and with them went the Warsaw Pact, Moscow's military counterweight to NATO. To make matters worse, the Soviet Union was forced to withdraw its troops from Eastern Europe. The result was chaos as the high command began to bring troops home but had no place to put them. Officers and their families soon found themselves living in tents in

Siberia at thirty degrees below zero. It was no longer a case of the high command attempting rationally to plan what was to happen with doctrine, it quickly became an effort to find a place to put troops from Eastern Europe. "By 1990 the primary job of the General Staff was simply to carry out these directives as expeditiously as possible and in a manner likely to preserve Soviet security interests."[45]

Faced with Gorbachev's argument against numerical superiority, the high command began to emphasize quality over quantity. If the armed forces could not expect to have the largest military, it wanted the best. This approach would have a number of ramifications. For example, officer efficiency reports were normally prepared every four years. However, a new policy was introduced requiring all officers be reevaluated based on "qualitative parameters." This meant assessing his technical competence, his knowledge of military science, and how he related to enlisted personnel. Those who failed the evaluation would be transferred to the reserves.[46]

While it would be wrong to speak of a rupture between Gorbachev and the military, by mid-1987 it was clear to both sides that while they agreed on many points they had different views of Soviet military doctrine.

By and large, the Soviet military accommodated and adopted without dissent the first two articles of the political leadership's reform agenda regarding doctrine—the rejection of superiority as a goal of policy and the desirability of depriving either side of the ability to execute a surprise attack. It was the third provision, the injunction against offensive military operations, that became a source of contention and debate.[47]

The military did not want to give up its offensive doctrine despite the comments cited above. Qualitative parameters were fine and needed, but the idea of putting the initiative in the hands of the enemy was hard to swallow. Something would have to be done to break the logjam.

MATHIAS RUST COMES TO THE RESCUE

In one of the stranger events in military history, a young West German civilian by the name of Mathias Rust did the seemingly impossible. On May 27, 1987, he flew a single-engine Cessna Skyhawk 172 through 700 kilometers of heavily protected Soviet air space and landed in front of the Kremlin, not far from

Gorbachev's office. Ironically, the episode took place on Border Guards Day. Gorbachev was out of the country, but when informed, he was furious. It was difficult to decide whether to call the affair a farce or a complete failure of the Soviet military's air defense forces. The bottom line, however, was that Gorbachev and the Soviet leadership had been humiliated. After all, Rust could have easily been a terrorist or a spy. It gave Gorbachev the opportunity he needed to put the military in its place. The high command had resisted his efforts to introduce perestroika into the military in a meaningful way long enough. Now he would take action. The next day, the Kremlin announced that both Sokolov and the head of the Air Defense Forces, Alexander Koldunov, were being replaced.

The high command was stunned. Since Brezhnev's time, they had expected to be consulted on key personnel matters. In their minds, the decision about who should fill these senior positions was a military matter. True, the general secretary made the final decision, but only after consulting closely with them. Now they had been blind-sided. However, as Dusko Doder pointed out, Gorbachev "knew the supreme importance of first impressions, and he acted forcefully, as if civilians had always been in charge of strategic issues."[48] He was not about to negotiate with the generals. He acted.

Sokolov's replacement was a major surprise to the generals. While General Yazov appeared on Western lists of likely successors to Sokolov, Gorbachev's appointment of the sixty-three-year-old general to head the Soviet armed forces was a shock. He was junior to most Soviet military leaders and, unlike the vast majority of them, had minimal experience in Moscow. The latter qualification had been considered a *sine qua non* for such high level appointments at least since Brezhnev's time. However, Yazov was a field commander, a soldier's soldier. While he would later turn against Gorbachev, Yazov's unique background and his lack of time in the halls of the Defense Ministry made him a perfect choice from the general secretary's perspective.[49] The last thing Gorbachev wanted was another Moscow bureaucrat.

Yazov was born on November 8, 1923, in the village of Yazovo in Omsk province. He joined the army in 1941 and was sent to a short course for infantry officers in Moscow. He graduated in 1942, a newly commissioned officer at the age of nineteen. He was wounded in World War II, but returned to duty after a short convalescence. By 1965 he was a full colonel. After graduating from the Voroshilov General Staff Academy in 1967, Yazov was given command of a division, and by 1970 he was a major general. From 1972 to 1974 he commanded a unit in the Caucasus and was then transferred to the Main Personnel Directorate in the Ministry of Defense. He later became first deputy commander of the Far East Military District, and in 1979 he became commander of the Central Group of Forces in Czechoslovakia. By 1984 he was commander of one of the USSR's prime military commands, the Far East Military District. In 1987, Gorbachev brought him to Moscow to take charge of personnel.

Yazov also differed from other senior officers because he was a long-time and enthusiastic supporter of the kind of change that Gorbachev was seeking in the military. For example, he had argued that officers had to "assume responsibility for decisions" and criticized those who thought that training troops to deal with high-tech weapons was only a problem for specialists.[50] Gorbachev first met him when he visited the Far East in July 1986. What surprised Gorbachev was Yazov's willingness to admit mistakes—something unheard of at that time. For example, when asked by Gorbachev about the state of discipline in the region, Yazov responded, "Discipline in the district had not improved recently and had even worsened in individual units and subunits. He presented accurate figures. Hundreds of officers and dozens of generals attended this talk. Now this talk is called in the district nothing other than a lesson in truth."[51]

While implementing perestroika in the armed forces would be difficult, given continued resistance by the rank and file, it was clear that Yazov strongly supported it. Yazov expected them to take the new policy seriously, and pressure on the armed forces was stepped up accordingly. For example, in February 1988 Soviet commanders were ordered to report to the Ministry of Defense on what steps they had taken to reduce disciplinary infractions. Then on October 13, 1988, at a special Politburo meeting, Gorbachev "heard and discussed a report on disciplinary problems in the Soviet Armed Forces. He ordered the military to take action immediately to effect a dramatic reduction in code violations."[52] A month later all commanders from division and higher levels met in Moscow and were told that their careers depended on how well they dealt with disciplinary violations. The generals and admirals were stunned: Who was Gorbachev to tell professional soldiers and sailors how to run their forces?[53]

Despite Yazov's support, however, Gorbachev continued to face major problems in getting the generals to accept his policies. "The few generals who were genuinely supportive of Gorbachev's initiatives were unable to control the ranks, however, especially the army's opinion makers," observed Zoltan Barany. "Although the generals rarely risked open defiance of Gorbachev's military reform initiatives, they successfully stonewalled their execution."[54]

THE IMPACT OF PERESTROIKA ON
THE MILITARY

Two aspects of Gorbachev's perestroika policy had major, long-term implications for the armed forces. First, he began speaking about *demokratizatsiya* (democratization). In the civilian sphere he sought to create a situation in which subordinates would not be afraid to criticize the actions of superiors. For example, members of parliament or the media would be prepared to criticize the actions of government bureaucrats, the very people who stood in the way of implementing his policies. The same was true of the military; subordinates would expose inefficiency and incompetent officers in the armed forces.

The second part of perestroika to bedevil the Army was *glasnost* (openness). In order for politicians, ordinary citizens, and others to be able to express their opinions, Gorbachev realized that they first needed the necessary information. How could anyone criticize an organization's failure to do business properly if the individual did not know that it was making mistakes? How could anyone criticize accidents (that were not really accidents) or excessive budgetary expenditures if information on neither (or a hundred other items) was available?

Under the rubric of glasnost something was happening in the USSR that had not been seen since Stalin's time: Party leaders were being openly criticized at Party meetings. In addition, the meetings were being televised. For many Soviets these discussions were the most interesting programs on TV. Many sat glued to their television sets night after night, unable to believe what they were hearing—open criticism of the way the political system was being run.

Gorbachev also called for competitive elections, and in September 1988 he obtained parliamentary approval for voting changes. He was also elected chairman of the Supreme Soviet, which permitted him to claim the title of president of the USSR. In November parliament approved amendments that created a new Congress of People's Deputies with 2,250 members. Gorbachev's strategy was simple: "As he toured the country and the world in late 1988 and early 1989, he described his strategy as a political vise. He was squeezing from the top and the popular fronts were squeezing from the bottom. Together they would crush the conservative bureaucracy."[55]

The generals considered both of these policies, democratization and glasnost, to be heresy. For example, how could a military be democratic? The military is by nature hierarchical. Privates do not criticize sergeants, and lieutenants do not criticize generals. Openly questioning the actions of superiors would undermine military order. Furthermore, a military organization like the Soviet armed forces was based on secret information: the number of its forces, the kind of weapons it possessed, its battle plans, etc. were all secret. Both democratization and glasnost created major problems for the civilian world, and they would eventually lead to the unraveling of the communist system. But when it came to the armed forces, the reforms turned the organization upside down.

While they probably did not fully understand the long-term implications of either policy, the generals tried to deal with democratization by keeping it within the military's party organization. In accordance with the Party policy of criticism and self-criticism, for example, a subordinate could (theoretically) criticize the actions of his superior at a Party meeting. This option helped avoid undermining the chain of command. The problem, of course, was that the senior officer wrote the subordinate's fitness report and a serious, hard-hitting criticism by the subordinate might have unintended, negative consequences for the junior officer. As a result, when criticism occurred during Party meetings, there was an air of unreality about it. Some action would be criticized and the senior officer would feign remorse and promise to do better, but the exercise was more theater than reality.

The situation was different, however, when it came to both informal organizations and the legislature. In 1989, for example, disgruntled officers created an organization named Shield (*Shchit*) because, according to its members, the Ministry of Defense was not looking out for them. In response, the Ministry set up officer assemblies in an effort to counter public criticism of the military, including that by members of Shield. Soon both groups would direct their criticism at the Gorbachev administration.

Military officers would also become increasingly active in the country's parliament. Officers had always been members of the Supreme Soviet, but prior to Gorbachev military membership in this "toothless" parliament had been perfunctory. Under Gorbachev, however, the situation changed. Parliament was open to members of the military—who now had to stand for election just like any other candidate. The problem with members of both informal organizations and the parliament was that many officers took their membership in these bodies seriously and believed that they had the right to speak their mind and to lobby for policies that were often opposed by the defense ministry.

While democratization was an irritant for the defense ministry, glasnost was a nightmare. Military officers were not only *not* used to washing their dirty laundry in public, most of them could not conceive of a situation in which their shortcomings would be discussed by the civilian press. Secrecy was the basis of military operations. What happened in the field, in the barracks, or on a ship was not the public's business. If a plane crashed, even as a result of military incompetence, it was the military's business. If salaries changed, that was also the military's problem. In short, the generals could not understand why civilians or dissident military officers should be given information that could be used against the Ministry of Defense.

Few generals thought Gorbachev would go beyond just democratization and glasnost and actually fire most of the military's senior officers. But during Yazov's tenure, some 1,200 generals were retired, producing nothing short of a major generational change.[56] By 1990, the average age of senior military officers had been reduced from 67.3 to 62.2 years.[57] According to Gorbachev, this was an effort "to renew and revitalize the staff of generals and the officer corps."[58] If Gorbachev hoped to see this change lead to a modification in the attitudes among senior military officers, he was disappointed.

Gorbachev dropped another bombshell on December 7, 1988, when he announced before the United Nations General Assembly that the USSR would unilaterally reduce its armed forces by some 500,000 troops. In particular, he had decided to withdraw six tank divisions from Eastern Europe, one-third of what Moscow had deployed there. Soon it became clear that the Soviets were serious about changing their doctrine, as training exercises began to concentrate on defensive tactics. Meanwhile, the Soviet Fleet "cut back on distant operations."[59]

The military began to take a number of steps aimed at restructuring or reforming the armed forces. First Yazov announced that the military would introduce a "contract" system for the Navy, with other services to follow. Under this system, a conscript would have the option of serving for two or three years beyond his initial term. If he decided to serve an additional two or three years, he would receive special training and a salary of 150 rubles a month "and higher." Yazov also spoke of the possibility of cutting the length of conscripted service and warned his colleagues that the armed forces faced additional cuts. He also announced that military-educational systems would be cut by 30–35 percent, that the number of officers studying at civilian universities would be cut by 30–40 percent, and that the system of command and control would be streamlined. As a result, staffs would be reduced by 15–20 percent and the number of flag officers would be cut by "no less than 30 percent."[60]

In November General Mikhail Moiseyev, who had replaced Akhromeyev as chief of the General Staff, stated that the military intended to introduce a reform plan in three incremental stages.[61] The first stage (up to 1994) involved the implementation of all arms control agreements signed by Moscow as well as a modification in operational and mobilization plans and the adoption of new legislation governing the military. The second stage (1994–1995) would complete cuts in the Soviet armed forces, reorganize the army's central apparatus, modify the internal structure of military districts, and reorganize military-educational institutions. Finally, during the third stage (1996–2000), a 50-percent reduction in strategic arms would be carried out, and the existing military structure would be modified. In the end, the military would have about 3.2 million men under arms. In 1989 the Central Asian Military District was abolished and Soviet troops withdrew from Afghanistan.

The critical aspect of this "reform plan" put forth by the General Staff was that it did not include a simultaneous conceptual modification of Soviet military doctrine. Even the Afghan experience carried little weight with the General Staff. As Michael Orr put it, "The experience of the Afghan War (1979–1989) did not alter the Soviet ground forces' preoccupation with large-scale conventional or tactical nuclear warfare. Counterinsurgency, peacekeeping, and the other tasks that Western armies now call 'Operations Other Than War' did not feature in Soviet military education."[62] True, the defensive aspect would be emphasized, but it would continue to be a military based on large numbers of troops and reserves capable of launching large-scale offensive operations primarily against NATO. In short, the General Staff was considering a reduction in size, not a modification in the way the Army would fight a war.

One of the most important effects of glasnost was that the revelation of abuses and crimes within the military led to a decline in public respect for the military. The Army was admired; after all, it had saved the country during World War II. Now, however, the populace was learning that service in the ranks of the Soviet Army was a barbaric experience. In addition, junior officers began to lose respect for senior officers. As Odom noted, "As glasnost spread they often expressed their disdain for senior officers quite openly. A lieutenant colonel in Kaliningrad went on a month-long hunger strike. Interviewed on Moscow television, he explained it as 'a protest against the reactionary generals who are a brake on military reform.'"[63] Public opinion surveys underlined the alarming decrease in public support for the military. In 1990 "only 59 percent of the Russian public expressed some confidence in the armed forces." In fact, public support had slipped to the point where Soviet officers were being attacked by civilians: "In 1989, 85 were killed by civilians, not in the line of duty but just because of their profession, and in the first quarter of 1990 another 21 were murdered and 189 injured."[64]

Meanwhile, Gorbachev and the high command were learning that loosening central control over the Army had a number of unwelcome effects. To begin with, it was difficult to control officers—once they had been given the chance to express their own opinions and to act independently of the high command. The high command intended the officer assemblies mentioned above to be easily controlled organizations, ones that would support the leadership. However, on November 12, 1990, Gorbachev met with an all-Union Assembly of Citizen Soldiers. Much to Gorbachev and Yazov's surprise and embarrassment, many of the 1,100 participants took the opportunity to blast Gorbachev because of his failure to take decisive action in rebellious parts of the country.

The speeches from the floor also included a torrent of complaints about the breakdown in the Soviet state's authority in the rebellious regions. Instead of hiding them from public view, Defense Minister Yazov had them printed in the military newspaper, *Krasnaya zvezda,* which could be bought anywhere in the country. Gorbachev was being criticized for failing to take effective action to preserve the political integrity of the Soviet state and for making too many decisions about defense spending cuts and arms control agreements too rapidly.[65]

As a colonel present at the meeting put it, "Today we have to say this straight out: Do you as President, the government, and the people need the Army at all: If so, things cannot remain as they are."[66] The idea of colonels or majors criticizing the head of state—and the head of the Party—was unthinkable. Yet that was exactly what happened. Others were even more critical of both the high command and Gorbachev. As a result, Gorbachev's prestige was damaged. He was being accused of doing nothing, while the Army was on the edge of disintegration.

GORBACHEV'S IMPACT ON THE MILITARY

Morale in the armed forces was declining. What had once been one of the most sought-after careers was quickly losing its luster. For example, junior officers were leaving the military: "70 percent of those retiring prematurely were under 25, and 77 percent were described as efficient, conscientious, and possessing initiative, with 90 percent rated as either excellent or good." Then a poll conducted in August 1990 indicated that "only 40 percent of officers regarded their jobs as even satisfactory, and 24 percent wished to change their career." The next year the number of officers asking for early discharge was equal to those joining.[67] Without a cadre of well-trained junior officers, a conscript army cannot hope to be combat ready, especially if it does not have a competent staff of NCOs. Indeed, their presence was absolutely critical if the Army hoped to maintain combat readiness.

Many of the most vocal critics of the high command were new members of the Soviet parliament. They openly challenged the defense ministry's plan for military reform. For example, when Yazov's name was sent to the Congress of People's Deputies in July 1989, for confirmation as defense minister, he was roundly criticized by military officers who were members of the Congress. Indeed, the criticism was so strong that Gorbachev had to come to his minister's defense.

One critical issue discussed in parliament was whether the Army should become professional immediately or should continue with its conscript base. The legislators who favored an immediate professionalization of the military were assisted by glasnost, which made public a problem that had long been a secret or at least not openly discussed in the media—the practice of *dedovshchina,* the bullying of junior recruits by their seniors. While *dedovshchina* had been a problem for some time, a phenomena known to every conscript who served in the armed forces, it was not spoken about in the media. Many civilians were unaware of it, but with the advent of glasnost stories of senior soldiers exploiting junior soldiers became a topic of conversation in the media on almost a daily basis. The brutal practice became even worse as military cohesion and control deteriorated.

Some analysts believe that *dedovshchina* was a result of the Gulag experience, where the stronger prisoners beat up the weaker. Others argued that it went back to the Kremlin's decision in 1967 to change conscript service from three years for the Army or four years in the Navy to two years in both. As a consequence of this change, conscripts were called up twice a year, fall and spring, and at any given time the Army consisted of four different groups, ranging from those who just entered the armed forces to those who were about to get out. The third group (the *deds*), in particular, harassed the first. The situation was made worse by the lack of a meaningful noncommissioned officer corps present in the barracks and tasked with the job of keeping order in smaller units. As a result the more senior conscripts (those in their second year of service) maintained order. Not only did they train juniors, but they disciplined them in the barracks as well. Such behavior included everything from stealing their food, money, clothes, shoes, etc., to rape and beatings. Officers often were involved as well. Odom reported the experiences of one former soldier:

The junior soldier washed the *ded's* laundry, cleaned his boots, washed his feet, cleaned his weapon, swept out the barracks, cleaned toilets, and performed numerous other services for the *ded*. On the work details, the *stariki* ["old men"]forced the younger soldiers to perform the heaviest and dirtiest tasks. To humiliate first year soldiers, *stariki* gave them extremely obscene and demeaning nicknames. When junior soldiers received food packages and money from home, the *stariki* openly stole them. At mealtime *stariki* frequently took a junior soldier's food for themselves. Homosexual rape was widespread.[68]

While the recruit had the right to file complaints, and while the system would generally respond if he did, the recruit's life would not be worth much once the guilty party finished his time in the stockade and returned to his unit. Officers were overworked and often held second jobs (like driving a taxi) to make ends meet. This meant it was impossible for them to monitor what went on in the barracks after hours. Many supporters of a professional military argued that if the military were professionalized, the problem would go away. In the meantime, *dedovshchina* had serious implications for the military's combat readiness. For example, a platoon commander during the Afghan War recalled:

When I first got to the unit in the commander of our platoon . . . would yell and cuss people out all the time. He would also hit people and even kicked a *starik's* teeth out. So one day when we were out in the mountains on operations, two of the *stariki* just pushed him over a cliff. They said he had slipped, and even though most of the platoon saw them, nobody reported them. Everybody hated his guts and was happy to get rid of him.[69]

Another case involved a young soldier assigned to a tank in Afghanistan:

I knew the young soldier very well; his name was Aleksey. When he would come to the base, he used to tell me that the *stariki* were abusing him viciously; beating him constantly and making him do the hardest work. If he couldn't accomplish it, the three *dedushki* would beat him twice as hard. He told me that they forced him to stand guard every night until dawn; he seldom slept more than two or three hours. They even tried to molest him sexually. His face was always marked by beatings. What could I advise him? I just told him, "Hang in there Alyosha, hang in there." Well, in the end, he couldn't take it anymore, and one night while the *dedushki* were sleeping sweetly he emptied an entire magazine into them and killed three of them.[70]

It is hard to overstate the impact this "tradition" had on the combat readiness of Soviet troops. It is one of the reasons why the Army's cohesion began to break down in Afghanistan.

Discipline and order in the military also began to deteriorate. In December 1990, for example, Yazov informed a closed meeting of officers that "about 500 conscripts had committed suicide in 1990, while 69 officers and 32 NCOs had been murdered. On that same occasion, the MPA chief, Colonel General Nikolai Shlyaga, said that 2,000 soldiers had died in the first eleven months of 1990."[71] Housing was also a major problem:

General [Dmitry] Sukhorukov gave an indication of it in April 1989, when he told a television audience that 45,000 servicemen and their families were without apartments in the next two years. Almost a year later, in February 1990, Marshal Yazov told an interviewer, "housing is the most acute problem today . . . More than 173,000 families of officers and warrant officers do not have apartments. At the same time another 74,000 apartments required upgrading.[72]

The situation did not improve. In December 1991, it was estimated that "at least 74,000 lived in the worst slum conditions, e.g., twenty-two families in a Leningrad hostel sharing two lavatories and wash basins and one kitchen (no hot water), with the children sleeping in ammunition boxes."[73]

Vladimir Lopatin, a former political officer in the Naval Air Forces, and others continued to argue that the best way to stop the chaos in the armed forces was to professionalize it. He blasted the military leadership, arguing that the Ministry of Defense was stonewalling the reform plan that he and his colleagues had suggested. Lopatin maintained that conscription was not working. As he put it, "Any further delay is likely to aggravate the crisis in society and the Army and poses the threat of the Army's disintegration." Using figures from a survey taken by the Main Political Directorate of the Soviet Army and Navy, he pointed out that overall interest in serving in the military was sharply decreasing. In 1975, for example, 78 percent of enlisted personnel had expressed "great interest in the service." By 1986 the figure had dropped to 63 percent, and by 1990 it was down to 12 percent. "And yet the Ministry of Defense assumes that it will be possible to retain all-Union universal military service for at least the next 15 years!"[74] Even the status of professionals was under attack. For example, in 1991 it was reported that pay was so low that "regimental commanders earned half as much as city bus drivers. Officially, it was admitted that a married junior officer with two children lived below the poverty line."[75]

In response to the calls for a professional Army, the high command argued that it was both unpatriotic and unrealistic. Akhromeyev attacked the idea of "voluntary service" as "unacceptable," stating that it violated the principles of "social justice" and warned that such an army "would cost our people far more than it costs at present."[76] Yazov followed up that July telling the country's legislators, "We cannot afford a professional army."[77] In November 1990 the high command reiterated the point in an article in *Voennaya mysl,* maintaining that the immediate transition to a professional military would not be possible for financial reasons.[78] By the end of 1990, the lines were clearly drawn. On the one side Yazov and Moiseyev remained staunchly opposed to the question of a professional army, while officer-politicians like Lopatin and his colleagues strongly backed the proposed change. This debate, however, would plague the high command for many years to come.

Vladimir Serebryannikov, a lieutenant general and a professor at the Lenin Political-Military Academy, argued that, from a military standpoint, militia formations were "inferior" to a regular army. He claimed that such units could not master modern military technology, thereby weakening the country. He believed that reliance on a small professional military to back up a militia was nonsense.[79] What if the country were to get into a major war with a country like the United States? A small military, however professional it might be and however good its weapons were, would not be sufficient even if it was backed up by a militia.

In the meantime, the Army faced problems in its efforts to retain a conscript Army. As the media published more and more revelations about *dedovshchina,* an increasing number of young men evaded the draft. According to Soviet figures, in 1988 there were 1,044 draft evaders, in 1989 there were 6,647, and in the first eleven months of 1990 the number "was up 85.2 percent over the first eleven months of the proceeding year. In addition, full time students in universities and all college-level institutions were given a deferment provided they finished their studies." If the institution had a military faculty, male students had to accept a reserve commission. However, since only two to four percent of reserve officers were called up, the vast majority of college students managed to avoid military service.

By 1990 problems with the draft were getting out of hand, primarily because many young men in various republics refused to report for the draft. For example, seven republics failed to meet their quotas: Georgia (27.5 percent), Armenia (7.5 percent), Lithuania (33.6 percent), Latvia (54.2 percent), Estonia (40.2 percent), Uzbekistan (87.4 percent), and Kirghizia (89.5 percent).[80] That fall the situation was even worse: "Only 78.8 percent of the total recruitment goal was reached." There were even problems in the Russian areas.[81] Many of the republics were trying to set up their own forces. The following year, Yazov reported that the military was short 353,000 conscripts, because some republics refused to cooperate. So the Soviet military began a practice that was to have serious and negative long-term implications for the Army. It compensated for the shortfall "by accepting more conscripts with criminal records and members of minorities who spoke little or no Russian."[82]

In addition to the declining quality of recruits, there were increasing problems with soldiers using illegal drugs. In a study conducted in 1987, 69 percent of soldiers "said that hashish was available; 22 percent of those serving in Afghanistan said that they could get heroin, and 11 percent said that LSD was available." According to the same source, "50 percent of Soviet personnel are said to be regular users."[83] If this was true, it is no wonder that the Soviet Army was far from combat capable when the USSR broke up.

Given the other problems in the military, it is not surprising that the desertion rate soared. In 1990 there were up to 500 desertions each day in construction units in the Far East. "An entire company of soldiers from a unit in Georgia ran away to Moscow, where they staged a demonstration in front of Moscow State University to protest their commander's sale of their labor to local collective farms for brandy." A year later, the list of those who were absent without leave was up to 2,500.[84] It is hard to have an effective military if a significant part of it has deserted or gone AWOL.

Corruption had long been a problem in the Soviet armed forces, but glasnost made it clear to the populace just how widespread it was. Take, for example, the issue of forced labor. It was traditional for Soviet officers to "loan" their troops to local farms as labor in return for a percentage of the crop, a strategy often indispensable for feeding troops.[85] The problem was that not all officers were honest. Many "loaned" out their troops and pocketed the proceeds. Then there were the officers who took kickbacks from parents in return for giving their sons the most desirable assignments. As one writer explained in the Party's main journal, "For the specific price or by means of patronage he filled many 'orders,' dealing with . . . conscripts and servicemen."[86]

There were also problems involving outright theft, especially of weapons. Between 1989 and 1990 weapons thefts increased 50 percent.[87] The problem was even worse in Afghanistan: "Soldiers readily stole ammunition, weapons, vehicle parts, and just about everything else in the Soviet Army's inventory to barter with Afghanis. Some types of Western consumer goods could be obtained this way, but drugs were in greater demand."[88] Indeed, according to another source, pilferage assumed a "mass character."[89] The most common "practice involves selling or trading military goods and equipment for drugs and food. Military goods stolen and bartered include boots, blankets, spare parts, tires, construction materials, gasoline, and even weapons and ammunition."[90] By 1990 the military prosecutor in Moscow reported a 40 percent increase in crime over the previous six months. Premeditated murders were up by 16.3 percent, serious bodily injury by 41.9 percent, and rape by 15.8 percent.[91] Overall, thefts rose "50 percent between 1989 and 1990."[92]

Glasnost also had a major impact on the evolution of Soviet military doctrine. As noted above, responsibility for this set of guidelines had been a monopoly of serving military officers since the mid-1960s. In 1987, at the same time Gorbachev was making it clear that he wanted a new, defensive military doctrine, two Soviet theorists, one a retired officer and the other a civilian academic, took on the General Staff. The authors, Valentin Larionov and Andrei Kokoshin, penned an article supposedly about the Battle of Kursk during World War II.[93] In this article the authors took a clear swipe at the high command's attitude toward the involvement of civilians in issues as complex as military doctrine by criticizing aspects of Soviet military doctrine:

> Rethinking historical experience, specifically the Battle of Kursk fought in the summer of 1943, when Moscow deliberately chose to assume a defensive posture—of its own free will, and not out of necessity. "This was the first case in the history of war and the military art, where the stronger side assumed the defensive. As is known, the classical formula for the military art ran as follows: defense is the strong type of military action; therefore the weaker side resorts to it." But the USSR was not the weaker part on this occasion; the Red Army "had no fewer than the Wehrmacht," and in a number of indicators was superior to it. [94]

In essence, the authors argued that despite significant differences the past and the present, the Battle of Kursk showed that a carefully prepared defense could be effective. Larionov and Kokoshin published another article in 1988 in which they differentiated among four types of defensive strategies. Without going into detail, the important point was that the authors were considered legitimate, knowledgeable commentators; a situation that forced the generals to respond. Yazov, for example, reacted to the first Kokoshin and Larionov piece by maintaining, "Defense, however, cannot defeat an aggressor." The point is not which side was right. Rather, the novelty was that the country's senior military officers were forced to listen to and deal with civilian analysts on an equal basis regarding one of the most sensitive aspects of Soviet military issues—doctrine.

Even more upsetting to the high command were the splits that began to appear in their own ranks. The idea of a senior military officer breaking ranks with his colleagues and siding with civilians had not occurred for a long time. In 1988, General Vladimir Lobov, first deputy chief of the General Staff, followed the standard military line: "The Soviet Union is building up its Armed Forces on the principles of adequate defense."[95] However, a month later, he criticized the Soviet military's tendency to overemphasize the role of surprise in modern warfare.[96] Another two months after that comment he blasted Stalin's strategy in World War II because of its overemphasis on the offensive. The result, he maintained, was a "deformation" of Soviet military strategy.[97] This was even true of the question of a professional military. For example, in early 1991, Colonel General Vladislav Achalov, a deputy defense minister, qualified his support for conscription by noting, "Many of the problems encountered by an officer, from a platoon commander to the minister of defense, will disappear in a professional army of their own accord."[98]

In August 1990 the Ministry of Defense sent a draft reform plan to Gorbachev, who sent it on to the Supreme Soviet, where it was expected to be adopted. Unfortunately, the draft would never be adopted because of the political turmoil that surrounded the Kremlin during 1991. From the standpoint of Soviet military culture, the worst aspect of the process was that the high command's monopoly over military doctrine had been broken. It now found itself in a reactive mode. The high command was forced to respond to Gorbachev's new policies or what the civilians said, and as a result the generals never were able to construct a coherent military doctrine. The 1991 war in the Persian Gulf further damaged the high command's control over the military doctrine debate. After all, the Iraqis had used Soviet doctrine and weapons and were beaten badly. Moscow had to come up with a new plan if it hoped to have a doctrine and weapons systems capable of matching those of the United States and its allies. In any case, the collapse of the USSR on December 25,

1991, ended the high command's efforts at military reform, at least under Gorbachev. They would have to try to maintain control of the process under a new president. The biggest problem however, was that the high command had a very restricted view of military reform. They believed it was simply a question of adjusting numbers. Not even the Afghan experience changed their thinking. "The experience of the Afghan War (1979–1989) did not alter the Soviet ground forces' preoccupation with large-scale conventional or tactical nuclear warfare. Counterinsurgency, peacekeeping, and the other tasks that Western armies now call 'Operations Other than War' did not feature in Soviet military education."[99] This failure to realize that the nature of war had changed would have the most serious implications for the Russian Army when it was faced with a war in Chechnya three years later.

In the meantime, the Soviet Army began to shrink in size. In 1986, the Soviet military stood at 5.13 million.[100] By 1991 it was down to 3.4 million, far more than the 500,000 unilateral reduction that Gorbachev had promised.[101] Despite these figures, Soviet sources claimed that the military itself did not know how many troops it had. According to *Pravda*,

> We are the sole army in the world which does not even know precisely how many types of "forces" it has; there are football and hockey and gymnastic and wrestling and shooting forces. I am far from the first to have engaged in this conversation, but there has been no progress whatsoever. The manual clearly names the army subdivisions: squad, platoon, company, battalion; nowhere does it record the right to the appearance of a such a subdivision, as for example, "soccer team" or "hockey team," whose chiefs carry the rank of colonel.[102]

Another form of internal control that the high command lost was the Communist Party structure. Indeed, it would turn out to be the critical structure holding the military together. In 1977 the so-called Brezhnev Constitution stipulated that the Soviet military was pledged to defend the USSR against external aggression and to safeguard the country's "socialist gains." In practice this meant helping preserve the Communist Party's monopoly on political power, which was guaranteed under Article Six of the Constitution.

Radical dissidents, led by Lopatin, argued that the Party should not play a favored role in the Army. Lopatin explained the situation in February 1990, "The CPSU's role must be characterized by a switch from directly supplanting state organs in defense leadership to implementing its own policy through servicemen who are Communists. This requires a resolute reduction in the number and staff of political organs, the introduction of a system of appointment by election, and reorientation of work toward elevating the servicemen's status and protection."[103] Lopatin was not calling for the total removal of the Party, but for a modification in its role. The Party's monopoly position should end, while the political organs would take on an educational, morale-boosting role.

Meanwhile, there was a discussion inside the Party on the proper role that it should play in the military and in society at large. A plenum of the Central Committee was held February 5–7 to draft a platform for the 28th Party Congress. The plenum called for a renunciation of the CPSU's monopoly of power and the creation of a presidency. The generals were strongly opposed. In voicing opposition to removal of Article Six from the Constitution, Moiseyev argued, "Many questions . . . arise in connection with Article Six of the USSR Constitution, and in particular with the role of political organizers in these circumstances."[104] Other generals sounded similar concerns. General Boris Gromov, the "hero" of Afghanistan, argued that the military could not "lie outside of politics," by which he meant the Communist Party.[105] General Akhromeyev, who was now an adviser to Gorbachev, argued that "a political struggle is under way in the country between those people who favor and those who oppose socialism. The opponents of socialism know that the main forces in their way are the Communist Party and the Armed Forces. That is why they are attacking them so virulently."[106]

The battle between the Ministry of Defense and the military reformers was finally settled when Gorbachev issue a decree in 1991 ordering the armed forces to create "military-political bodies: to carry out state-oriented educational tasks; the 'bodies,' according to the explanations subsequent to the president's announcement, were to operate in parallel with Communist Party military organizations already in place."[107] De-partyization had not become a reality, but the Party's monopoly over things such as morale, training, promotions, and political indoctrination had ended. The critical problem from the military's standpoint was that the Party's continued presence in the military was critical for cohesion. Given all of the ethnic problems that had arisen, the Party was one of the few structures holding the military together. Without the Party, the high command worried that the military would disintegrate further. This was a major reason why General Moiseyev had vigorously argued against the abolition of Article Six.

One of the more interesting developments that occurred as a result both of glasnost and the participation of the military in areas such as arms control, was the participation of senior military officers—for the first time—in political events. Admiral William Crowe, who was then chairman of the U.S. Joint Chiefs of Staff, invited Akhromeyev to visit the United States. When he came, Akhromeyev brought with him a large number of his senior deputies. As Crowe noted,

> You noticed, he [Akhromeyev] said, that I didn't call on my people very much. The reason, as he explained it, was that they had little understanding of the political world, either at home or abroad. They knew, for example, nothing about arms control or the Soviet-American relationship. Although they were four-star generals and admirals, their training had been like his, extremely one-sided. In retrospect he was not happy with his training. It hadn't, he thought, prepared him for higher responsibilities in political circles. He had to learn those skills on the job after he became Chief of Staff. That was what had moved him to bring his vice chiefs along. He wanted to open their eyes to an area of the world they knew so little about. "I thought these fellows ought to get out of town," as he put it.[108]

Akhromeyev realized that if he was to bring the Army into this new world of perestroika and glasnost they had to be familiar with how the civilian world or, in this case, the world of arms control and U.S.-Soviet relations operated. As time went on, the high command would become more and more involved in the political process.

USING THE SOVIET ARMY AGAINST THE SOVIET PEOPLE

In addition to his "chaotic" approach to reforming the country, Gorbachev alienated the military with his decision to use the military not once, but three times, against the Soviet populace and then blame them for carrying out his orders. The incidents occurred in the capital cities of three union republics: Georgia, Azerbaijan, and Lithuania.

Tbilisi, 1989

In April 1989, the military was ordered to send troops to Tbilisi, Georgia, in response to strikes and demonstrations that threatened to get out of control as the demonstrators began to number in the hundreds of thousands. Soldiers found themselves in action, and they reportedly used truncheons and sharpened shovels on civilians without warning. In the end, at least eighteen civilians were killed with untold others wounded. At a minimum the Army's standing in society was severely undermined. "The image of Soviet soldiers clubbing unarmed Georgian women to death, needless to say, was emotionally explosive for the public, not just in Georgia but in most other non-Russian national republics."[109] Then the political leadership, namely Gorbachev and other politicians, fought among themselves over who was responsible. In the end, the Army, in the form of Lieutenant General Igor Rodionov, who commanded Soviet forces during the operation in Tbilisi, was blamed. Rodionov tried to defend himself before the Congress of the People's Deputies, strongly denying that any soldiers had clubbed demonstrators to death using their shovels. He argued that the military had no alternative but to use force to protect itself from the demonstrators.

The most important result of the incident in Tbilisi and the subsequent report on the affair was that it infuriated the military. Why should the military willingly use force against civilians when the civilian leadership, who the military fervently believed endorsed their actions, ran and hid the moment it was time to accept responsibility?

The key institutional lesson drawn from the Tbilisi events was that it was detrimental to the prestige and integrity of the armed forces for the army to play a role in internal political disputes. This lesson came to be known as the "Tbilisi syndrome." Minister of Defense Yazov said that officers were psychologically "fettered" by the "Tbilisi syndrome," which caused hesitation in carrying out their orders and duties in emergency situations.[110]

Baku, 1990

In January 1990 the Soviet military again found itself called upon to use military force against Soviet civilians. The issue was relations between Azeris and Armenians that had led to conflict over the autonomous oblast of Nagorno-Karabakh, located in the republic of Azerbaijan. The oblast was populated almost entirely by ethnic Armenians, and they wanted to become part of Armenia. Gorbachev refused and soon thousands of demonstrators took to the streets. The Party leadership hesitated, not sure how to handle matters. Eventually the Army was called upon to intervene and restore order, especially in Baku, the capital of Azerbaijan. Shortly thereafter, an investigator arrived. He immediately informed Colonel Alexander Lebed that he was there to arrest the many soldiers who had committed "criminal" acts. Lebed sent the man packing and refused to turn over any of his troops. As a result of this event, the Army became convinced that it could not trust civilians. They would send them into action and then, if things did not turn out the way they wanted, they would blame the military.[111]

Vilnius, 1991

Finally, there were the events in Vilnius. Nationalism was becoming an increasing force for change throughout the Soviet Union, and this was especially true of Lithuania. On March 11, 1990, the Lithuanian parliament declared the republic's independence. Moscow declared the Lithuanian parliament's action illegal, and on April 18 Gorbachev began an economic blockade of the republic.

Next, the scheduled conscription call-up turned into a fiasco, especially in the Baltic region. Massive numbers of young men from the Baltic republics refused to serve, and local authorities protected them. As a consequence, Moscow announced on January 7, 1991, that airborne troops would be used to enforce conscription and warned local authorities not to interfere. Then on January 13, the National Salvation Committee, a front group for the Kremlin, accused Lithuanian nationalists of using radio and TV stations to engage in anti-Soviet propaganda. Contrary to what some analysts in the West believed, the paratroopers were not involved in the subsequent attack. Interior Ministry troops were dispatched to the TV station, where they confronted unarmed civilians who had surrounded the building. The troops removed the demonstrators, and, in the process, sixteen unarmed civilians were killed and many others were wounded. Once again, the civilians left the military in the lurch. The next day Gorbachev claimed that it was the local commander's fault. "It was a terrible political performance which severely damaged Gorbachev's legitimacy all across the political spectrum."[112] This was particularly true of the military, which was criticized even though it had not been directly involved. Where was the military's commander-in-chief when they needed him? The message to the troops was clear: Gorbachev did not care what happened to them.

MILITARY CULTURE

Given the conservative nature of Soviet military culture, it is not surprising that the high command disliked Gorbachev. It is perhaps ironic that officers like Akhromeyev initially agreed with Gorbachev on the need for a policy like perestroika. Akhromeyev understood only too well that if the USSR was to compete with the United States, it would have to shake-up its economy and that was what perestroika was intended to do. The problem, however, was that none of the high command realized where it would lead. They had no idea it would get out of control and radically upset their world.

To begin with, Gorbachev and other civilians interfered in that "Holy of Holies," military doctrine and force structure. Who were these civilians to tell the high command how to structure its forces? Not since Khrushchev had a civilian told the military to follow a specific doctrinal policy. As they saw it, Gorbachev showed little or no respect for their expertise and the many years they had spent as professional officers. As a result, they resisted, even if only passively. They gave the impression of going along and there were times when they had to, such as downplaying nuclear war. However, the generals stubbornly refused to give up their belief in a mass army, and for many reasons, Gorbachev did not push them to make a major change in this area. Their approach was to do the minimum necessary by reducing forces while avoiding the order to come up with a new conceptual approach to military doctrine and strategy.

What was just as bad, Gorbachev embarrassed the military. His firing of Sokolov and Koldunov in the aftermath of the Rust incident, followed by his removal of the "old guard" from senior positions in the military, upset many officers. They did not like having their dirty laundry washed in public. The appointment of Yazov as defense minister was especially upsetting. He was "jumped" over a number of officers senior to him, which was a clear violation of military culture, only because Gorbachev had been impressed by him during a visit to the Far East.

In particular, the high command detested Gorbachev's policy of glasnost. They objected to it for two reasons. First, glasnost undermined the generals' secretive approach to military matters. Publishing internal problems faced by the Army only made the situation worse: learning of the extent of problems such as *dedovshchina* convinced many young men to avoid military service. It also led to a drop in public respect for the armed forces, an organization that had hitherto been highly regarded. The generals could have better dealt with the problem by creating a meaningful NCO structure to replace the political officers who were gradually losing authority, but the idea of giving that kind initiative and responsibility to enlisted personnel went against Soviet military culture.

Democratization made no sense to the world of military culture either. The armed forces is a hierarchical organization. Trying to democratize it undercut the authority of senior officers. Relatively junior officers like Lopatin and his colleagues were now on the same level as the General Staff. They were trying to force the military to change its personnel and force structure. The generals gave in, at least insofar as they began to think of a contract system, but they did very little to implement it. They were opposed to the idea of a professional military.

And then there were budgetary cutbacks. The high command was now paying a heavy price for having long absorbed a large part of the country's budget. Georgii Arbatov explained that before Gorbachev, "The military and its attendant industries were given a completely free hand, carte blanche . . . and were prepared to only give the rest of us a few alms."[113] The problem for the high command was that it did not have the wherewithal to maintain the military it had while facing budget cuts. How could they make the kinds of changes Gorbachev demanded when he was taking money away from them? Gorbachev even went so far as to publish the size of the budget, something that certainly violated the military's penchant for secrecy.

CONCLUSION

To be fair to Gorbachev, he was living in a hurricane, trying to make fundamental changes in the way the USSR operated in an effort to save the country. The military was important only because he quickly realized that it was using up a significant part of the country's resources, and that if he hoped to restructure Soviet society he had to get control of it. He needed the money that the military gobbled up, and he needed to project a benign external image so that the rest of the world would not fear the Soviet Union while he worked to restructure it.

Gorbachev only had a bit more than six years to try to reform one of the most conservative organizations in the USSR. Nevertheless, the military believed that Gorbachev's leadership style left something to be desired. The high command believed he treated the military as it if were just another part of the system without realizing that it was unique in many ways. Changes introduced in the educational system have a significant impact on how students are taught, but the educational or medical or agricultural systems do not have the hierarchy, the cohesion, the unique culture, and the isolation from the rest of society that the military possesses. They also do not have a monopoly over the more complex forms of violence, as is the case in the Army. Soviet military culture worked on the basis of order and planning. It likes a predictable, stable world. It expects to be told what to do and what kind of resources it will have to complete the mission. From their perspective, the main impact Gorbachev's policies had was to create chaos and disorder. To the generals, it was almost as if Gorbachev had little or no idea what was happening in the military and, if he did, he decided to ignore it. It would take care of itself.

Many military men felt betrayed by Gorbachev. He was presiding over the collapse of the country. It made little difference whether he understood the military or not or whether he was responsible for it. He had both ignored and undermined the Soviet military as an institution. Gorbachev had failed to demonstrate leadership. The generals realized that the USSR was heading into a unknown world, and, in many cases, their understanding of politics was naive at best. But they expected order and direction. And without it, there was little likelihood that an organization as conservative as the Soviet Army would change. The result was that the high command's mind-set remained fixed in the pre-Gorbachev period rather than coming to grips with the new realities of the last years of the USSR.

Gorbachev's failure to court the Army would cost him dearly when conservatives unleashed a coup against him. The military would not fight against him, but it would soon become clear that in the struggle between Gorbachev and Boris Yeltsin, the armed forces preferred Yeltsin.

CHAPTER THREE
YELTSIN AND THE CREATION
OF THE RUSSIAN MILITARY,
SEPTEMBER 1991 – DECEMBER 1994

We have almost no combined units in the west and south, so it turned out.
Boris Yeltsin

Mikhail Gorbachev's idea of perestroika led the high command to believe that the reforms would lead to technological parity with the West. In time, however, it became clear that Gorbachev did not have a "plan" for improving the country's military. The generals and admirals believed that he was determined to dismantle the armed forces so that he would have sufficient funds to deal with problems in different sectors of the economy. Gorbachev's biggest problem was that he failed to understand that the Communist system could not be reformed. It was based on centralized control, and once that glue that held it together failed, the entire multiethnic system would collapse.

The generals were especially hard-hit by Gorbachev's "reforms." First, perestroika undermined the military-industrial complex on which the military depended. Second, glasnost had a disastrous impact on military cohesion and combat readiness. Third, the military was unaccustomed to the daily criticism now emanating from the civilian media. Public respect for the military dwindled. Most upsetting, many officers believed that the armed forces were on the verge of collapse, and the generals saw Gorbachev and his policies as part of the problem—not the solution. This opened the door for Boris Yeltsin, the president of the Russian republic. The military had limited contact with him, but what they saw of him was encouraging; they believed he would do a better job of protecting their interests.

YELTSIN'S LEADERSHIP STYLE

Yeltsin was stubborn, arbitrary, and unpredictable.[1] He was also impulsive and would make decisions on the spur of the moment. He was undisciplined and his behavior could be erratic. He was irascible and his primary—indeed, his total—focus was on his political power, on guarding his position. He also was not interested in creating new political institutions, and that applied to the military and its many problems. His goal was to destroy the old system, to make it impossible for a communist regime to ever take control of Russia again. As far as the Army was concerned, Yeltsin did not believe it would be needed, given the end of the Cold War.

Many of Yeltsin's personality traits conflicted with Russian military culture. His impulsiveness and unpredictability flew in the face of high command procedures. The generals required clear instructions on what the political leadership expected them to do and an assurance that resources would be there when the time came. Regarding military reform, the generals expected the president to tell them what he wanted from them, and assure them that he would support them both financially and politically. Generals are trained to keep "their eye on the ball," and they expected the president's word to count for something. If he asked them make plans to deal with event X, they would begin to do so. But Yeltsin's erratic and undisciplined behavior made that impossible.

YELTSIN ENTERS THE PICTURE

Yeltsin used the negotiations over the future configuration of the USSR to begin his campaign against Gorbachev. The military was to play a very important, if seemingly passive, role in Yeltsin's battle against the president, and he had been courting the generals for some time. It soon became obvious that while "Gorbachev remained the legal supreme commander until December 1991, in practice, Yeltsin was making the important decisions."[2] If anything, the January 1991 debacle in Vilnius, when the airborne troops were criticized for actions taken by the Interior Ministry forces, convinced the military that Gorbachev was untrustworthy. If any more proof was needed, the Union Treaty provided it. The treaty, which effectively ended the USSR as a sovereign entity, convinced many of the generals that Gorbachev had lost his senses. He was preparing to give the country away!

The Union Treaty negotiating process raised many questions that needed answers, including: Assuming the country split up, what powers would the central government retain? What guarantee was there that all of the republics would sign the agreement and abide by it? How would inter-republic disputes be resolved? What were the implications for the Soviet military? How could there be a unified military if the country was broken up into fifteen different republics? What about nuclear weapons? Who would be in charge?

Yeltsin made a special effort to widen his contacts within the military in 1991. For example, "On 31 May 1991, the presidential candidate Yeltsin toured the Tula region with [General Pavel] Grachev and dispensed a mixture of promises and actual gifts such as wrist watches to soldiers he met including drivers."[3] He also promised to pay for a new 500-unit apartment complex for the Tula division's officers.[4] Then for the June 12 Russian presidential election he selected Colonel Alexander Rutskoi, a genuine military hero based on his service in Afghanistan, as his running mate. In the process, Yeltsin convinced the Army that, unlike Gorbachev and his chaotic, confusing approach to dealing with the country, he was a decisive leader who would pay careful attention to the armed forces and their many problems. Toward that end, he worked hard to find senior officers he could trust to run the Army. "Yeltsin's solution was to put the army under the command of people he trusted," writes David Betz, "and to grant the military considerable autonomy in coping with the hard times from its own means as it saw fit."[5] He worked to develop friendships, especially with the paratroopers and their commander, General Pavel Grachev, a man who would play an important role during the August 1991 coup.

Then Yeltsin flew to Estonia during the Baltic crisis and criticized Gorbachev's handling of events in that region. According to Yeltsin in July 1991, he specifically asked Grachev, "Pavel Sergeyevich . . . if our lawfully elected government in Russia were ever to be threatened—a terrorist act, a coup, efforts to arrest the leaders—could the military be relied upon?"[6] Much to Yeltsin's relief, Grachev said he was prepared to play a critical role if civil disturbances broke out in the Moscow area. Yeltsin then announced that he opposed the use of Russian military personnel against civilians outside of Russia proper. Yeltsin also formed an alliance with retired military officers who could serve as liaisons to the Army. Thus while the military was not necessarily on Yeltsin's side, it was at least neutral toward him, while it had serious doubts about Gorbachev's leadership ability and his willingness to stand up for the army in a crisis. Yeltsin had done his homework.

Meanwhile, Yeltsin and Gorbachev were at odds. Yeltsin had become a member of the Congress of People's Deputies for the Russian Soviet Federated Socialist Republic (RSFSR), and in May 1990 he was elected chairman of the new RSFSR Supreme Soviet. He proceeded to attack Gorbachev's policies, and in February 1991 he went so far as to demand Gorbachev's resignation. Yeltsin's supporters also organized demonstrations against Gorbachev. Gorbachev was being pushed into a corner. On the one hand, he had appointed a number of conservative officials to senior positions in the Soviet government, individuals who urged him to crack down. He had the option of calling in the military and/or security services to restore order. What if he did and there was widespread resistance? Did Gorbachev want that on his conscience?

YELTSIN, THE ARMY, AND THE COUP

The military leadership was in a quandary. [7] In an effort to defuse the ethnic crisis that was worsening daily, Gorbachev had proposed the Union Treaty. It would have provided the republics with considerably more independence while maintaining a modicum of central control. A meeting involving the leaders of the fifteen republics was held at a Soviet government dacha at Novo Ogarevo, located near Moscow, and an agreement was reached on April 23, 1991. As a result, it appeared that Gorbachev's efforts to keep the country together would be successful.

Meanwhile, it was becoming almost impossible to get recruits from the republics to serve in the military outside of Russia unless they were Russians, and there were even problems with draftees inside Russia. There was not much chance of maintaining a viable Army absent the hundreds of thousands of recruits needed to man it. Some of the republics were even demanding the creation of their own militaries. To make matters even worse, as noted above, the Communist Party's special authority (i.e., Article Six of the Constitution) had been abolished.

The conservatives, led by KGB Chief Vladimir Kryuchkov, Defense Minister Dmitry Yazov, and Interior Minister Boris Pugo, tried to have a bill enacted in the "lame duck Union Parliament to enhance the powers of Union Prime Minister [Valentin] Pavlov."[8] Gorbachev ignored them. Meanwhile, all three men pressed the president to crack down, imploring him to declare a state of emergency. Gorbachev continued to ignore them, and on August 4 he left Moscow for his annual summer vacation at Foros in the Crimea. The Union Treaty was scheduled to be signed on August 20. But conservative Communists were not about to stand still and permit the USSR to collapse.

The conservatives were not only convinced that they had to act to prevent the signing of the new Union Treaty, they "believed they had the power to do so."[9] After all, Yazov was on their side, and all the other side had was "Democratic Russia and its allies [which] were unwieldy, undisciplined, and unsophisticated."[10] Given the accumulated military grievances against Gorbachev, it seemed likely that the military would come out in strong support of the August 1991 coup plotters. Yet they refused, for a number of reasons. To begin with, the Soviet and Russian military has a long tradition of staying out of politics. The Soviet military had been through decades of indoctrination, political socialization that emphasized the importance of civilian control. To take only one example, General Albert Makashov, commander of the Volga-Urals Military District, tried to get the Army involved in the plot by using the Communist Party, but he was unsuccessful. His colleagues refused to rally to his side. As noted in the preceding chapter, the Soviet military was not only relatively autonomous, it was also apolitical. Individual officers might take an interest in politics, but the to the vast majority, politics was *terra incognito*.[11] What the military really wanted was a politician who would take charge and act decisively.

The military was also astounded at the ineptness shown by the coup plotters. Military officers are known for their planning prowess; they regularly plan operations down to the second. In this case, however, they could only shake their heads in wonderment at the incompetence of the plotters: the failure to seize Yeltsin at his dacha outside Moscow, the fact that a number of the plotters were drunk part of the time, and their inability to ensure control of the military even with the involvement of Defense Minister Yazov. Marshal Yazov acted in a very unmilitary manner because he seemed unable to make up his mind about what to do during the coup. Military officers are taught to be decisive.

The combination of poor planning and Yeltsin's efforts to woo the Army paid off when the coup was launched on August 19, 1991. It ensured that important segments of the high command were not prepared to support the plotters. For example, officers like Grachev, Alexander Lebed, Boris Gromov (who controlled Interior Ministry troops), and Marshal Yevgenii Shaposhnikov (who commanded the Russian Air Force) were expected to play crucial roles. Without their cooperation, the coup could not—and did not—succeed.

In the end, the most valuable role played by these officers was to ensure that the Army did *not* become involved. In addition to Interior Ministry troops, Grachev and Lebed were expected to ensure that the airborne forces were ready and available at the designated time, while Shaposhnikov's job was to make sure that the troops needed in Moscow (including non-airborne forces) were airlifted to the capital.

On Monday August 19 Yazov told his senior officers that Gorbachev was incapacitated and that, as a result, a State Committee on the State of Emergency (GKChP) had been formed to seize power until the president was healthy enough to resume his position. In the meantime, Yazov warned his colleagues that public disorder was possible. Therefore, the military had to be in a position to "maintain order" if problems arose. He summoned Colonel General Nikolai Kalinin, the Moscow military district commander, General Vladislav Achalov, and Grachev, "ordering them to move their troops into Moscow. Kalinin was to bring units from the Tamanskaya and Kantemirovskaya divisions, Achalov was to assign an airborne unit to cordon off the Ostankino television station, and Grachev was to bring the airborne regiments from Tula, Kostroma, and Ryazan."[12] The generals' primary task was to ensure that troops were in their proper positions. He added, in fact emphasized, that force was to be avoided at all costs. Accordingly, the troops began to move into position. Yazov believed that a show of force—armored units on the streets of Moscow—would intimidate Muscovites. He was in for a surprise.

That afternoon, General Valentin Varennikov joined a group sent to the Crimea by the Emergency Committee to confront Gorbachev. The president was told to join the GKChP or resign. He refused and claimed that General Varennikov " 'behaved in the crudest manner' and rebuked him saying, 'The people are not a battalion of soldiers to whom you can issue the command right turn or left turn, march and they will do as you tell them.'"[13]

Meanwhile, preparations went ahead for an attack on the White House, home of the Russian parliament. According to the plan,

> the Alpha unit's "A" group was to try to infiltrate the White House, and, if that failed, to blast its way in, followed by a second, or "B" group. The second group was to identify, bring out, and document those people detained. These groups totaled 260 men plus a reserve of 200. Additional KGB forces were assigned blocking roles. A MVD political unit was to help clear an approach path to the building for the KGB elements. The deputy minister of the MVD, Colonel General Boris Gromov, was to have MVD firefighting units available in case of a conflagration. Finally, airborne troops were to wall off the White House at some distance from its perimeter and also to prepare to break through into the ground floor in the event the Alpha unit failed or had trouble.[14]

From a military standpoint, the main flaw in this plan was the lack of coordination. Three different military bureaucracies were involved, and they were not talking to each other. To make matters worse, the troops involved had no idea what they were doing. It was standard Soviet practice for political officers to carefully prepare troops for normal operations, let alone something as sensitive as a coup, but they were not doing their job. It was a recipe for disaster.

Yeltsin was fully alert to what was transpiring around Moscow. In order to counter the plotters, he contacted key military figures who themselves were worried about the civilian casualties that a coup would inevitably produce. On Monday morning he reached Marshal Shaposhnikov through an intermediary. Shaposhnikov made it clear that he did not support the coup and began to delay carrying out orders. He even called his air force commanders around the country telling them to cancel the alert that Yazov had ordered. He later spoke with Grachev and informed him that he would not support the coup. Grachev said he too was opposed and added that he had spoken with Boris Gromov who would likewise not support the coup. Finally, Yazov decided to call off the assault on the White House, where Yeltsin and his supporters were holed up. Later that day, Shaposhnikov called Yazov and asked him to go further by denouncing the coup. He was supported by several other senior officers. After thinking matters over, Yazov informed the GKChP that he was withdrawing the military's support for the coup.

Much to his chagrin, Gorbachev, who was under house arrest at his dacha in the Crimea, did not play a significant role in the events in Moscow. In fact, in many ways he became an afterthought. It was Yeltsin who was in charge. For example, several tanks moved in front of the White House, and their crews and their officers came over to his side. Yeltsin then climbed on one of the tanks and made his famous speech of defiance, announcing that neither he nor others defending the White House were prepared to give in to the coup plotters.

Still, the military faced a dilemma. Which order should they follow? This is always a critical question for military professionals. When informed of the problem, Yeltsin responded by issuing a formal decree (*ukaz*) stating that the GKChP was illegal and that as the popularly elected president of Russia, he was taking temporary command of the Army—until Gorbachev returned.[15] While this decree satisfied some officers, others supported the GKChP, believing that it had the best chance of restoring order in this beleaguered country. The result was potentially very dangerous. The officer corps was split and it could have led to a civil war. However, the Tbilisi Syndrome remained alive and well. The armed forces did not want to again be blamed for causing civilian casualties, therefore they did not do anything.

Meanwhile, Yeltsin was focused on power. He realized that the best way to destroy Gorbachev's authority was to further undermine Soviet state structures.

After all, Gorbachev was president of the USSR, and if the USSR could be destroyed, then he, as president of the Russian republic, would be in a much stronger position. As a result, on August 20 he issued a decree giving Russia control over the USSR's economy as of January 1, 1992. He followed this up with another decree that stated that Russia would henceforth pay Soviet forces stationed on Russian territory. This move was a stroke of genius, because soldiers were beginning to worry about where their next meal was coming from. At least one politician cared about them! The decree also noted that Russia would set up a military of its own, although it did not specify a date. To add insult to injury, on August 22 Yeltsin outlawed the Communist Party and seized all of its assets. There was little left of the state and the party Gorbachev was supposed to be leading.

As the coup was collapsing, people began to wonder about the fate of the generals, like Mikhail Moiseyev, chief of the General Staff, who had supported the coup. Yeltsin again showed himself to be a master politician. Instead of sending them off to jail and creating resentment among the officer corps, he issued Decree No. 64, which essentially stated that they would no longer be allowed to serve in the armed forces. An investigation into the actions of all senior officers was carried out by a commission headed by General Konstantin Kobets. As a result, "thirty generals from the high command, nine deputy ministers of defense, ten military district and fleet commanders, eight heads of major [Ministry of Defense] departments, and three other lower-ranking commanders, and 316 additional generals who actively supported and promoted the coup were retired."[16]

Given the gravity of the situation, Yeltsin could have locked up the people who had supported the GKChP and thrown away the keys. After all he, not the parliament, was now in charge of military affairs. However, he chose to be lenient. His leniency no doubt pleased many of the senior officers who understood how their colleagues ended up on the wrong side in this very confusing situation. Yeltsin's action also brought a new, younger generation of generals to the fore. He would rebuild the Army by putting officers loyal to him in positions of authority. Yeltsin wanted a cadre of generals he could count on in a crisis. He was well aware that if they owed their positions to him, they would be more likely to support him. Meanwhile, on December 5 he repeated his earlier pledge to pay the salaries of Soviet military personnel, even those located outside of Russia.

Not everyone was happy with Yeltsin's treatment of the military. Some thought he was too lenient. For example, Vladimir Lopatin, a member of the Supreme Soviet, remained an outspoken opponent of the military high command.

He had driven Yazov to distraction with his call for a militia-based military[17] and he had continued his efforts to "democratize" the high command. He maintained that nothing had changed under Yeltsin. He also argued that he had information that many of the generals who had remained in their positions or were advanced to take the places of those who were dismissed had supported the coup. He further claimed that, contrary to Shaposhnikov's order, political activity (i.e., Communist Party activity) was continuing inside the military. He even went so far as to compare Yeltsin's relations with the Army to Gorbachev's. Thus he claimed that the *old* administration was still in charge despite the change of faces. For practical purposes, Shaposhnikov and Yeltsin ignored him, just as they did the parliament in general.

Shaposhnikov had a very difficult task. He was trying to hold the Army together while the country was falling apart. He understood only too well the implications of serious splits in the military. He was counting on political leadership to help him. Shaposhnikov said that Yeltsin was decisive: it was clear where he stood. But Gorbachev not only frustrated him, he flip-flopped all over the place. For example, on December 8 Gorbachev phoned Shaposhnikov several times asking if he had heard anything about Yeltsin's discussions in Belarus with other republic leaders concerning the future of the Soviet Union. At one point, Gorbachev warned Shaposhnikov not to "meddle" in political matters. Shaposhnikov was growing tired of Gorbachev and his indecisive manner. When Gorbachev called the next day, Shaposhnikov took the unprecedented step (for a serving military officer) of telling off his commander-in-chief.[18] Then, on December 11, Gorbachev and Yeltsin spoke before senior military commanders. As Shaposhnikov recalled, Gorbachev "did not say anything of substance, and at the end, expressed his regret that he had not paid more attention to the Armed Forces. I thought to myself after his appearance on television. Wouldn't it have been better if he had retired earlier—after his return from Foros?"[19] Yeltsin had won the Army over to his side, after all he controlled the purse strings. Gorbachev would not have been in a position to support the military even if he had been decisive. Meanwhile, the key question facing Yeltsin was simple: Would he deliver on his promises? Senior military officers were counting on him.

Despite their preference for Yeltsin over Gorbachev, Soviet generals and admirals worried that his actions would split the military into fifteen different entities. They were beginning to worry that he was not as determined to keep the USSR together as they had wished. On the other hand, the creation of national guard units might not be all bad. It could relieve them of future responsibility for internal events such as those in Tbilisi, Baku, and Vilnius. What the generals really feared, however, was that the national guard units would quickly become separate armies. They did not intend to sit by and watch everything they had given their lives to fall apart. Officers like Shaposhnikov, whom Gorbachev had appointed to replace Yazov as defense minister, believed that if the country hoped to remain a significant military power, to be able to project military force and protect itself, all of the republics must live together under the country's nuclear umbrella and keep their air defense forces unified. The same was true of the Army. Yeltsin publicly agreed: "I firmly declare that along with these formations, unified Union Armed Forces must exist . . . Any division of strategic arms among the republics is completely out of the question."[20] Unfortunately, as often happens in politics when the situation is very fluid, events took on a momentum of their own. Ukraine soon announced it was setting up its own military. It was obvious to the Soviet military leadership that this was just the first of a number of similar actions by the other republics. As a result, it was becoming clear that the USSR's days were numbered, and that also applied to the Soviet Army and those who served in its ranks. For example, on September 6, the State Council, a body created to manage the political transition from the dying Union to some new form of inter-republican cooperation, recognized the three Baltic republics as independent countries. Two weeks later, Gorbachev ordered Shaposhnikov to discharge all draftees from Lithuania, Estonia, and Latvia.

While republics like Ukraine were setting up their own armed forces, Soviet military personnel were becoming stateless. If they remained in the military in Ukraine, they would be forced to become citizens of Ukraine. But if they left Ukraine and moved back to Russia, they were not guaranteed a place in the Russian Army (which did not yet exist) and what would they do about housing?[21]

Leaders also had to decide what Moscow should do with the Soviet military machine. Who was in charge? Who should the country's officers obey? Should they listen to Shaposhnikov, who was head of the "joint" post-Soviet forces? He was in Moscow, but the troops might be in Uzbekistan or Armenia. What should be done about the hundreds of thousands of soldiers stationed outside of Russia? What about their weapons systems? After all they belonged (in theory at least) to the joint Soviet armed forces. In October, Shaposhnikov went before the State Council to argue that it was becoming increasingly difficult to keep the Soviet military together as a unified military. Then "at the State Council's November 4 meeting, he cautioned that unilateral actions by the republics were destabilizing the armed forces and urged the presidents to adopt a five-year plan to govern joint military reform and reconstruction."[22] Nothing meaningful was accomplished as the internal situation in the USSR continued to deteriorate.

THE MILITARY'S PROBLEMS WITH YELTSIN

Despite their initially positive attitude toward Yeltsin, based on his apparent concern for the armed forces and willingness to help the generals and admirals make the transition from the communist to the post-communist world, the country's senior military leadership quickly decided that he was not interested in them or the Army. Yeltsin's only concern was to keep the political support of the generals and, to that end, he lavished praise on them. He needed their loyalty in case he had to use them to stay in power, as occurred in 1993. He would promise them almost anything. Delivering on his promises, however, was another matter.

Yeltsin was convinced that the Cold War was over and that the threat facing the USSR had diminished. Who was going to attack Russia? Why worry about Russia as a superpower? Its biggest problem was that it might collapse internally. As a result, scarce funds had to be spent on social and economic problems. The military could wait. In the meantime, Russian military superpower status would lose its significance. The Kremlin had nuclear weapons, and Yeltsin believed they were sufficient to deter any potential foe.

Because he was primarily focused on keeping the generals on his side, Yeltsin was not ready to force them to come to grips with the realities of the post-Cold War era. He permitted them to continue to live in their make-believe land of superpowers. Major changes in military force structure or personnel policies would cost considerable money, something he wanted to avoid. While the generals complained—sometimes publicly—of the military's dire straits and even openly opposed him on issues such as invading Chechnya, the idea of a military coup never seemed to be under consideration. Some generals became politically active, but they did so as individuals, not as an interest group. Efforts to build a coalition of current and former military officers consistently failed.

The result of these two different trends was that the generals and admirals were left alone. They continued to focus on fighting a war against NATO, one that they believed would involve masses of soldiers as in World War II. Meanwhile, it was becoming obvious to the rest of the world that the army of the future would inevitably be smaller than the Soviet Army, but the Russian generals disagreed, maintaining that conflicts would continue to be tank heavy, backed up by massive numbers of reserve troops. Psychologically, the generals were still tied to the past.

Permitting the generals to live in the past, however, exacerbated problems. The budget was cut severely, while the high command refused to reconceptualize their strategy. They recognized the need for military reform—or at least paid it lip service—but they resisted a significant modification of force structure, strategy, or operational procedures. The budgetary cuts Yeltsin imposed on the Army would have driven any senior officer to distraction, but in this case, the high command would have fared better had it been more pragmatic and willing to plan for a considerably smaller, more flexible, and highly maneuverable military. In the long run, the problems that the country's generals faced when the Soviet Union collapsed were nothing compared to the situation the armed forces would find themselves in under Yeltsin.

The decision to scrap Article Six of the Constitution put the Main Political Administration (MPA) in a difficult situation. Shaposhnikov's view was simple: abolish the Party and the MPA. Indeed, he believed all political activities should be eliminated within the military, and the Army should be apolitical. He emphatically wanted to get rid of the party. "In fact, the day before he was appointed, he suggested to the assembled MoD [Ministry of Defense] military collegium—as it advised Moiseyev on what to tell Gorbachev now that the attempted coup was over—that 'de-partyization' should be recommended. Moiseyev agreed, but General [Nikolai] Shlyaga, the former MPA chief objected, rebuking Shaposhnikov, 'You are a young man, still hot tempered.'"[23]

Shaposhnikov was not alone. Other officers had openly quit the Party. "The Air Force had the worst record in this regard."[24] Shaposhnikov pushed a reluctant Gorbachev to get rid of the Communist Party's monopoly in the military. One of the most outspoken opponents to eliminating the Party was Colonel General Albert Makashov, the aforementioned commander of the Volga-Ural Military District. As early as June 1990 he had angrily told Gorbachev that Communists in the army were totally opposed to getting rid of the Party. Gorbachev also did not believe the Party should be removed from the military. Nevertheless, under pressure from Shaposhnikov and others, on August 30, 1991, he issued a decree prohibiting political activities in the Army.[25] The problem, however, was what to do with the thousands of political officers in the military. Many of them knew nothing but political work. No one knew what the MPA was supposed to do now. Some believed that it could be used to fight corruption, crime, and problems like *dedovshchina*. But others feared that it could also be resurrected as an arm of the Communist Party at some time in the future.

The generals also feared anarchy. They had seen what happened when Article Six was removed and the MPA began to lose influence. Like it or not, the political officers carried out an important function in the military because of their direct work with soldiers.

Yeltsin was sympathetic to Shaposhnikov's pleas and on September 1, 1991, he issued Order No. 418, liquidating the MPA. According to Shaposhnikov, a commission was created to evaluate those individuals serving as political officers with an eye toward whether or not they should remain in the military in other capacities. Line officers were overjoyed. As Shaposhnikov explained it, the problem with the MPA was that no one ever knew what its task was. It depended on the individual political officer. In one case, the political officer operated as the commander's deputy and did an excellent job of supporting him and taking care of the troops. In another instance, however, he attempted to politicize matters and tried to ignore commanders.[26] Two former political officers were then given the responsibility of evaluating 92,500 political officers to determine which ones could work in a non-partisan environment. Officers who were deemed loyal and competent were asked to stay on in the Army. Those who were not were given their walking papers. In the end, about half of the MPA personnel were retained. "It chopped the group of MPA generals down from 345 to about twenty."[27] If they were going to remain in the military, they would have to become professional, competent officers able to perform the duties of a line officer. Most of them joined the new department of military, educational, and personnel affairs. They were supposed to work with soldiers to improve morale and help personnel as psychologists and as personnel and educational officers. Unfortunately, even now no one knew what these officers were supposed to do. The Army would pay a heavy price in coming months and years for this ambiguity. For all practical purposes, these officers would have only minimal contact with the average soldier and therefore be of almost no use in helping maintain morale, discipline, and order.

Defense Minister Yazov had set up officer assemblies on August 1, 1989, as a way of paying lip service to Gorbachev's policy of democratization. These were regular meetings where the high command would listen to the officers' complaints and suggestions and then decide which ones to implement. The problem, however, was that like most "democratic" institutions in the USSR, officer assemblies had more to do with show than reality. The overwhelming majority of those who took part were generals, personnel not likely to create problems for the high command.

After the fall of the Soviet Union, however, there was renewed pressure to hold more officer assemblies. But this time the push was for a more democratic forum, one where the real concerns of officers would be heard, considered, and acted upon. Shaposhnikov agreed, and on January 17, 1992, 5,000 officers who were especially concerned about the future of the Soviet armed forces descended on Moscow. When it was Yeltsin's opportunity to speak, he played to the officers' fears, arguing that while there would be changes in the defense budget, his administration planned to focus its attention on personnel problems. As an example, he announced that his government would build 120,000 apartments for officers. As he explained, "For the first time in the entire history of our Army in Russia, a people-oriented military budget was adopted." Sixty percent of the budget would go to personnel, while 40 percent was intended for hardware.[28] While there were some disgruntled voices, Yeltsin had appealed to the officers using the issues that concerned them the most—their futures and personal lives—and pledged to take care of them.

Shaposhnikov had a problem when it came to dealing with Yeltsin. First, he made it clear that he was opposed to the use of the military against civilians. He stated that he would oppose soldiers firing on civilians as long as he was defense minister: "I will never permit our Armed Forces to be used against its people either to settle inter-ethnic or political disputes."[29] Second, conscious of the past, Shaposhnikov told Yeltsin that any orders involving the use of the military against civilians should be in writing. Third, Yeltsin was likely well aware that the general also would have opposed his budget cuts—and would have said so publicly and loudly. Needless to say, Yeltsin did not want such a strong leader for the armed forces. He wanted someone he could control. Shaposhnikov was not that officer.

In the meantime, Yeltsin took notice of Pavel Grachev. Like most senior officers, Grachev favored Yeltsin over Gorbachev. Yeltsin's hard work to win their favor was beginning to pay off. Yeltsin had given the generals, including Grachev, the impression that he intended to "take care" of them in the future. Second, Yeltsin also came across as a man who was decisive and courageous. While some probably thought that Yeltsin's standing on a tank in front of the White House to oppose the coup was grandstanding, the generals respected him for his courage. Not knowing what the military or internal security troops might do, he had the backbone to take a stand—literally.

Grachev was a different kind of officer. First, he was only 44 years old, and he was the commander of the country's elite airborne troops. He was a decorated hero from the Afghan War. The problem was that it was one thing to command the airborne troops; it would be something very different to run an organization as complex as the Russian Army, especially in light of the country's almost total lack of political institutions and money. Most important from Yeltsin's standpoint, however, he appeared to be a loyal officer, one who would carry out whatever orders Russia's president might give, even if they were distasteful.

CREATION OF THE RUSSIAN ARMY

By March 1992 it was clear that the Commonwealth of Independent States was leading nowhere. It was a confederation of states, but from a military standpoint, Yeltsin and the Russian high command recognized that it was time to create Russia's own armed forces. But how? The Soviet military's weapons and personnel were spread all over the former USSR. On March 16 Yeltsin signed an order, On the Ministry of Defense of the RF [Russian Federation] and the Armed Forces of the RF. This led, on April 4, to the establishment of a State Commission, under the leadership of Colonel General Dmitry Volkogonov, that was tasked with preparing the ground for the creation of a Russian Army.

On May 7, Yeltsin signed the orders that officially created the Russian Army. Shaposhnikov suddenly found himself without a job, as the Soviet Army no longer existed. Meanwhile, Grachev was promoted to army general, and became first deputy defense minister—and acting defense minister. Two weeks later, Grachev was named Russia's first minister of defense.

To put it simply, Grachev inherited a mess. As one source put it, "The Air Defense had lost the majority of its bases and the army had lost most of its first line troops and weapons—up to 70 percent of its latest weapons, according to General Grachev."[30] To make matters worse, many of the units resembled "Swiss cheese because of all the holes there are after soldiers simply went back to their home countries in the Caucasus or Central Asia."[31] And the military was not happy. The Army was becoming frustrated. Alexander Lebed, at that time commander of the 14th Army in the so-called Trans-Dniester Republic, a secessionist enclave of Moldova, blasted the Yeltsin regime when he noted, "It's time to stop fooling around in the swamp of little-understood politics . . . "It is time to get to work; the interests of the state must be defended."[32]

One of the first issues to face the Russians after the creation of the Russian Army was the question of who was in charge—Yeltsin or parliament? The issue came to a head in the drafting of the Law on Defense. Parliament wanted to play an equal role to make sure that Yeltsin would not use the military against it. Toward this end, it focused on personnel appointments, arguing that it should have veto power over the appointment of senior officers. It refused to pass the law on defense until Yeltsin agreed to its position on personnel appointments. As Barylski noted, parliament "granted the president the power to nominate the minister of defense, the chief of the General Staff, the deputy ministers of defense, and the service and territorial commanders; *however, they were to be appointed only with the consent of Parliament.*"[33]But Yeltsin ignored actions by parliament that he did not like. As a result, he removed the words in italics from the document, but the Duma would not budge. The final bill was signed into law on September 24, 1992, and stated that the president had to get parliament's consent prior to such appointments. While he was opposed to this language, Yeltsin was not concerned, because he had already made the key appointments. This issue would be revisited in 1993 when a new constitution was adopted.

THE MILITARY AND THE CONFRONTATION WITH PARLIAMENT

By early 1992 it was becoming obvious that a major struggle for power was underway between Yeltsin and the RSFSR Supreme Soviet. Ruslan Khasbulatov, the speaker of the Supreme Soviet, was determined to make parliament into the center of power in Moscow at the expense of the president. The problem, however, was not just the jockeying for power. The increasing conflict was also a result of the "ignorance on each side of how to be a civilized counterweight to the other," as Shevtsova noted.[34] Yeltsin made a few concessions to parliament, but they did not satisfy the legislators. Then the Seventh RSFSR Congress of People's Deputies, meeting in December 1992, took a number of steps aimed at limiting Yeltsin's authority. Yeltsin was furious and appealed to the nation, arguing that he could not work with the parliament. He maintained that the only way to resolve the dispute over how much power the two sides should have was by a referendum: "Give the people a way to demonstrate which side they trust more—the president or the parliament."[35] Finally the two sides agreed to hold a referendum on April 11, 1993. The parliament would draft the constitution, but the president had the right to make changes before it became public. If the two sides could not agree on a draft constitution, the competing versions would be put before the Russian public.

By the beginning of 1993 it was clear that Yeltsin and parliament were still far apart, and neither side was ready to compromise. This raised an obvious question: What would the military do in the event of a showdown? When the issue was raised in late February, Grachev made it very clear that as far as he was concerned, "I will not permit the incidents that occurred previously and were permitted—I am talking about drawing the armed forces into a war against their own people."[36] Fearful that a clash between the two sides was just a matter of time, Grachev organized an officers' assembly on March 5. He went out of his way to argue that the military would stay out of politics and that he, as defense minister, would do everything possible to keep it aloof from the political struggle. As he put it, "Any attempts to appeal to the Armed Forces in the political struggle are criminal and are fraught with the most serious consequences."[37] The problem, however, was that, like it or not, the military was facing a highly unstable situation. The lines of authority between the legislative and executive were not only unclear, they were fluid. While Yeltsin followed up on Grachev's comment by stating that he had issued orders to the military *not* to become involved in internal politics, the reality was that the temptation for either—or both—sides to try to make use of the Army when crunch time came would be irresistible.

The battle between Yeltsin and the parliament soon worsened. On March 12 parliament took back the special powers that Yeltsin had been given on October 1991. In practice, this meant that he could no longer legally issue decrees that had the force of law. He would have to have parliament's approval. Then parliament rejected Yeltsin's plan to hold a referendum on April 25. Yeltsin responded by stating that he would go ahead with the referendum despite parliament's opposition and that his decrees no longer required parliamentary approval; in other words, he was in charge. The Constitutional Court ruled Yeltsin's action unconstitutional, which led Khasbulatov to suggest that Yeltsin should be impeached. Briefly it appeared that Khasbulatov and Yeltsin had worked out a compromise, but it was rejected by the parliament. Yeltsin then began to consider the possibility of dissolving parliament. In the end a compromise "of sorts" was reached. The April referendum would be held, but it would contain four questions: Do you support the president? Do you support the government's social and economic policies? Should there be early elections for the presidency? Should there be early elections for parliament?

When the referendum was held, "58.7 percent expressed confidence in the president, and 53 percent supported his social and economic policies. Only 31.7

percent of the voters favored early presidential elections, while 43.1 percent of voters favored early parliamentary elections."[38] It was a victory for Yeltsin.

Throughout the battle between president and parliament, Vice President Alexander Rutskoi and Yeltsin were constantly at odds. He was the only politician in Russia who came close to Yeltsin in popularity, which made Yeltsin see him as a threat. How could Yeltsin get rid of the general without alienating the military at the same time?

Yeltsin made his move on May 7. The Constitution gave the president the right to determine the vice president's duties, so Yeltsin announced that henceforth Rutskoi would not have any assigned duties. He was a vice president in name only. To add insult to injury, on September 1, Yeltsin had Rutskoi locked out of his Kremlin office, claiming that the vice president was under investigation for corruption. Then on September 21, Yeltsin issued Presidential Decree No. 1400, which dissolved parliament and introduced presidential rule. He also announced that elections for new representatives, as well as to approve a new constitution, would be held December 11–12. The parliament responded by swearing in Rutskoi as Russia's president. On September 22 weapons were given to individuals who were prepared to defend the parliament building, known as the White House. A confrontation was now inevitable. On September 25 militia and Interior Ministry troops moved into position to blockade the parliamentary building.

The Army was in a position to determine the outcome of the standoff between Yeltsin and parliament. But before examining how the conflict unfolded, some background is necessary. In February 1993 the parliament had passed the Law on Military Service, an action strongly opposed by the high command. The law not only cut obligatory military service from two years to eighteen months, it also introduced a wide variety of exemptions that would cut down the number of young men eligible to be drafted and would have a very negative impact on the Army.

Yeltsin, meanwhile, was playing a duplicitous game. While he made no effort to stop the deferments, he continued to woo the Army. As Stephen Foye pointed out, Yeltsin took advantage of a meeting with the high command in June to "praise them for restoring control, rebuilding cohesion, and raising morale in the army."[39] Yeltsin met again with Army leaders in June to discuss the situation in the Army. Yeltsin gave them a pep talk. He openly discussed problems and prospects for the military, telling them, "The Russian armed forces were achieving organizational viability within their new contours. The tremendous change from the unitary armed forces of the Soviet Union to some fifteen different national armies took place under extremely difficult conditions."[40] The generals appreciated the attention and respect Yeltsin appeared to be showing them.

Well aware of the possibility of a clash between parliament and Yeltsin, Grachev called his deputies together on September 20, one day before Yeltsin suspended parliament. While no specific orders were issued, the commanders were warned of the impending crisis and told to be ready to do whatever was necessary. Then, in an effort to distance the military from the use of force in the event of civil unrest, Grachev assembled his deputies on September 22. He went out of his way to make the point that the military would not get involved in the dispute between Yeltsin and parliament, emphasizing that he had told commanders to stay out of the dispute unless he gave them written orders. However, the military might need to become involved if the confrontation led to violence. As he put it, "The army must be left in peace, outside politics. It guarantees Russia's security and will not meddle in questions of internal security up to the point where political passions cross into general confrontation. If the blood of innocent people is spilled, the Army will not remain neutral."[41]

In an effort to ensure Army support, Yeltsin issued a statement that was published in the main military newspaper, *Krasnaya zvezda*. "Dear Soldiers of the Russian Armed Forces! My Sons!" it began. "I appeal to you at a critical moment for Russian statehood and our Fatherland." He called on them to remain united and to avoid being dragged into a political battle by parliament. He ended by noting, "Remember that the prevention of national collapse and civil war and the prospects for the revival of a great Russia depend on your firm, responsible position."[42] Yeltsin was clearly concerned about the military, and he wanted to be sure that they would support him rather than parliament. To make sure that Army officers understood that he was serious, he stated that any officer who did not support the law—meaning Yeltsin—would be removed from duty—immediately! According Barylski, the latter action was successful. "Only some forty to fifty active-duty personnel rallied to Parliament. Some 2 million did not,"[43] giving a clear victory for Yeltsin. Still, there was the question of actually using the military, because it was becoming clear that the militia and Interior Ministry troops were not up to the job.

On October 2, Yeltsin ordered Grachev to begin moving troops into Moscow. According to Yeltsin, when he spoke to Grachev on October 3, the general informed him that "army troops were ready to come to the assistance of the police at any moment."[44] Later that day, Yeltsin said that Grachev had told him that Army troops had begun moving into Moscow. Yeltsin soon learned from the police, however, that the Army had remained outside of the city. He was furious. He believed he had to do something dramatic. He had to shake the generals up.

Meanwhile, on October 3 there were large demonstrations by supporters of parliament. Rutskoi and Khasbulatov began calling for a march on the Kremlin to get rid of Yeltsin and his supporters. A second group began to march on the Ostankino radio and television center. Yeltsin's hand was forced. He had no alternative but to respond, but how?

It was at this point that Yeltsin said that he went to the Defense Ministry "to find out what was really happening."[45] When he arrived, an emergency meeting of the collegium of the Defense Ministry was underway. Yeltsin entered the room and looked around at the grim expressions on the faces of the generals. "They obviously understood the awkwardness of the situation: the lawful government hung by a thread but the army couldn't defend it—some soldiers were picking potatoes and others didn't feel like fighting."

Despite their hesitancy to get involved, a plan was proposed, one that the military officers believed to be viable. Orders were issued to bring in ten tanks, an action that required the Army's participation because the Interior Ministry troops did not possess any tanks. At this point Grachev spoke up. As Yeltsin recalled, Grachev then asked,

'Boris Nikolayevich, are you giving me sanction to use tanks in Moscow?' I looked at him in silence. At first he stared me right in the eye, then dropped his gaze, Chernomyrdin, unable to contain himself, turned to Grachev, 'Pavel Sergeyevich, what are you saying now? You've been assigned to command an operation. Why should the president decide what precise means you require for it?'[46]

In effect, Grachev was asking for a written order, an action that should not have come as a surprise, given the high command's past experience with politicians in such a situation. Grachev had to face his colleagues, who were only too mindful of the past misuse of the military by irresponsible politicians. Now, however, the country's president was prepared to sign an order, saying, "I'll send you a written order."[47] The Army now had a formal, written order, ordering it to use force for the sake of domestic politics. Unlike Gorbachev, Yeltsin had assumed personal responsibility for what happened.

At 6:30 the next morning, tanks began firing on the White House. Yuri Voronin, the deputy speaker of parliament, called the Ministry of Defense where he spoke with Colonel General Dmitri Volkogonov, who told Voronin what he did not want to hear: Namely, that Yeltsin was the country's president, that he had issued a lawful order in writing, and that the Army would carry it out—end of story. The military's job was to neutralize opposition in the White House, a task it carried out successfully in a relatively short amount of time. The actual arrest of those who had seized the White House was left to the country's security services. Rutskoi and Khasbulatov, as well as Generals Achalov and Makashov, were arrested and sent to Lefortovo Prison.

Why did the military support Yeltsin? After all, Rutskoi was a general and a Hero of the Soviet Union. There were a number of reasons why the majority lined up behind Yeltsin. First, Yeltsin was the president and controlled the careers of officers like Grachev. Yeltsin had appointed him, and that fact alone meant that if parliament had won, Grachev would have been fired. Second, there were people on parliament's side who were trying to get parts of the military to back the parliament, and the high command was obsessed with keeping the armed forces united. Third, Yeltsin had offered to raise soldiers' salaries, while the parliament had turned down the Army's request for more pay and fewer deferments. Fourth, the generals could not afford to be neutral. If they had, it would have sent a confusing signal to the rest of the Army. It "would have raised doubts in the minds of commanders about whose orders should be obeyed and would have led to the very split in the officer corps that Grachev and the high command were working to avoid."[48] Finally, and probably most important, Yeltsin understood the military. He had carefully cultivated his contacts with it and told the generals what they wanted to hear. He promised to help the military rebuild and gave the generals the impression that he was prepared to do what was necessary to make it an effective foreign policy tool in the future.

The most important aspect of the use of the Army in October 1993 was that it meant that the armed forces had crossed the Rubicon. In 1991 they had carefully avoided becoming directly involved in the coup attempt. This time, however, military units had actually been used to determine the outcome of a domestic political struggle. "No longer could it remain neutral in a time of intense political struggle . . . A tradition had been broken and a precedent set."[49]

AFTER THE CONFRONTATION

The October crisis demonstrated that the military did not want to play a role in solving domestic political problems. With this in mind, Grachev ordered officers to stay out of politics in the future. The Communist Party had been abolished, and he believed that the only way the military could survive was by becoming apolitical. He claimed that politics was a profession different from the military, and that military officers had no business being involved in it. The military served the entire country—people of all political persuasions. As a consequence, they were not to become involved in politics. It was a clear warning aimed at ensuring that the military would not split over political issues. As Barylski noted, "Officers could not afford to ignore his warning that those who want to build successful military careers should not attempt to combine them with politics."[50] If they decided to run for a position in the legislature, they did so at their own risk.

Meanwhile, Yeltsin called for a referendum on a new constitution to be voted on in December. The military was encouraged by *Krasnaya zvezda* to vote yes. Almost no military officers entered the simultaneous parliamentary elections, and while the rank and file voted yes, their vote was primarily against the existing situation. It was obvious that soldiers and officers were tired of the confused and chaotic situation in the military. They wanted change and direction from civilian authorities.

Most important from the military's standpoint, Yeltsin's new constitution removed legislative controls over the military. It placed the military directly under the control of the president. After the constitution was approved in December 1993, even the appointment of senior officers became the president's prerogative. And in January 1994 Yeltsin issued a presidential decree that "subordinated all 'force organs' to the president."[51] The problem, however, was that Yeltsin's primary interest in the Army—despite his many promises—remained ensuring its loyalty in case of a domestic problem. This is why he went to great efforts to appoint officers he trusted. He had no idea of what kind of a military he wanted or how he intended to rebuild it. Indeed, as Baev pointed out, "Grachev's mandate as provided by the President was to restore the controllability of the Army and secure its loyalty, but not to reform it."[52] However, Yeltsin promised to improve funding and to work to ensure that the military-industrial complex did not collapse. He also continued to heap praise on the Army. In October 1994, for example, "He spoke of Russia as a great power and said that he highly values the leadership of the Ministry of Defense."[53]

MILITARY REFORM

While Yeltsin did not seem overly concerned about it, the high command clearly realized that military reform was a necessity. The Army could not hope to carry out its tasks unless structural changes were made. They were hoping that Yeltsin would appoint a powerful defense minister to represent their interests. Unfortunately, Yeltsin appointed Grachev. According to Colonel Yuri Deryagin, who was involved in the process, "By appointing General Grachev as the new defense minister, the president for all practical purposes has buried military reform."[54] Grachev's task was to come up with something that would look like a military reform plan, but one that would not irritate Yeltsin.

Accordingly, Grachev devised a three stage plan. The first, which was to be completed in 1992–1993, would

> set up a Ministry of Defense of the Russian Federation; finalize the target numerical strength and structure of the Russian Armed forces; determine a system to control them and establish the sequence and time frame for their reform process; create a legal basis for their functioning, with due regard for the norms of international law and existing international agreements; and design a system of social guarantees for servicemen, members of their families, and people discharged from service.[55]

During the second stage, which was to last two to three years, Russian troops would complete their withdrawal from outside of Russia. A reduction in personnel would be carried out, bringing the overall strength of the Army down to 2.1 million by 1995. In addition, a mixed system of conscripts and professionals would be adopted. Finally, during the third period, which was to take three to four years, all troops would be withdrawn from the Baltics, structural and organizational reforms would be introduced, and the overall size of the military reduced to 1.5 million.[56] The problem with this plan was that it was a replay of the proposal previously put forth by Yazov.

Grachev believed that the 1991 Gulf War had demonstrated that the Russian idea of a static defense would not work due to the effectiveness of high-tech weapons. The offense now had the upper hand. Second, as much as the Army wanted to stay out of internal politics, it was clear that the military had to be in a position to intervene quickly, if that became necessary. As the plan stated, the

Army was authorized "to remove the effects of internal social, ecological, and other 'upheavals' and also to provide support for border guards and internal security troops."[57]

Like Yeltsin, Grachev did not believe Russia's threat came only from NATO. Instead, it could come from any direction and the only way Moscow could respond would be by dispatching highly trained, lightly equipped troops. This meant airborne, naval infantry, and motorized forces, in addition to army aviation and the necessary support forces. According to Grachev, "this presupposes the existence of small but powerful groups of forces, ready to take immediate action wherever a real threat arises."[58] The mobile forces would be based on the five airborne divisions and three independent brigades from the Soviet Army. The large, million-man-strong strategic reserves would be available in the event of a major war. While Grachev may not have been aware of it, military analyst Pavel Felgenhauer reported that other generals, led by General Mikhail Kolesnikov, were working hard to undermine his mobile force plans.[59]

Meanwhile, Grachev and Yeltsin came up with a new idea for Military Doctrine, which they believed would give the impression that reform was under way. After all, that was Yeltsin's main concern. The new doctrine was promulgated on November 2, 1993, in Decree No. 1833 and, with the events of the previous month in mind, included a reference to the potential need to use the military internally, thus legitimizing the use of the military on the domestic front. Yeltsin did his best to highlight the "progress" that he claimed was taking place in the military. Image was everything to him. For example, on November 14, 1994, he argued, "The mobile forces are being completed, a new concept for building up the Armed Forces and other Russian troops is drawing to a close, and Pavel Grachev is the best defense minister of the past decade."[60]

The simple fact was that nothing was happening other than Grachev's attempt to build up the airborne forces. According to Felgenhauer, generals at the Defense Ministry called Grachev's plan "toilet paper."[61] A poll taken among 567 colonels and forty-eight generals in 1994 indicated that "just over one percent considered the reforms to be working, about 30 percent thought they had accomplished nothing, and over 60 percent thought they had changed the army for worse."[62] The new doctrine did not provide the kind of detailed guidance that the generals needed to work on force planning. The only good thing about it, from the high command's standpoint, was that it kept the politicians off their back.

YELTSIN'S IMPACT ON THE RUSSIAN ARMY

The Russian Federation inherited a military that was in dismal shape. The withdrawal of Russian forces from Eastern Europe had destroyed Russia's best troops. The Group of Soviet Forces in Germany was made up of category-one divisions. They were disbanded, sent back to Russia, and often unceremoniously dumped in a very inhospitable part of Russia—perhaps Siberia—with no accommodations for the soldiers, the officers, or their families. They were expected to fend for themselves at a time when there were no funds or assistance from the political authorities.

It soon became obvious, even to the non-specialist, that major restructuring as well as widespread shortages and dislocations were inevitable. But Yeltsin and Grachev did not deal seriously with the many problems confronting the military. Indeed, Yeltsin's failure to pay attention to the military, along with the conservative generals' refusal to come to grips with the changed conditions, only served to make the situation worse. Take, for instance, the budget. Despite Yeltsin's earlier promises, the budget collapsed, leaving no money for the generals to manage the changes that had to be made. In 1991 it stood at $324.5 billion. The next year is was down to $86.93 billion; in 1993 it was $74.1 billion, and in 1994 it was $71.7 billion.[63] To make matters even worse, the military did not even get the meager allocations it was promised. For example, in 1993 the budgetary shortfall was one billion rubles, in 1994 its was 12.2 billion rubles.[64] These cuts and shortfalls had a devastating impact. In 1994, Grachev commented, "Our budget for 1994 was corrected in an attempt to tackle, first, the social problems of 120,000 homeless officers, thousands of people without jobs. This will consume 50 percent of our resources."[65]

There were also major problems with recruiting and retaining personnel. At one time, competition for officers' schools was intense. Gaining a commission in the Soviet Army opened the door to a very prestigious career. In 1989 there were 1.9 applicants per space. By 1993, number of applicants per space was down to 1.35.[66] Just as bad, in 1987 4.1 percent of students at the military schools were expelled for failing to study. In 1993 the number was up to 13.4 percent.[67] An August 1990 poll of the Army revealed that "only 40 percent of officers regarded their jobs as even satisfactory, and 24 percent wished to change their career."[68] That was not surprising, considering that a junior officer's family was living below the poverty line unless the wife was able to work.[69] The situation was even worse three years later. Some "92 percent of officers polled 'had no faith in tomorrow,' 50 percent noted worsening living conditions, 35 percent an increased lack of social protection, and 34 percent a loss of both prospects and saw no point in continuing to serve."[70] Yeltsin claimed he was helping, and to his credit the armed forces received a number of pay increases. The problem, however, was that they had little impact, because inflation ran far ahead of their pay increases. Officers were leaving in droves. For example, as part of its downsizing, in 1992 the Ministry of Defense's plan called for the discharge of 36,000 officers. In fact, some 59,163 left the military voluntarily.[71] The same thing happened in 1994; while the plan called for the discharge of 19,674 officers, some 60,033 left voluntarily.[72] In fact, between 1992 and July 1994, "over twice as many officers left the army than was forecast (155,000 rather than 71,000). Over half were under the age of 30, a very serious loss of cadre—officers who would have been the cutting edge of any plan to implement military reform."[73] This meant that there was a serious shortage of experienced junior officers. More than 28 percent of them had served in their positions for less than a year.[74] Junior officers are the ones with closest contact with the troops. Their military skills and dedication (or lack thereof) have a major impact on how well and effectively soldiers fight. No one could not blame them for leaving. Why remain in a military that was forcing its troops to live below poverty levels? Unfortunately, the lack of experienced, trained junior officers would be obvious when the Russian Army was called on to fight in Chechnya in 1994.

The problem in recruiting officers was duplicated in the enlisted ranks. Moscow had the draft, but thousands of young men did their best to avoid it. In 1992 draft avoidance was double what it had been the previous year. In Moscow, a city where few wanted to serve in the Army, only 7 percent were drafted. This meant that by June only every tenth or eleventh young man was entering the military. Given the size of the Army, it was not long before the manning level dropped. According to one source, it was down to 50 percent, and by October some units had only 8 to 10 percent of the personnel required.[75] In an effort to make the military more attractive, on January 1, 1993, the Ministry of Defense decreed that young men would not have to serve outside of Russia proper without the individual's consent. But it did little good. In February Grachev complained that only 416,000 (23 percent) of draft-age youths were eligible to be drafted—a shortfall of 986,000.[76] The quality of conscripts also continued to decline. As Grachev stated in 1994, "Last year 34,000 conscripts had a criminal record." Only 76 percent of those called up had completed a secondary education.[77]

Even worse, from the standpoint of unit cohesion, was the continued presence of *dedovshchina*. The lack of professional NCOs meant that the soldiers continued to be left to their own devices in the barracks, with the younger soldiers being trained and disciplined by the more senior ones. Not surprisingly, there were problems. In February 1993, Grachev admitted, "Bullying has been and, indeed, still is an urgent matter."[78] Three months later, he claimed, "A recent analysis has shown that the number of hazing incidents in the Army and in the Navy, especially linked with the death of servicemen, has dropped by 40 percent during the first months of this year as compared with the same period of 1992."[79] Grachev's optimistic comment was refuted the following year by a report from the Academy of Sciences that concluded, "For any man entering the Army, there was an 80 percent probability of his being beaten up (30 percent in a particularly savage or humiliating form), and a 5 percent chance of being the victim of a homosexual rape."[80]

Opposition to the draft was widespread throughout Russian society. The Cold War was over, and the military was a mess. Why send young men in to join it, especially given the prevalence of *dedovshchina*? Many Russians wanted to abolish the draft completely. In response, the Yeltsin government agreed to cut mandatory service from two years to eighteen months and alternative service was written into the Constitution, although it would not become a reality until several years later due to military resistance. The generals strongly opposed the cut in service time, because it meant that 320,000 men would be discharged at one time, both the eighteen-month and the twenty-four month classes, but only half of them could be replaced by new recruits.

Thus the high command faced a serious problem. Yeltsin's decision to cut conscript service to eighteen months, together with increased public opposition to the draft, meant that the high command would have to come up with an alternative approach. The answer was to focus on the idea that Yazov had proposed: to create a segment of enlisted personnel who would be professional soldiers—*kontraktniki*—serving on contract. This program began on December 1, 1992. The idea was to have 10 percent (about 100,000 troops) of the Army be professional soldiers by the end of 1993. The proportion would gradually increase to 30 percent by 1995 and 50 percent by 2000.

At first, the process appeared to be going well. By April 1993 there were 45,000 troops serving on contract, and by June it was up to 110,000. However, there were problems. For example, in 1993 alone, 15.8 percent of the contracts were cancelled. There were two primary reasons. First, the quality of many of those who signed up was low. In many cases, they "signed a contract out of desperation," often because they could not find any other job. Second, the *kontraktnikis* were soon disillusioned not only because of the low pay, but due to their living conditions, which were not much different from those of recruits. There was little the Army could do. The Ministries of Finance and Economic Development did not provide the Ministry of Defense with the extra money needed to fund such a program.

Meanwhile, the moral and social fabric of the military began to deteriorate. Corruption was a serious problem, and in 1992 there were 3,923 reported thefts from weapons depots.[81] The problem was so serious that Yeltsin himself mentioned it, "The embezzlement of weapons and military hardware with a view to their resale has acquired menacing proportions."[82] Grachev also brought up the issue. He stated that 459 men were dismissed for selling military weapons and equipment, while 3,711 had been disciplined and criminal charges were leveled against thirty-one.[83] The best known case of corruption involved General Matvei Burlakov, the last commander of the Group of Soviet Forces in Germany, who was accused on taking kickbacks in exchange for selling off Soviet assets at low prices. He was even accused of providing Grachev with a Mercedes. Instead of being fired, he was given the post of deputy defense minister. He was subsequently accused of having played a part in the assassination of Dmitri Kholodov, an investigative reporter who was looking into reports of corruption in the Group of Soviet Forces in Germany, and was dismissed and retired. Charges of corruption had begun to touch Grachev himself.

More traditional crimes were also a problem. According to one source, "the number of premeditated homicides increased (by 71.4 percent; 26 servicemen have already died), as well as rapes (up by 60 percent), thefts of state property (by 125 percent) and personal property (by 300 percent), and crimes associated with the acquisition, possession, and sale of narcotic substances (by 80 percent)."[84] Not surprising, discipline also began to collapse. In the Far East a number of sailors were permitted to starve to death on a remote island base when their command forgot about them. Then there was a report that a soldier on guard at a strategic missile site went berserk and killed several of his comrades.[85] These were minor events compared to what happened on May 14, 1993. On that day an ammunition dump in the Far East blew up, an explosion that Russian sources claimed had the explosive power of a nuclear weapon. "An investigation showed that [the blast] was the result of 'negligence and lax discipline on the part of the guards.'"[86] Numerous statistics can be offered to show the rise of crime and corruption in the new Russian Army, but the point should be clear by now: there was a serious collapse in both areas.

Training was also being neglected. In fact it was almost non-existent, and senior Russian officers saw no way out. As the chief of the Main Directorate of Combat Training commented, "For me to predict some kind of breakthrough in this area in the near future would be, at very least, unprofessional."[87] This lack of training hit pilots especially hard. They were getting only 25–30 hours a year. In one case a commander went out on a limb and ordered 26,000 tons of fuel on credit at the personal cost of 11 billion rubles.[88]

Problems with equipment were also severe. In the first place, Moscow had only received a small part of what had been the Soviet Army. According to one estimate, "Some 70 percent of the most up-to-date technology and weapons of the former USSR remained outside Russia."[89] To make matters worse, 70–75 percent of the equipment and weapons inherited by the Russian Army from the Soviet military was outdated. Forty percent of repair facilities, including 80 percent of those that serviced armored vehicles, were outside of Russia. In many cases, Russian forces had begun to use their reserves. In 1993 only 20 percent of Russian tanks were combat ready. By 1994 the situation had deteriorated to the point that

> troops' material provision has been cut by nearly 60 percent as a result of which approximately 70 percent of games and maneuvers had to be scrapped: combat flying practice had been reduced sharply; from 100–120 hours to 30–35 hours a year; and only one to two divisions are deemed fully combat-ready in each military district, and one to two ships in each fleet.[90]

The situation facing the Navy was just as bad. A top admiral reported that the Navy had received less than half the money it required. He added that it could only use about one-third of its shipyards, because the others were in desperate need of repair. This meant that ships had to stay in dock four or five times longer than normal.[91] Furthermore, by October 1994, eighty-five nuclear submarines had been tied up because they were too expensive for the Navy to operate.[92] Because of budgetary cutbacks arms procurement also fell. For example, between 1991 and 1994 procurement dropped by more than 80 percent.[93] The Russian military would have to make do with what it had, because it was not getting any new weapons at the time and it was unlikely to get any in the near future.

Combat Readiness

It was clear to almost everyone, both Russian generals and Western observers, that Russian combat readiness had dropped. In 1992, the high command believed that over 70 percent of the Army could not perform the "basic task of stopping a combat vehicle in its designated place."[94] The Russian Army was in sorry shape. It was said that Russian military units resembled Swiss cheese due to their many gaps and holes.

Looking at the Strategic Rocket Forces, normally considered to be the most combat-ready force, one source argued that they were in such horrible shape, "they were about to lose their combat readiness. In fact . . . the command posts and control centers were in worse shape than the missiles."[95] Furthermore, "a survey of Russian commanders in 1994 showed that 70 percent do not believe that their units are able to perform combat assignments under real life conditions."[96] General Vladimir Semenov, commander of Russian Ground Forces, noted that the combat readiness of his troops was limited and complained that the ground forces were not receiving new equipment.[97] This meant, that "outside of the elite airborne and peacekeeping formations, units are generally undermanned by about 50 percent, keeping only one combat ready division in each military district."[98] The bottom line was that the military was falling apart. To quote one expert, "The army's moral decay, declining discipline and reliability and failing cohesion are not only undermining military effectiveness, however. They pose a threat to the very existence of the army, and to the state as well."[99]

MILITARY CULTURE

The military was disappointed with Yeltsin. Most important, they resented Yeltsin's decision to force them to become involved in the 1993 attack on parliament. Grachev was able to get a signed order, and that was better than under Gorbachev. Nevertheless, the military had been forced to become involved in domestic politics.

Second, Yeltsin was not serious about introducing a major change in military doctrine and strategy. That was obvious with Grachev's appointment. But then his reform plan was nothing more than a reprint of Yazov's proposal. It contained nothing new, and certainly there was no effort to force the generals to come to grips with the new reality of the post-Cold War world. They would have probably opposed whatever he and Grachev came up with, but this plan was laughable. It did nothing except put the spotlight on Grachev's airborne units.

Finally, despite their repeated efforts to explain the depth of the problems the Army was facing in its attempts to operate on a day-to-day basis, Yeltsin paid no attention. Did he not realize that he was presiding over the "collapse" of the Russian military? In almost every instance, the military was falling apart. Desertion, crime, corruption, *dedovshchina,* officer retention, and training were all disaster areas. The budget had been slashed beyond anything the generals had anticipated.

Generals and admirals were fully aware that the president's primary concern was to stay in power. After all, that is the supreme concern of every politician. However, they expected him to focus on the larger aspects of the polity, such as the long-term reform of the military. If the president hopes to use the military either internally or externally, it must be in a position to carry out his orders. As far as being irascible is concerned, generals and admirals grow up in a very abrasive and difficult environment. As a result, Yeltsin's use of tough language to criticize the military was nothing new. However, much depended on how it was done. The military believes that criticism should take place in private, away from the media.

Finally, the generals are professionals, having spent the better part of their lives learning how to use and employ the most destructive and violent tools available to a nation-state. As a result, they expect the president to respect them in the decision-making process. They assumed he would lay out the guidelines, but also take their proposals and suggestions seriously. Interfering in military operations or ignoring their advice when it came to launching military actions is something they strongly oppose. In addition, the generals expect the president to "take care" of the armed forces. This is particularly true in a transitional period. The military supported Yeltsin, and they expected him to support them.

CONCLUSION

Given the collapse of the USSR and the structural and personnel problems that accompanied it, it was inevitable that the process would have a negative impact on the combat readiness of the Russian Army. The best magician in the world would not have been in a position to avoid the many problems associated with this collapse—and Yeltsin was no magician.

The problem was not only the collapse; it was the lack of presidential leadership that made the situation worse. While there is no doubt that Yeltsin needed the military for his struggle against parliament, he could have been more assertive. For example, the military needed strong leadership, and he could have picked a better man to be defense minister. There was much talk of a civilian to hold the post, which some military officers opposed. However, everyone knew that Grachev was not up to the job, an opinion he would confirm to even his strongest supporters when it came to the war in Chechnya.

Second, much of the problem went back to money, the devastating collapse of the budget primarily because of the government's inability to institute an efficient and effective taxation system. A good percentage of the taxes were not being collected, another problem that Yeltsin seemed insensitive to. To quote Leon Aron, "Almost a decade of improvisation and political expediency between 1987 and 1996 had produced an arcane system of more than 200 overlapping federal and local taxes and a crushing tax burden often amounting to more than 100 percent of individual and corporate incomes."[100] Then there was the widespread corruption that was not only present in the armed forces as noted above, but throughout Russian society as well. There was always a way to avoid paying taxes, which meant there was little or nothing available to spend in the armed forces.

Third, Yeltsin showed very little leadership. He did nothing to push the military toward creating a military structure to reform the Russian military, whether it meant structure or doctrine. For example, the Ministry of Defense and the General Staff were constantly at odds over both conceptual and operational matters. Eventually, Yeltsin would make the mistake of separating them and placing both of them on an equal status under his office, but instead of moving to enforce order in the military establishment, he permitted chaos to reign.

The sad, almost irresponsible result of Yeltsin's inattention to the military during his early years in power was that it would lead to the deaths of thousands of young conscripts and their junior officers in Chechnya. But that was the price that would have to be paid for a lack of leadership on the part of Russia's first president.

CHAPTER FOUR
CHECHNYA, MILITARY DISINTEGRATION, AND YELTSIN, NOVEMBER 1994–JUNE 1996

Russia no longer has an army—what it has is only military formations of boy-soldiers which are hardly capable of achieving anything.
General Alexander Lebed

Few observers expected that the Russian Army would come close to collapse in the little-known Russian Republic of Chechnya. Yet that is what happened, and while the generals must share some of the responsibility for the disaster, the bulk of the blame lies with President Boris Yeltsin. Indeed, there is little doubt, that his policies vis-à-vis the military—regardless of his reasons—were the primary reason for its disastrous performance.

Throughout this period, Yeltsin would continue to make promises to the generals, but he seldom kept them. The military itself continued to deteriorate. It was starved for money, while deferments meant the best recruits were unavailable. Meanwhile, crime, corruption, and *dedovshchina* continued to get worse, while weapons deteriorated further, the quality of officers went down, planes were not able to fly, tanks were abandoned for lack of spare parts, and ships could not go to sea.

It was reasonable to think that Yeltsin might reward the military handsomely for its willingness to support him in his battle with parliament in October 1993. He knew the military was in a desperate situation. The high command also knew that the Army was falling apart, a point that Defense Minister Pavel Grachev made in mid-November 1994:

Unless there is respect for the Army, unless the very approaches to its financing are changed, unless the armed forces are provided for without interruption, unless staffing by conscription is changed, unless social programs provide for them, and unless legislation is improved, there will be in the near future an irreversible loss of combat ability, a real disintegration of the army.[1]

However, Yeltsin did not care about the military. He was more concerned about staying in power, and the military was only important for attaining that goal. He showed no compunction in slashing the military budget. Although in 1993 he had pledged to increase the budget for the Army, which then stood at $74.1 billion, and to reform the military-industrial enterprises and research organizations, in 1994 the military budget dropped to $71.7 billion. The next year it dropped all the way to $46.6 billion, despite the ongoing war in Chechnya.[2] Not surprisingly, the Army felt betrayed. At the same time, Yeltsin began to put greater emphasis on Internal Ministry troops by increasing their financing and salaries. His primary concern was to strengthen those forces that would help keep him in power. In his mind, there was no external threat, so why waste money on the Army?

For his part, Grachev pushed hard among his uniformed colleagues to keep the military out of politics. As Baev put it, "Defense Minister Grachev's 'strong recommendation' that members of the military should not stand for parliamentary elections also bore fruit, minimizing the influence of various self-appointed 'political commissars.'"[3] This is exactly what Yeltsin wanted him to do. The president's primary concern was to control the military, and he was not afraid to criticize them in the process. For example, in mid-November 1994, Yeltsin noted that he was "not completely satisfied" with the level of combat readiness in the armed forces.[4]

CHECHNYA DECLARES ITS INDEPENDENCE

Chechnya is a small republic in the Caucasus region, about the size of Connecticut. Historically, the Chechens and the Russians have often been at each other's throats. The Russians battled the Chechen tribes for years until they were finally conquered in the nineteenth century. The Chechens tried to gain their independence in 1917, when Tsarist Russia collapsed, but the Red Army intervened. Then during World War II, Stalin had most of the Chechens removed and sent to Central Asia, because he feared they would collaborate with the Nazi invaders. During the process of resettlement hundreds of thousands of Chechens died. When Khrushchev permitted them to return to their homeland in 1957, they did so with a strong feeling of animosity against everything Russian. Stalin may have been the evil man who signed the order to deport them, but in Chechen eyes it was the Russians who had carried out the order. Resentment remained deep even while Chechens learned to coexist with the Russians in the post-war years.

For their part, most Russians returned the sentiment. They disliked the Chechens. Russians who encountered Chechens on the street in Moscow would complain that the people were untrustworthy; they were criminals, crooks, members of the mafia, and drug smugglers. In short, Russians did not believe that Chechens could be trusted. They were ungrateful for the assistance the Russians had provided them since the end of World War II, and Russians believed a Chechen would stab a Russian in the back or slit a Russian throat without blinking an eye.[5]

The purpose of the above comments is not to support one side or the other. Rather, it is to demonstrate the deep-seated dislike—even hatred—between the two peoples. From the Chechen side this feeling manifested itself in a desire to separate themselves from Russia; possibly through complete independence. In fact, Chechnya began its push for independence on August 21, 1991, only hours after the collapse of the August coup attempt, and its leaders declared its independence from Russia on September 6. A former Soviet Air Force general, Dzhokhar Dudayev, was invited to become president, and on October 27 he was elected president by popular vote. He then proclaimed his intention of gaining independence for Chechnya, and on November 2 the Chechen parliament declared the republic's full independence.

Yeltsin's response was to immediately declare a state of emergency in Chechnya. On November 10 the Russian Supreme Soviet convened in Moscow to deal with the president's decree, which it ultimately denounced on November 11. Yeltsin warned Dudayev that he had three days to disarm and that, if he did not, Moscow would act. Yeltsin, as he often did, paid no attention to the parliament and dispatched 600 Interior Ministry troops to Chechnya.[6] He had no intention of putting up with Dudayev's call for independence. Like it or not, Yeltsin was determined to keep Chechnya part of Russia. Yet the dispatch of the troops ended up humiliating the Russians. When the planes landed in Grozny, the Russian troops were met by Chechen soldiers who surrounded, disarmed, and confined them in the airport. They were subsequently put on buses and sent back to Russia.

Meanwhile, there was the issue of the Russian Army stationed in Chechnya. Not surprisingly, the (previously Soviet, now Russian) forces were confused. To begin with, there was the question of whom they worked for: Gorbachev as president of the USSR or Yeltsin as president of the Russian Republic. Even after the end of 1991, when Gorbachev and the Soviet Union had left the scene, there was confusion because the Russian Ministry of Defense had yet to be established. The Chechens, meanwhile, wanted the Army—Soviet, Russian, or whatever—to leave. Ultimately, the situation differed from unit to unit: "Some bases were overrun, including that of the 566th Regiment of Interior Ministry troops in Grozny, between 6 and 9 February 1992; others handed over their arms in return for being allowed to leave in peace; and finally the Russian Defense Ministry under Pavel Grachev itself made a deal handing over many arms to the Chechens in return for a promise of safe passage."[7]

Altogether Dudayev obtained 50 percent of the Russian Army's assets in Chechnya. There were enough different kinds of weapons—including tanks—to build a small army and outfit a number of militia groups, which is precisely what Dudayev did. These weapons would be used against the Russian Army when Yeltsin ordered it to invade two years later.

Meanwhile, Dudayev worked hard to undermine Russian control over Chechnya. But Moscow would not countenance Dudayev's maneuvering, given its desire to control the oil pipelines coming from the Caspian Sea and traveling through Chechnya. The Kremlin needed the proceeds from the pipelines to help rebuild the country. As Barylski explained, "It was imperative that Moscow demonstrate its ability to defend the pipeline route from Azerbaijan to Novorossiisk which passed through Chechnya."[8] Second, the idea that a part of Russia could declare its independence, thereby destroying Russian state sovereignty, was unacceptable to Yeltsin. Today it was Chechnya, but Russia was a multiethnic state and if Chechnya were permitted to leave the Federation, it would only be a matter of time before another republic followed suit.

THE RUSSIAN MILITARY AND CHECHNYA, PART I

One of the key military areas where the high command made little effort to rethink matters in the aftermath of the Cold War was low-intensity conflict. The Army did not understand such conflicts or how to fight them. This was particularly surprising, given Moscow's experience in Afghanistan in the 1980s. But if the military learned from that disastrous conflict, it was only at the tactical level. The problem, as Roy Allison pointed out, was that the Russians continued to see conflicts in state-to-state terms. The Kremlin believed that there would be local conflicts, but they would always involve one state against another. The idea of unconventional or substate warfare, as it is understood in the West, did not seem to dawn on them. "Russian military thinking found it

difficult to internalize forms of conflict involving irregular operations, especially those undertaken by substate military formations. It was easier to view
irregular operations as an extension of state policy."9 At a time when a revolution in warfare was needed, the most the high command would concede was
the need to create formations capable of fighting small states. The importance
of socio-political factors—like winning the hearts and minds of the local
population—never seemed to occur to the generals. The idea was to smash an
opponent, to advance until the entire area was occupied, and to then put down
any resistance with brute force. Human life, either that of Russian troops or
the local population (collateral damage), was not an important concern for
many of the generals. In the West, the idea that combat would lead to a high
percentage of civilian or military casualties would cause generals to modify or
rethink military operations. However, this was not normally an important
concern for the Soviet/Russian high command.10

Meanwhile, it was 1994. Yeltsin now had a new constitution, and he planned
to enforce it throughout the Federation, starting in Chechnya. He decided it
was time for the Kremlin to act. He did not intend to continue to put up with
Dudayev's refusal to accept Moscow's rule. If nothing else, there was talk that
the Russians were having so much trouble with Chechnya that they would not
be able to keep the tiny republic in the Russian Federation; that Chechen rebels
would throw the Russians out and declare their independence. Moscow had
billions of dollars at stake. Something had to be done to reassert Russian rule.
By September, plans were being formulated for a possible Russian invasion.
Two months later, on November 26, a column of Russian tanks moved into
Chechnya disguised as Chechen rebels. The action fooled no one, and they
were soon taken prisoner by the Chechens. Both Yeltsin and the military were
humiliated—again.

On November 29, 1994, Yeltsin issued an ultimatum. The Chechens had forty-
eight hours to disarm. If they did not, Yeltsin said he would declare a State of
Emergency and send in the Army. Not surprisingly, Dudayev rejected Yeltsin's
ultimatum. Yeltsin did not declare a State of Emergency, since that would have
required parliamentary approval. Instead, he relied on the Security Council, a
body he had created and staffed with his supporters, who unanimously supported his policy. From Yeltsin's standpoint, he was commander-in-chief of the
armed forces, and he was not about to permit the Duma to get in the way.

At this point Grachev began to play a major role. Grachev was well aware
how bad the situation was inside the Army. He had gone to the Security
Council and appealed for more money to fix its many problems. He let the

politicians know that the budget had been so low that the military had not been able to carry out training exercises for the last two years. He noted that the draft was a mess, that weapons and equipment were in poor shape, and that morale was low. He was told to make do with what he had.

The Security Council then named Grachev to be in charge of overall Chechen policy as well as any potential military operation in the republic. He set up an operational headquarters to plan for military contingencies. This put him in charge of the internal security troops, the border troops, and other forces in addition to the regular Army. Unfortunately, the Security Council retained overall authority over the operation. This meant that Grachev would have the Council looking over his shoulder at all times. Grachev was then dispatched to negotiate with the Chechens, but the Security Council restrained his flexibility to the point where his hands were tied. Finally, in a last-ditch effort to break the deadlock, Grachev and Dudayev met on December 6. Only the two of them were present in the room. There seemed to be progress. For example, Russian prisoners were handed over on December 8. The Duma followed up by suggesting mediation, and Gorbachev offered to be the mediator.

Yeltsin refused the offer and stripped Grachev of his Chechen portfolio. There had been the possibility of a compromise in Chechnya, but Yeltsin undermined Grachev and then he took away his responsibility for dealing with Chechnya, a slap in the face that most military officers would find shattering. Given the lack of confidence the president showed in them, many would have resigned. However, Grachev decided to be a good soldier and do what he was told. This was a major tragedy for the Russian military. Grachev was now in charge of military operations, a position for which he was not qualified. To make matters worse, the Security Council retained overall control of Chechen policy.

Despite Grachev's knowledge of how bad things were in the Army, he supported Yeltsin to the point of claiming that an invasion of Chechnya would be an easy operation. He said he did not expect resistance. He famously remarked that he could "take Grozny with one airborne assault regiment in two hours."[11] It is hard to fathom how he could have made such an unrealistic statement. He had been given a top-secret directive by his staff ten days prior to the war. This directive reportedly stated that the Army's combat readiness was low, that it faced major problems in mobilizing troops, that operational capability was lacking, and that the troops were untrained. Training had not taken place at the regiment or division level in over two years. The majority of battalions were only manned at 50 percent and there were serious problems with the quality of conscripts. In short, the Army was in a mess. Military analysts were stumped: "Knowing the situation so clearly, Grachev's bold prediction that he could take Grozny with a single airborne regiment in two hours is incomprehensible. Perhaps Grachev privately understood the true problems in the force but put on the face of public bravado to support the presidential directive he had received."[12]

In addition to a desire to please the boss, there was another possible explanation for Grachev's naiveté when it came to invading Chechnya. Perhaps he was a prisoner of the high command's failure to understand how complex and difficult substate conflict is. Since Chechnya was not a real state, he apparently believed that its ability to stand up to regular military units was nil. The Chechens would turn tail and run the first time they saw his mobile, regular military force, according to this line of thinking. If nothing else, Afghanistan should have taught him that scenario was not about to occur.

Many military officers thought that Grachev should have told Yeltsin, "Enough. I resign." They knew that the war made no sense, and that it would only lead to the unnecessary deaths of hundreds if not thousands of Russian soldiers. General Makhmut Gareyev probably spoke for a number of officers when he observed, "It can be confidently said that if [World War II hero Marshal Georgii] Zhukov had been the Defense Minister in 1994, the war in Chechnya would not have occurred. In any case, he would not have offered his assurances that execution of the mission in Chechnya would be a simple matter. The same applies to the day-to-day affairs of the Army and Navy."[13] But Grachev was no Zhukov, either in his willingness to stand up to the country's leader or in his brilliance in planning military operations.

THE ARMY INVADES CHECHNYA

It is hard to communicate just how bad off the once-vaunted Russian Army was as it prepared to launch an invasion of Chechnya. For example, officers were standing guard duty because units were so understaffed. In fact, almost all units were at cadre status, meaning they had only 10–20 percent of their total allotted staff. In effect, the military was faced with organizational chaos. The only way they could put a military force in the field was to pull units from all across Russia. Naval infantry units from the Northern and Pacific Fleets, airborne units, troops from the Border Guards, some regular infantry as well as reservists were called up from all over the country. This created a situation in which "many soldiers had never fought or trained together."[14] Soldiers were simply thrown together in a unit and sent off to do battle. However, training is critical because it not only builds unit cohesion, it helps the commanders to know what to expect from different individuals and teaches the soldier both how to do his job and the importance of trusting the soldier next to him. To get an impression of just how bad the situation was, note Timothy Thomas's comment:

> In the 81st Motorized Regiment of the 90th Tank Division, out of 56 platoon commanders, 49 were yesterday's [civilian college] students. More than 50 percent of the men sent to war had never fired live shells with their tank cannons, and had no idea of how to do so. Military cooks, signalers, and mechanics were appointed to shoot anti-tank guns and missiles as well as machine guns.[15]

There was also almost no preparation of intelligence information. As any military officer is well aware, intelligence is critical in any military operation. The Kremlin's failure to collect the information and to do an intelligence assessment meant that when the Army invaded, it did so blindly. It had no idea of what to expect. This is one of the main reasons why the Russians did not expect such strong resistance from the Chechens. Nor was there any targeting information for armor, artillery, or air assets. As impossible as it seems—since Chechnya is part of Russia—the maps were totally inadequate. If that were not enough, Moscow chose the worst time of the year to launch the invasion. In fact, there was no reason why the operation had to be launched in December. The fog and low clouds hampered air operations. Neither fixed-wing aircraft nor helicopters could see their targets. The untrained drivers would have had a difficult time keeping their tracked vehicles on dry roads, but they were faced with ice and snow, factors that made the movement of troops even more difficult. Yeltsin could have waited for another four or five months until the weather would have been better, but he refused.

Grachev's plan was divided into three stages. The first was supposed to begin November 29 and last eight days. Its purpose was to prepare the jump-off locations from which the attack would be launched. Stage II was set for December 7–9. Russian forces would approach Grozny, the capital of Chechnya, from different directions while protecting communications assets and carrying out reconnaissance. Four days were planned for Stage III, during which Russian forces would encircle the capital city. By December 14 Russian troops would be in Grozny.[16] While the plan sounded fine on paper, professional military officers knew that it was fantasy and said so.

Colonel General Eduard Vorobyev, deputy commander of Ground Forces, was sent to the field headquarters at Mozdok, North Ossetia, where he took over "temporary" command on December 18. "After studying the situation" he reported to General Mikhail Kolesnikov, chief of the General Staff, that he did not believe the operation had been properly prepared. He asked to have offensive operations postponed. However, on December 20, Grachev phoned Vorobyev and ordered him to officially take over command of the operation. Vorobyev refused and in an interview commented:

> When I heard all these people, and met them personally, I decided the operation was not prepared. There were no reserves organized, which is the most important part of an operation. They had not considered weather conditions, the snow, rain, mud, and slush. The strength of these forces was based on aviation, which could not operate in such conditions, they could not work in the fog and they could not use their laser weapons. They could not drop bombs. Helicopters could not fly and could not provide the corresponding support.[17]

In short, he did not believe that the troops were prepared to carry out the operation. One day later, in front of other officers, Grachev demanded that Vorobyev resign. Vorobyev immediately handed in his letter of resignation, and Grachev appointed the very ambitious Lieutenant General Anatoly Kvashnin to command Russian forces.

Vorobyev was not the only senior officer to express his displeasure with the Chechen operation. General Yevgenii Podkolzin, the commander of airborne forces, was intentionally cut out of the action, because Grachev feared he would also oppose the operation. In addition, three deputy ministers of defense, Generals Boris Gromov (the hero of Afghanistan), Valeri Mironov, and Georgii Kondratiev were left out of the key planning missions because Grachev did not trust them. Not surprisingly, that opinion carried over to the Main Military Collegium, which was excluded from planning for the action because, according to Baev, Grachev was worried that it would give Gromov an "opportunity to consolidate the 'dissidents.'"[18] Grachev forced all three deputy ministers to resign. Gromov was particularly strong in his criticism of the way Grachev and Yeltsin were using the Army. "Both the state of the army and its status in society upset me in every respect. The armed forces are today in a state of depression for both objective and subjective reasons . . . There is the simply amoral attitude shown today toward the armed forces officers . . . That attitude should be one of respect. Care should be taken of those people."[19] In the end, a total "of 540 generals, officers, and NCOs resigned rather than serve in the 1994–1996 Chechen War."[20] According to Colonel Vitaly Shlykov, by April 1995, 557 officers had been fired, and criminal proceedings had been begun against eleven of them.[21]

Not surprisingly, given his outspoken nature, General Alexander Lebed was particularly vociferous in his criticism of both Grachev and Yeltsin. On one occasion Lebed publicly stated, "Grachev must go, if only to safeguard the honor of the army and its morale."[22] He expanded his criticism to include Yeltsin when he commented:

"The whole world has come to know the main Russian military secret" the reforms of the armed forces under the leadership of *the best defense minister of all times and peoples* has ended up with their complete collapse. It is terrible and bitter to understand Russia no longer has an army—what it has is only military formations of boy-soldiers which are hardly capable of achieving anything.[23]

He was not the only general to criticize the decision-making process. General Kondratiev publicly complained, "All issues are being decided by Pavel Grachev's inner circle . . . It seems likely that the president has not been informed about the true state of affairs."[24]

Despite Vorobyev's refusal to take command and the resignation of a large number of officers, the army gradually began to get on board. What else could they do? Hundreds of officers had resigned and with little or no effect on Grachev or Yeltsin. They were determined to proceed, and that meant that Russian soldiers, however unprepared, would soon find themselves in a war. The military's decision to go along with Yeltsin was helped by his decision to accept "the moral and political responsibility for the operation, thus relieving the generals and officers of the fear that they would be turned into political scapegoats."[25]

But even when the country's senior officers decided to go along with Yeltsin's policy, morale problems continued to be a serious issue throughout the invasion. As journalist Anatol Lieven reported, regular military officers were upset at the prospect of fighting a war against Russian citizens. They had no problem with fighting "Chechen bandits" nor did they think that Chechnya should be allowed to become independent. However, even with Yeltsin's willingness to accept formal responsibility for the operation, the Tbilisi Syndrome was alive and well. The soldiers feared that once again they would be asked to use force, that there would be civilian casualties, and that they would be blamed. "They said that in the meantime they had held an officers' assembly and resolved not to advance any further, because it was not clear to them who had ordered the intervention in Chechnya or what its goal was. 'A mutiny? You could call it that,' a lieutenant-colonel from the motorized infantry told me."[26] The situation would get so bad, Felgenhauer reported, that "many officers in Chechnya confessed to me in mid-January 1995 that at the beginning of that month the Russian army was on the very of refusing to obey the ridiculous orders of its commanders and government."[27]

THE ATTEMPT TO TAKE GROZNY

By December 11, the Army had begun to assemble its forces. There were 23,700 troops (19,000 Army, 4,700 Interior Troops), 80 tanks, 208 ACVs, and 182 guns and mortars. Meanwhile, the Chechens had 98 tanks, over 150 ACVs, and up to 300 guns and mortars.[28] On the morning of December 11, 4,000 Russian troops (a combination of Army and internal security troops) began an advance in three columns. The three columns were to move from different directions, meet, and seal off Grozny at the same time. All three columns would have to work with Prussian efficiency in order for the operation to be successful.

As they proceeded toward Grozny, snipers shot at them, and there were roadblocks and other efforts to stem their advance. General Ivan Babichev led a column coming from the east through Ingushetia. Instead of running into guerilla warfare, he ran into crowds of Ingush civilians, some of whom were armed. They blocked the road and destroyed some of the Russian vehicles. Lieven, who was traveling with Babichev, recalled:

On 13 December [Babichev's] column reached a point near the village of Davidenko on the main road to Grozny, where it was confronted by a crowd of Chechen women who performed the zikr on the road and told the Russians that to advance they would have to drive over them. At this point, Babichev, with the backing of an assembly of officers, announced in my presence that he would not kill civilians and refused to advance any further.[29]

Babichev's actions were morally commendable, but from a military stand-point he was not following orders, another sign of the depth of the problems in the military. Grachev was furious. On December 21, he stormed into a meeting at Mozdok and chewed out military personnel for not being more ag-gressive. It was not until December 25 that the blockade of Grozny was com-plete, and even then there were major gaps in the Russian lines through which the Chechens were able to bring in supplies and fresh troops. The city would not be completely sealed off until February 22, 1995.

On December 31, 1994, Russian forces began storming Grozny, which to the Russians represented the heart of the rebellious republic. As noted above, Grachev thought it would be an easy operation. The soldiers who entered the city did not expect a fight. He believed they were up against a group of disor-ganized, untrained crooks who would run at the first sight of Russian tanks. But that was not the case. First, the eastern and western groups that were sup-posed to attack simultaneously, failed to move. This made it possible for the Chechens to focus all of their resources on the main Russian attack. Second, the Russians tried to attack using tanks, without infantry cover. They as-sumed tanks would be able to blast their way into the city. As any student of armor tactics knows, the use of armor without covering infantry is a recipe for disaster.

The 6,000 Russian troops that entered Grozny on December 31 soon learned that the Chechens were far better prepared to fight in an urban en-vironment and much better motivated than they had anticipated. The Che-chens knew the environs of Grozny far better than the Russians, and they also understood Russian weapons; after all, most of them had served in the Soviet Army. The Chechens also had modified buildings to provide them with better positions from which to attack the Russians. The Chechens split into small squads of fighters rather than concentrating their forces in one area. They might be in basements or sewers, on the roofs of buildings, be-hind barricades, or beside the road. Ambushes and snipers were every-where. They would fire and then quickly move to another location. The Chechens had also pre-sighted their mortars and artillery so they were ex-tremely effective in firing at Russian forces. They planted roadside bombs along expected Russian advance routes. There are also reports that the Che-chens had obtained Russian battle plans in advance and that they were able to listen to Russian communications because the Russian made no effort to encode them.[30]

The battle for Grozny—to use the American expression—was a "turkey shoot" for the Chechens. They trapped Russian units in the street while destroying the armored vehicles that were not made for street fighting. According to a Chechen cited by Lieven, "the Russian soldiers stayed in their armor, so we just stood on the balconies and dropped grenades on their vehicles as they drove by underneath. The Russians are cowards. They just can't come out of shelter and fight us man-to-man. They know they are no match for us. That is why we beat them and will always beat them."[31]

Based on the preceding comment, the Russian troops clearly had poor leadership. What soldier sits in a vehicle while someone drops grenades on him? Such dismal tactical operations are not surprising, however, given that junior officers were also poorly trained and lacked combat experience and that, as in the past, the Russian Army lacked trained NCOs.

There were also morale problems. There was no one to replace the political officers of the Soviet Army, whose task was to tell the troops why they were fighting, what the goal was, and why they were putting their lives on the line. Coordination among the various units also was poor. The Russians were relying on troops from three different bureaucratic entities: the Defense Ministry, the Interior Ministry, and the Federal Security Service (FSB). The Interior Ministry troops did not possess tanks or artillery and so were not trained to fight with them. Yet they were critical for the Army. Then there were the air assets. Their ability to operate was constantly obstructed by the weather. There were also cases of fratricide as pilots mistook Russian forces for the enemy. Russian losses were catastrophic. Consider the following:

> According to an interview with a participant of the operation, the 131st Motorized Rifle Brigade (MRBde) and the 81st Motorized Rifle Regiment (MRR) took the brunt of the losses. In one column alone 102 out of 120 armored personnel carriers and 20 out of 26 tanks were destroyed by Chechen anti-tank fire, and all six "Tunguska" surface-to-air missile systems were also destroyed. Seventy-four servicemen, including a corps' operations officer, were captured. The commander of a division surface-to-air missile platoon, LTC Aleksandr Lezenkom added that "they were not trained to fight in cities and an enormous amount of armored equipment, thoughtlessly left in narrow streets without any cover, was not protected by the infantry . . . there is a lack of even basic co-operation between different subunits and their commanders and subordinates."[32]

Within only a few hours, hundreds of Russian soldiers were dead, and dozens of Russian tanks had been destroyed. At the conclusion of the battle for a railway station, early in the attack, "one correspondent counted seventeen burned-out tanks and armored vehicles in front of the radio station."[33]

It was not until January 19 that Russian forces successfully captured the presidential palace, their original goal. Outside of Grozny, the Chechens continued the war by using guerilla tactics. On January 25, the Security Council declared that the military phase of the war was over. Operational command was transferred to the Interior Ministry. General Anatoly Kulikov, a deputy interior minister, was placed in charge, although Army troops continued to fight.

By mid-February it was clear that discipline had broken down in both the Interior Ministry and Defense Ministry troops. To be fair, it is important to note that the Chechen way of fighting was brutal and begged for retaliation. For example, Chechens would spread-eagle captured Russian soldiers in windows and fire around them, daring the Russian troops to shoot back.[34] Well-trained and disciplined troops, despite such horrendous behavior, are taught to not stoop to the level of the other side. The problem was that, at times, the Russian forces resembled rabble. Note the following description: "During the battle in the city, if the men on the BRTs saw someone on the street, they'd shoot at them like game. They don't do that now, unless they're very drunk, but if they don't like the look of you, they will stop and arrest you, or maybe just beat and rob you."[35] It was not the Russian Army's finest hour.

On February 13 Russian and Chechen forces reached a cease-fire agreement. The agreement prohibited the use of heavy weapons such as artillery, aviation, and mortars. On March 1, Grachev again came out with another of his highly publicized claims, arguing that the Russian Army would shortly capture the remaining key Chechen strongholds. The Russian Army did indeed push on, with little concern for collateral damage—even if it meant killing Russian civilians living in Chechnya. By May 1995 they had achieved considerable success and had pushed the Chechen rebels into the mountains in the southern part of the republic. The battle then became a classic guerilla war, with both sides engaging in hit-and-retreat actions. There would be major dramas, such as when the Chechens seized a hospital in Budennovsk in June 1995, taking nearly 2,000 people hostage. The Russians eventually attacked the hospital and hundreds of Russian civilians died in the process. The Russians then suffered the humiliation of being forced to allow the Chechens to return to Chechnya.

The last major battle of the First Chechen War took place in August 1996. Led by Shamil Basayev, the Chechens set out to seize several cities including Grozny. They sealed off the city, thereby making it very difficult to reinforce Interior Ministry troops in the city. Military forces came to their rescue, but it was a very bloody and difficult battle. It lasted two weeks and "total Russian casualties for the battle included 500 dead and 1,400 missing and wounded."[36] The war was finally ended by a cease-fire agreement negotiated by Lebed and Chechen leader Aslan Maskhadov on August 22.

ASSESSING THE RUSSIAN MILITARY'S PERFORMANCE IN CHECHNYA

There are a number of reasons for the Russian military's poor performance in Chechnya. First, Russian soldiers did not know why they were in Chechnya. Indeed, there were even reports that many of the soldiers did not know *where* they were when they arrived in Chechnya.[37]

Second, while the naval infantry and airborne forces are highly trained, they are not trained to operate together. Furthermore, having them work with barely trained reservists or officers just commissioned from civilian universities guarantees problems. Different communication systems, different tactics, different weapons systems, putting them together with these hastily combined forces inevitably led to operational problems. One result of these ersatz units was that they were unable to carry out the missions assigned to them. Another was that Russian soldiers died as a result of "friendly fire" incidents caused by poorly trained colleagues.

Third, the units were given equipment that had been poorly maintained, which also guaranteed problems. "During the road march into Grozny, two out of every ten tanks fell out of the formation due to mechanical problems. Most of these tanks were T–72s that had been previously overhauled two or three times."[38]

Fourth, the Russian military completely misread the kind of war they would be fighting. Their focus was on state-level conflict, even if it involved small states. As a result, they expected a conventional war that would be a cakewalk. However, it turned out to strain all of their resources. The war was brutal, and the Russian Army paid a heavy price for its failure to recognize the substate nature of the conflict. Thousands of Russians died. According to Colonel General Volkogonov, by February 24, 1995, 1,146 men had been killed and another 374 were missing and presumed dead.[39] This is not to suggest that the Russians did not learn or try to change tactics. After the chaos of the first days, it became obvious to the commanders that something had to be done. The major problem, however, was that the troops were insufficiently trained. It is one thing to take a group of highly trained troops and lay out a new tactical approach. They know what to expect from one another and are experienced enough to make critical changes in approach. However, that was not the case with the Russian Army in Chechnya.

Fifth, while poor communications equipment can be blamed for some of the confusion, the lack of a clear chain of command, something that is a *sine qua non* for militaries all over the world, was critical. From 1994 to 1996 "there were over eight changes of senior command" within Russian forces in Chechnya.[40] It is difficult enough to maintain bureaucratic control over military forces under the best of circumstances, it is even more difficult when politicians interfere, when different branches or units fight for control within the same organization, and when different organizations (e.g., Interior or Defense) get involved. Troops must know whom they work for and who is giving orders. It is also critical that the various units share intelligence and information. Because of confusion in the chain of command, this did not happen. Information is power, and the rival organizations were often unwilling to share it with other forces they saw as competitors. Finally, there were numerous occasions when those in authority did not give clear and concise orders. Commanders often did not know what was expected of them.

The bottom line was that the war in Chechnya destroyed the military's already questionable reputation. Michael Orr hit the nail on the head when he observed:

An army with over 70 divisions in its national order of battle struggled to raise a handful of deployable units. Officers and men who had never served together before were sent into battle in "composite regiments." The reputation of the Army never recovered from the disaster of the battle for Grozny in the winter of 1994–1995. Some units were performing better by the end of the war, but, although some generals have since claimed they were on the point of victory by August 1996, the soldiers on the ground and most Russians were only too relieved when the war ended in an ignominious withdrawal.[41]

One long-term impact of the Chechen War was that many Russian officers came to believe that Yeltsin was incompetent, that he had no idea how to use military force effectively. The war made no sense no matter how you looked at it. Furthermore, the debacle convinced the generals that their president did not care about them or their sacrifices. Senior officers also began to believe that those who had resigned prior to the war were right. Furthermore, they felt Grachev was culpable for having led them into this mess.

This raises the question of responsibility. There are a number of explanations for what happened in Chechnya. First there is Yeltsin. While the chaos that accompanied the change of administration, and the shift from one political system to another, is understandable, there was no excuse for his starving the military and then expecting it to go to war. Three years with no significant military exercises, outdated and dilapidated weapons and equipment, combined with grossly understaffed units should have convinced any outside observer that the Russian Army was in no position to fight in Chechnya. If that were not enough, the willingness of so many senior officers to end their careers rather than participate in fighting the war reinforced the idea that something was amiss. On top of everything else, the president interfered. Yeltsin and his civilian aides told the army what it could and could not do on several occasions. Then there was his personality, his stubbornness. While Lilia Shevtsova did not necessarily have the military in mind, they would have agreed with her assessment: "From December 1994 to the spring of 1995, Yeltsin became more irascible. Unable or unwilling to listen to reason, he would not consider compromise. Despite the failures, costs, and bloodshed in Chechnya, and although he may already have understood that he was caught in a political trap, he could not admit a mistake, and he stubbornly continued along the same path."[42]

The generals also had little respect for Grachev. There is no doubt that all officers in all militaries are under very strong pressure to carry out the orders they receive, regardless of how much they detest them. However, for whatever reasons, Grachev was *not* willing to stand up to Yeltsin. Furthermore, as an airborne officer he should have known and understood the enormity of the problems facing the Russian military if it attacked Chechnya. In the view of a large number of senior military officers, he should have stood up to Yeltsin the way General Vorobyev did.

Then there was Grachev's role in planning the operation. He was clearly in over his head. Suggesting that the operation would be over in two weeks was worse than silly, it was criminal; it condemned hundreds of Russian soldiers to die in the attack on Grozny. While we will probably never know what was said privately between Grachev and Yeltsin, sending troops off with so little preparation was irresponsible. Even an amateur military strategist would have been able to predict failure. But Grachev's primary concern appeared to be staying in the president's good graces.

YELTSIN AND THE MILITARY POST-CHECHNYA, PART I

Instead of praising the military for its sacrifices in fighting the war in Chechnya, Yeltsin criticized it sharply. For example, on February 16, 1995, he blasted the military in his annual address to the Duma, calling its performance "unsatisfactory." His solution was simple: the military needed to adopt a new reform plan, one that would solve its current problems. Toward that end, he demanded that the generals adopt reform measures and he assigned Security Council member Oleg Lobov and Prime Minister Viktor Chernomyrdin to come up with a reform plan. He also promised to set up a presidential commission on military reform. The he criticized the Army again on February 23, claiming, "The army is slowly beginning to get out of hand—the conflict in Chechnya convinced us once more that we are late with reform of the army."[43]

Few generals or admirals would have questioned the need for reform. They all understood its importance. Something had to be done. The problem with reform, however, was that it required money that Yeltsin was not prepared to part with. As Grachev remarked at the time, "If there is money, there will be reform."[44] Indeed, from the standpoint of those who had to care for the troops, the situation was desperate. To quote Colonel General Yevgenii Podkolzin, the commander of the airborne forces, "If we don't have the money to normally feed the soldiers and house the officers, all this talk about reform is worthless . . . If we had the same material basis as the Americans, we would not be talking today about any reform."[45] To make matters worse, Yeltsin was asking the military to begin the reform process while it was still fighting a war in Chechnya.

The generals refused to accept Yeltsin's suggestion that it was Chechnya that put reform on the priority list of things to do. Colonel General Igor Rodionov, who was at that time the outspoken chief of the General Staff Academy, argued that there while there was a need for military reform, it was not caused by the Chechen War. It predated that war.

Recently there has been a lot of talk that the military conflict, or as it is often called in the press, the war in Chechnya is almost the main reason why military reform is called for. The combat readiness of the armed forces and the skills of their commanders are being measured on the basis of military operations, failures, and mishaps in the Chechen conflict. There are attempts to adjust even the organizational and personnel structures of the armed forces of the future in such a way as to make them suitable to solving tasks analogous to those in Chechnya-type armed conflicts. Here we have an old illness: only that is frightening which frightens us now. From here comes the exaggeration of the dangers that are by far not the main ones. The Chechen tragedy no doubt has had its influence on the military construction processes. It sped up the understanding by both the political leadership and society of the need for reforming in the military realm of the country's activities. But the events in Chechnya are not the cause for military reform. It ought to be well understood by all those on whom the future defense of the country and its armed forces of the twenty-first century depend.[46]

In other words, Yeltsin should have understood that the problems the military faced were not just a result of the fiasco in Chechnya; rather the fiasco in Chechnya was a result of the failure to reform the Russian military as the generals believed necessary. The generals also refused to accept Yeltsin's attempt to foist the blame on them, and they took great exception to the increased attention he was focusing on the internal security forces. To again quote Shevtsova:

In 1991 there had been 186 army divisions; by 1996, there were one-sixth as many, and only ten divisions were battle-ready and fully staffed. Simultaneously, however, there had been an enormous increase in the number of internal troops. The Soviet Union had had about 8 million people under arms; the Russian Federation Defense Ministry and the interior troops now numbered 7.5 million, even though Russia's population was less than half that of the Soviet Union.[47]

In mid-January 1995 Yeltsin placed the Ministry of Internal Affairs in charge of the federal armed forces in Chechnya. Not only were the interior troops getting more attention from the president, there was also considerable resentment over the way command authority was allocated. The generals believed that this was not a military operation, but if they were going to go into combat, they believed they should have been in charge throughout. But command authority switched back and forth with interior troops officers commanding Army forces, when they knew very little about military tactics and many of the Army's weapons systems.

From a purely military standpoint, the generals were also to blame for the absence of a "lessons learned" exercise in the aftermath of the First Chechen War. In most cases, after a war, especially one that is lost, the generals and admirals sit down and study what happened. Why did this occur, why did that not take place, what went right, and what went wrong? It should have led to a major soul-searching on the part of Russia's generals, especially if the Army was about to launch a major reform program. But they refused to accept the fact that substate conflicts were a new reality. They believed that Chechnya was an aberration. They refused to see it as a new kind of war. Indeed, the feeling among the high command was so strong that, as Shlykov argued, military academies[48] were prohibited from teaching courses on it.

Publicly, Yeltsin seemed to accept the Army's request for more funds. On June 28, 1995, speaking at a graduation ceremony he stated, "A lack of resources was partly to blame for the slow pace of military reform, but it should get moving." He also claimed that he would put a stop to the fall in the military budget. "In the 1996 budget we have laid down the principle that the allocation of resources for national defense must be preserved at the level of 1995."[49] But in fact, the 1996 budget actually fell. Where it was $46.6 billion in 1995, in 1995 it was $42.1 billion.[50] This cut came at a time when the military owed 715 billion rubles for food alone, a situation that was forcing it to go into its wartime food reserves. Unfortunately, 90 percent of those food reserves had been eaten up by the beginning of 1996. The military could not even feed its troops.[51] If Yeltsin was providing the military with more money, it would turn out to be one of the best-kept secrets in Russia. As a result, his standing inside the military was low, as Timothy Thomas noted, when he observed:

> Some 3,000 servicemen stationed in Novosibirsk were surveyed and asked what quality a Russian president must possess. Some 81 percent said he must have the ability to impose order in the country. For servicemen, this also includes an army properly financed, one with a proper manpower level, one outfitted with new types of weapons and military hardware, and one that did not get it into situations such as Chechnya.[52]

Recognizing the problems he was facing in getting Yeltsin to provide the kind of financial support the Russian Army needed, Grachev reversed his previous stand on keeping the military out of politics. Hoping to get military officers sympathetic to the military's needs elected to the Duma, Grachev encouraged serving and retired officers to run for parliament. If enough of them were elected, it would mean that serving military officers, individuals who understood the depth of the problems faced by the Army, would be available to vote on critical issues. If that happened, perhaps then the Duma would be more willing to provide the Army with the money it needed.

Accordingly, Grachev and the Ministry of Defense (MoD) selected 123 active-duty and retired military officers to run for seats in the Duma in the election to be held on December 17, 1995.

> In the MoD's view, the current Parliament does not understand and sincerely take to heart the problems of the military and the state's defense capability. These included the budget and the war in Chechnya. The majority in Parliament has been hostile to the Minister of Defense and reluctant to fund military programs as requested. Grachev believes that Russia needs a cadre of military specialists in the Parliament who can prepare and substantiate various proposals on military problems and persuade deputies to support the Ministry's programs.[53]

The military mobilized their media outlets, most notably the Army newspaper, *Krasnaya zvezda,* "which suggested that the armed forces needed to ally with the industrial-military complex and become a more active political lobby."[54] In fact, Grachev's efforts were a failure. Of the twenty-two military men who were elected to the Duma in 1995, only ten were serving officers, and only two of them were from Grachev's list. Many of them did not agree with Grachev's policies and several resigned from the military in protest. The electoral failure was not surprising. First of all, Grachev was part of the problem. For example, in a survey conducted in Moscow and St. Petersburg in 1996, 17 percent saw Grachev and the "least likeable military leader." Moreover, respect for the military had fallen considerably in the aftermath of the Chechen War. In the same survey noted above, for example, only 22 percent believed that the Russian Army was strong enough to defend the country, with 60 percent claiming that it was not, and 18 percent were unsure.[55] Voters who have little confidence in the Army are not likely to elect its members to represent them in the country's legislature.

YELTSIN AND THE 1996 PRESIDENTIAL ELECTION

Yeltsin knew he was in for a difficult reelection campaign in 1996. He began the year with an approval rating of only 5 percent.[56] McFaul argued that despite this low approval rate, the populace was polarized between those who wanted the old Soviet-era system back and those who wanted change. Yeltsin was the candidate of change. He was further supported by large infusions of money from the oligarchs, and his campaign was run by Anatoli Chubais, who made the election into a referendum on communism. "Voters had to understand (or be made to believe) that they were choosing between two systems, not two candidates. To succeed in implementing this strategy, the Yeltsin campaign had to once again cast Yeltsin as a democrat."[57] Faced with the need to win over the Russian populace, Yeltsin put the military in second place. His primary concern was to control them, to be sure that they would not represent a political threat, and, in the meantime, he was more than prepared to ignore their interests.

Yeltsin openly criticized the high command in his State of the Federation speech in February 1996. He accused the military of failing to reward professional competence. He also said that civilian control over the military would be strengthened. Neither action was intended to bridge the widening gap between Yeltsin and the military. The speech was followed by a campaign that bore a strong resemblance to the old communist political education program. Grachev told the military to study carefully Yeltsin's State of the Federation speech. Turning members of the military into eager voters would not be easy. To quote Barylski, "Yeltsin could force Grachev to make the official military press toe the political line and he could even make officers parrot it; however, he could not control how they would actually vote without violating fundamental democratic principles such as the secret vote, which the military supported."[58] But even Grachev understood that Yeltsin's policy was not working. As he warned, "It is not wise to keep testing the military's patience and push it to the breaking point."[59]

Meanwhile, Yeltsin did not hedge his bets. On April 24, 1996, he convinced the Duma to pass the Law on Defense. It represented a total takeover by the president of control of the military. Under the new law, "The Duma has no role whatsoever in the review of military appointments, the definition of national defense policy, or the use of military force at home or abroad."[60] The president was almost completely in charge of the armed forces: personnel issues, defense policy, and decisions such as when to deploy military force. One of the reasons for Yeltsin's increased concern for control over the military may have been a result of comments from Grachev and Interior Ministry head General Anatoli Kulikov, who "expressed doubt about the ability to guarantee the loyalty of troops in case street clashes broke out."[61] He was doing everything possible to ensure that, however contentious the election might be, he would control the Army.

If there was ever a case of playing to the voting public, knowing that the promise would never be carried out, it was Yeltsin's Decree No. 722, which ordered the Defense Ministry to end conscription by the year 2000. No one in uniform believed that it was a realistic or reasonable goal. As Lebed put it, "It is a purely populist decree and nothing will be achieved."[62] General Rodionov, who would replace Grachev, called it "dangerous and irresponsible electioneering rhetoric that at best would never really be implemented and at worst could cause the final downfall of the Russian army."[63] It went over well with those Russians who tried to avoid military service and those who favored an all-volunteer Army, and it made the military's job of recruiting even harder.

Yeltsin won the first round of the election, but he did not have the 50 percent plus one vote he needed to win the election outright. It was clear to Yeltsin's supporters that he stood a very slim chance of winning a run-off if the other three candidates (Communist Gennadi Zyuganov, nationalist Vladimir Zhirinovski, and General Alexander Lebed) were to unite against him. He needed to find a way to divide and conquer them. From Yeltsin's standpoint, the least objectionable of the three was Lebed. The general was increasingly popular and charismatic, and did not have the kind of personal baggage that the other two carried. Lebed was very ambitious and wanted power, so Yeltsin turned to him to help him stay in power. Lebed was happy to join the Yeltsin administration, as presidential national security advisor and secretary of the Security Council. After all he was well aware that Yeltsin was sick and in view of the elimination of the office of vice president in the 1993 Constitution, Lebed believed he would be in a good position to take over as president.

In June, in a further effort to win public support, and please Lebed, Yeltsin fired Grachev. In addition to appeasing Lebed, it helped remove defense issues from the election campaign. Grachev was so disliked both in the Army and outside of it, that he would have been a natural target. In his place, Yeltsin appointed a Lebed protégé, General Igor Rodionov. Yeltsin also permitted him to fire a number of Grachev's deputies. Yeltsin won the July runoff election with 53.82 percent of the vote. To many in Russia, Lebed was not qualified for his position, and he was certainly not a team player. However, the Kremlin believed that most voters saw him as the lesser of two evils (the other being the Communists). Despite Lebed's emergence as a major political force, he did not represent the military. He had run for president as an individual, one who was strongly interested in politics and military affairs, but not as a representative of the General Staff or Ministry of Defense. Indeed, there were a number of areas in which Lebed and his military colleagues had strong differences of opinion, for example, on the question of the importance of airborne troops. Most important, despite Lebed's high-profile position, the military as an institution had remained out of politics.

THE GENERAL STAFF AND THE MINISTRY OF DEFENSE

The normal military chain of command calls for all military organizations to be subordinated to a central command authority. The General Staff has a variety of functions, but even if they are operational, they are normally subordinated to the defense minister. Given his fear of the military, it is not surprising that Yeltsin was concerned about this arrangement. It created a possibility where a unified Ministry of Defense and General Staff could combine forces against him in a political crisis.

With his authority over the military very much in mind, Yeltsin held a meeting on January 11, 1995, that was attended by Prime Minister Chernomyrdin and the heads of the two chambers of the Federal Assembly, Vladimir Shumeiko and Ivan Rybkin. He told them that he intended to detach the General Staff from the Ministry of Defense and create two parallel structures, both of which would work for him. General Rodionov discussed this proposal in an article:

> The assertion is made that in attaching the General Staff directly to himself, the President will be able to neutralize it, and, if necessary, forcibly suppress any external or internal threats to the security of the current political regime ...

Any reorganization of headquarters of the Armed Forces inevitably weakens command and control throughout the entire period of the reorganization process. "How long will this last?" Experience tells us that in Russia reforms do not happen quickly. Can we begin this process in the current complex situation? Will it not result in the ultimate destruction of the state's military system? Who developed the proposals for such a restructuring of the system of military command and control? Why will even the highest-ranking military leaders and top specialists only learn about the decision from the newspapers?

> Second, pulling the General Staff out of the Defense Ministry will immediately cause the creation of a different administrative structure, since not a single ministry, as practice has shown, can get by without them. Will the Defense Ministry in its new form really correspond to its name better than it does now?[64]

Lest the reader get the impression that Rodionov was alone in his expression of concern, General Makhmut Gareyev, considered by many to be one of the finest military minds in Russia at the time, similarly wrote:

> In countries where there is no developed civil society, the direct subordination of military departments to the president, as the supreme commander-in-chief, results in a situation where the army turns out to be in a special position, outside of civil and parliamentary control, and often all relations between the minister of defense and the head of state, or party, are built on principles of personal loyalty, which is not only dangerous in the political sense, but harms the army, for, as much as any organization that is hidden from the light of day and the public eye, it begins to decay without noticing or covering up its flaws.[65]

Despite the military's opposition, the 1996 Law on Defense did exactly what Yeltsin had threatened to do. Article 13, paragraph 2 of that law stated, "Oversight for the Armed Forces of the Russian Federation is carried out by the Defense Minister via the Defense Ministry and the General Staff of the Armed Forces, which is the main body of operational supervision for the Armed Forces."[66] Over time this would create constant confusion and at times even chaos as the line of authority became blurred. When the chief of the General Staff and the defense minister had differences of opinion, it left open the possibility that the former would ignore the latter—which is exactly what happened. After all, it was the General Staff that had operational authority and implemented the defense minister's orders, and it could always modify them as they passed down the chain of command to the troops.

TROUBLE IN THE RANKS, NOVEMBER 1994–
JUNE 1996

Morale in the Army continued to fall. In December 1994 Deputy Defense Minister Valeri Mironov commented, "Nihilism, lack of spirituality, and moral degradation have reached an extreme point that poses a danger to both army and navy combat readiness and the security of society and the state."[67] Those were not good circumstances in which to begin the Chechen War. In fact, the situation inside the armed forces only got worse during this period. Shortages increased, and, as the war in Chechnya demonstrated, the Army was totally unprepared to fight that kind of war—or any kind for that matter. It was totally deficient both physically and mentally.

As noted above, the drop in the military budget was especially significant. While it was estimated at $71.7 billion in 1994, the military allocation dropped to $46.6 billion the next year, then to $42.1 billion in 1996.[68] Given a drop of that magnitude, it is not surprising that the military soon found itself out of just about everything from food to bullets, from gas to fly its planes to fuel to sail its ships. As a result, the entire fabric of the military began to decay.

First, the Army continued to have serious problems attracting and retaining junior officers. In 1995, for example, over 50 percent of students at officer schools left prior to commissioning.[69] "By 1995, the Russian army was reported to be facing a shortfall of officers as high as 25 percent with the greatest problems at junior officer levels where the shortfall was as high as 45 percent."[70] Or as Grachev warned, "It was forecast that we might lose 2,500 officers this year in the rank of lieutenant to captain, but as many as 11,000 have already gone."[71] The next year it was reported that 50 percent of all junior officers had left for business as soon as their obligated service time was up.[72]

The situation was not much better among more senior officers. For example, in 1995 a survey was taken of officers attending the Gagarin and Zhukovsky Academies (usually at the major or lieutenant-colonel level). "Eighty percent ... were pessimistic about the future, and 87 percent were disturbed about the decline in the prestige of military service. Most were ambivalent about future military service, and 40 percent wished to resign. Incredibly, only 3 percent expressed an intense desire for continued service."[73] Even worse, Deborah Ball conducted a survey among Russian officers that indicated that there were questions concerning the potential reliability of field-grade officers in the event of an internal crisis.[74]

The reasons for their dissatisfaction were obvious. Housing was a major issue. As a result of budgetary cutbacks, the military had to reduce the number of square meters of housing it intended to build in 1994 from 80,000 to 60,000. In 1995 instead of 100,000 square meters, it would only be able to build 40,000, thereby leaving 180,000 officers without apartments.[75] There was also a problem with pay. Officers were given pay raises at six-month intervals, but these raises seldom kept up with inflation. Then there was the issue of actually getting a paycheck. It was almost always late. Most officers expected their pay to be several months late, a disastrous situation for a soldier who depended on his paycheck to support himself and his family. By 1996 it was reported that "80 percent of all officers had gone without pay for five months or more."[76] As a result, officers increasingly found it necessary to take second jobs to make ends meet, even though military regulations forbade officers from taking second jobs. However, the practice of "moonlighting"

is winked at by senior officers; indeed, according to *Red Star* [*Krasnaya zvezda*], commanders now often organize job opportunities "on the side" for their officers. A good posting is one that offers the best outside job opportunities, for example, the military academies in Moscow. The majority of officers are forced to take demeaning manual jobs and because their work is illegal they cannot complain about pay.[77]

In 1995 it appeared that there might be light at the end of the tunnel. The government agreed to index wages, thereby saving the officers from inflation. However, the Finance Ministry offered a 25 percent increase, while the Ministry of Defense argued that officers should get a 208 percent pay raise. As a result the officer corps became further demoralized. "Society has withdrawn the respect and prestige they normally accord to officers, and junior officers are resigning from the Army in droves. Older officers are being forced into premature retirement."[78] Why continue to serve with no respect, no pay, no decent housing, but still be expected to work long hours and face the dangers of fighting the Chechen War?

The draft remained a major problem and gradually worsened, not surprising in view of the War in Chechnya. To deal with this problem, on April 7, 1995, the Duma reversed its earlier decision and lengthened conscription time from eighteen to twenty-four months. The longer time period was also made retroactive for those drafted in 1993–1994. Students graduating from institutes of higher learning also became subject to conscription. This meant that college graduates would have to spend one year in the armed forces, regardless of whether they had participated in reserve officer training courses.[79] Drafting bodies was one thing—their health was another. In 1996, for example, 15 percent of those who were drafted had restrictions on where they could be stationed due to poor health.[80] Draft evasion was also a major problem. For example, in spring 1996 there were 26,000 draft evasions, in spring 1997 there were 32,000, and in the autumn of that year 40,000. What was most upsetting to the Army was that of the 66,000 draft evaders, only 110 were prosecuted. Clearly, Yeltsin and the civilian world were not taking the problem seriously.[81]

It was not surprising that young men did not want to serve in the Army. Conditions were horrible. For example, by mid-1995 the Army was complaining that it could not buy enough food and that "by winter many garrisons in the North could simply starve—but [the generals] were told to borrow some money from commercial banks."[82] The concern about starvation was not misplaced, because in the latter part of 1995 there were reports of twenty soldiers dying of malnutrition.[83] Food began to be rationed, and the Army again had to draw on its war reserves just to feed the troops. The next year there were warnings, "The soldier does not have enough to eat. He is hungry. And it is painful to see young guys in uniform begging in the streets."[84] These are some of the reasons why desertion remained a serious problem. "From January to June 1995, 3,000 servicemen absconded, raising concern for the crisis situation in the military."[85] According to one Russian source, "No one wants to serve in the Army. This is an axiom in Russia."[86]

The major problem with getting young men to serve was the continued prevalence of *dedovshchina*. C. J. Dick identified the problem when he observed, "The atmosphere reigning in army barracks can easily be compared to the microclimate in correctional labor camps."[87] In an effort to deal in part with the problem, the high command continued to push its effort to recruit more professionals. That policy too had its problems.

According to Moscow Television, between 1993 and 1995 "about 50,000 contract servicemen resigned."[88] Why did so many quit? There were a number of reasons. First, some were forced out due to poor quality, refusal to follow orders, etc. The major problem, however, was money. For example, in September 1995 the average Russian salary was 550,000 rubles. A contract servicemen, however, made only 278,000 rubles (including supplements). Yet at this time the subsistence wage in Russia was 300,000 rubles, and that number could be two or three times higher, depending on the part of the country.[89] In addition, their facilities were not appreciably better than that enjoyed by conscripts.

Why would an individual join the Army if he was going to be paid a pittance, not enough to support himself, let alone a family, and then be forced to live like a recruit? The answer was simple: few did, and those who did quickly left when they discovered the reality. Not only were they treated no better than a recruit, but they were almost guaranteed to be sent to Chechnya.

There was also a problem with moral decay in the military. In 1994, for example, an investigation showed that Chechen fighters were able to purchase weapons and ammunition from Russian soldiers fighting in the republic. Theft was also a becoming a major problem. By the end of 1994, one source reported, "In recent years the number of thefts [of arms] has increased by a factor of 25. While in 1987–1988, a little more than 100 items were stolen, now this is thousands of gun barrels, including not just pistols and rifles but machine guns, grenade launchers, portable surface-to-air-missiles, air-to-air missiles, and armored fighting vehicles."[90] By 1995 it was reported that, while the overall crime rate in Russia had risen by 5.6 percent, in the military it was up by 30 percent.[91] The situation throughout the military was so bad that the Military Procurator appealed to Yeltsin to set up military police to help deal with the problem. As Graham Turbiville observed, "Given the growing levels of random and organized criminality in the Russian military—and the corruption at all ranks, branches, and services—the creation of an effective military police force or other political system is clearly critical for creating a cohesive military institution."[92]

The Russian peacekeeping force in the former Yugoslavia, supposedly made up of handpicked troops, was also deeply involved in corruption. They were "the undisputed champions of illegal activities."[93] For example, in April 1995, the UN dismissed Russian Major General Alexander Perelyakin as head of the UN peacekeeping commander in a Serbian sector of Croatia. A Belgian battalion in the region had complained that the Russians had been involved in "smuggling, profiteering, corruption, negligence, and collaboration with local Serb militias." In Bosnia, UN forces "discovered Russian airborne forces selling UN fuel to both Muslims and the Serbs on several occasions, and speculation concerning their trafficking in other goods (to include small arms) was rife."[94] The corruption was so rampant in the armed forces themselves that one observer commented, "Corruption is so all-pervasive that social and official (as opposed to personal) honesty becomes simply irrational, irrelevant, unpraised, and unexpected.[95] Corruption was also widespread in the military commissariats to help young men avoid the draft. Alexander Golts commented that the paying of bribes to members of the commissariats and physicians was so rampant that it involved 87 percent of the youth and that "It is an industry with the turnover of tens of billions of dollars."[96]

COMBAT READINESS

Given the foregoing, it is not surprising that combat readiness continued to drop. Even the elite Strategic Rocket Forces had serious problems. An article discussing the problem in the SRF noted, "The command posts and control centers were in worse shape than the missiles."[97] In fact, by the end of 1994, the country's senior generals were complaining that the military could not carry out its tasks—and they had in mind more than just the war in Chechnya. To quote a Russian observer:

> The actual situation is as follows: the troops are manned by 45 to 50 percent; troops' material provision has been cut by nearly 60 percent, as a result of which approximately 70 percent of games and maneuvers had to be scrapped; combat flying practice had been reduced sharply; from 100–120 hours to 30–35 hours a year; and only one to two divisions are deemed fully combat-ready in each military district, and one to two ships in each fleet.[98]

In 1995 it was reported that only 20 percent of the entire fleet of tanks was usable, and that "the supply of combat aircraft had fallen twenty times."[99] It is hard to conceive of a combat-ready military when training funds are drastically cut. In fact, by 1995 they were down 90 percent in comparison with 1991.[100] The situation was so bad that pilots often spent most of their time sweeping runways. Indeed, many of them were reassigned to other branches because there was nothing for them to do.

Weapons modernization and purchases were also a major problem. For example, where in 1991 the air force had purchased 585 aircraft, in 1995 it bought only two![101] The same year the Army had received only twelve new battle tanks. It should have received 300 just to keep its armor at its current level.[102] To get an idea of how bad the situation was, consider the following: in most developed countries "between 60 and 80 percent of all weapons are new; in Russia the figure is 30 percent."[103] With no new weapons—in fact, with the Army unable to replace what it was using up—and no training, it was not surprising that there were major problems with combat readiness. Things were bad and getting worse.

MILITARY CULTURE

Yeltsin had disappointed the high command in the aftermath of the 1993 confrontation with parliament. The military had come to his aid, but his numerous promises all went unfulfilled. The generals were even more disillusioned by the middle of 1996. Yeltsin had forced them to go to war (even if it was inside Russia) at a time when almost all of them knew that an attack on Chechnya was suicide. The military was in no position to carry out such a mission. Many of the generals took the unprecedented step of resigning rather than leading troops into what they correctly assumed would be a "turkey shoot." But the president paid no attention to them. He showed little respect for the professional expertise of these men who had devoted their lives to the profession of arms. In the end, hundreds of Russian soldiers died, all because the president ordered them to attack, and the country's most senior general went along with him at a time when Grachev should have known better and should have warned Yeltsin that there was little chance that the attack would succeed. Instead, he boasted that it would be a cakewalk. Indeed, the disgust felt by most of the country's senior generals toward Yeltsin was only matched by their dislike for Grachev. He was inept, inexperienced, and most of all a blatant opportunist. They would all rejoice when he was unceremoniously sacked in mid-1996.

Then to further undermine their respect for their commander in chief, Yeltsin criticized them for the Army's poor showing in Chechnya. The audacity! He forces them into a war that could have been postponed for several months and for which they were not prepared. Why did they have so many problems? Because of Yeltsin's policies toward the Army. Had he not starved the military for funds the armed forces might have done a much better job. But to blast them for their poor showing when it had been his policies that created the situation was criminal in their minds.

The high command was also upset at Yeltsin's interference with the chain of command. By making the General Staff and the Defense Ministry parallel organizations equally subordinate to the president, he was creating a situation that would end up haunting the military, especially when Anatoly Kvashnin became chief of the General Staff. The generals did not always agree with policies advocated by the defense minister, but he was the defense minister, and they believed it was dangerous for two lines of authority to be created. Who were the generals and soldiers to obey in a crisis?

Yeltsin's first rule—like that of all politicians in all countries—was to stay in power. The generals understood that. But they objected to his tendency to "play" with them, as he did with his promise to get rid of the draft by 2000. They knew he did not have a plan and without a well-thought-out plan, the idea was silly. It was a political promise made at their expense, one that he did not intend to keep.

Meanwhile, the generals were well aware of what was happening to the Army. It was decaying from within and it was falling further and further behind the rest of the world and especially the United States. Yeltsin made one promise after another and, as they soon learned, he almost never kept them. While they understood that he had other priorities, it soon became all too obvious that he had little respect for them or their troops and that he was only interested in retaining their loyalty to avoid a challenge to his political power.

CONCLUSION

It would be wrong to place all of the blame for what happened during the preceding period at Yeltsin's door. After all, Grachev was a general and while he spoke out on the Army's behalf, he went along with Yeltsin's decision to invade Chechnya. Having said that, the continual problem throughout this period was—once again—the lack of presidential leadership.

First, while Yeltsin could not expect to have a sound budget until he got a tax reform bill passed, it was disingenuous for him to expect the Army to remain combat capable at a time when he was starving it of funds. That was even truer in light of his buildup of Interior Ministry forces. How was it that he could find money for them, but nothing was available for the Army—and what was available was constantly cut or not delivered on time?

Second, while Yeltsin did not focus on issues like strategy, a strong president would have sat down with the generals in an effort to understand how the military was responding to the end of the Cold War. What was it doing to balance size, weapons, personnel, and training with new threats? Had Yeltsin done so, he would have realized early on that his options with regard to Chechnya were more limited. He might have forced the military to come to grips with the new world of substate conflict. There is no guarantee that this approach would have led to a better showing in the First Chechen War, but it would have forced some very conservative, tradition-bound generals to take another look at how they were going to war. In short, Yeltsin was not obligated to take a careful look at the intricacies of military operations, but if he had, he might have made better policy choices.

Third, Yeltsin's tendency to ignore the military permitted the Army to avoid dealing with a variety of internal problems. The generals were right in arguing that military reform costs money—no money, no reform. However, had he pushed them to come up with a meaningful military reform plan—and stuck with it—they would have been forced to deal with issues such as *dedovshchina,* NCOs, crime, corruption, etc. in a more meaningful fashion. As it was, he let them off the hook by making boisterous claims that military reform was just around the corner, claims that the generals knew were exaggerated and had little or no relevance when it came to make substantive changes in how the Army operated.

Finally, Yeltsin did not learn from his mistakes in dealing with the Army. Unfortunately, as the future would attest, he paid almost no attention to them. He would repeat those same mistakes many times over. He was not interested in the armed forces, unless it came to staying in power or protecting the country from secessionist republics like Chechnya.

CHAPTER FIVE

YELTSIN AND THE MILITARY, JULY 1996–DECEMBER 1999

> As long as Yeltsin is in power, Russia will be dying.
> *Lieutenant General Lev Rokhlin*

From the military's standpoint, Yeltsin's last two and a half years in office were even worse than the first four years. He continued to use the military for his own personal purposes, without treating it as a serious organization in need of reform and reorganization. He constantly made promises: higher salaries, more money for the military, support for military reform. But he failed to live up to his promises, just as he had in the past. He did not treat senior officers with respect; instead, he publicly humiliated them. Most upsetting from the position of the high command was his continuing refusal to provide the military with the leadership it needed to deal with its severe internal problems. Issues like crime, corruption, *dedovshchina,* training, etc., only got worse, leaving the military in an incredible mess when he suddenly resigned on December 31, 1999. The Russian armed forces were a far cry from the military he had inherited in 1991. If its situation was serious when he became president, it would be nothing short of catastrophic by the time he left.

RODIONOV TAKES OVER

On July 17, 1996, Yeltsin appointed Colonel General Igor Rodionov as defense minister. While General Alexander Lebed's endorsement of Rodionov was important, he was also well thought of by senior military officers. As one General Staff officer put it, "It was the best possible decision . . . He enjoys deep respect both among the troops and in the central apparatus of the Ministry of Defense."[1] Many officers remembered that it was Rodionov who had been in charge of Soviet troops during the massacre in Tbilisi under Gorbachev. The Sobchak Commission had found him responsible for the brutal use of force in Georgia, but few in the military accepted that verdict. Rather, they saw him as a scapegoat for the sins of politicians like Gorbachev. Equally important, many in uniform remembered he had stood up for the Army by criticizing the Yeltsin government for failing to make military reform a priority when he was head of the General Staff Academy. As he put it, "If military reform is now at an impasse and the Armed Forces per se (i.e., the Army and Navy) have been reduced to a desperate state, this is primarily the fault of the country's political leadership, which has completely removed itself from the management of military reform."[2] Harsh words from an officer who hoped to be the country's defense minister, especially when they could only have been aimed at President Yeltsin and Defense Minister Pavel Grachev. Rodionov was convinced that Yeltsin's tendency to improvise when dealing with the military was a disaster. He was not being realistic in his approach to military reform. Most Russian generals, especially those at the General Staff Academy, believed that all aspects of military operations could be planned, but to be effective they had to be well thought-out and they had to be given a solid structural framework. Rodionov therefore believed that the country had to come up with a plan to deal with the military of the future. And in many ways his different background and personality made him the right person to deal with the issue.

Rodionov was unusual for a number of reasons. First, he was not opposed to civilian involvement in military matters. Rodionov believed they should participate at least at the strategic level. Furthermore, he was smart enough to realize that if civilians did not understand operational and tactical operations, they would constantly be making decisions that undermined the military's ability to carry out its mission. Mutual understanding was critical. Ignorant civilians were a threat to the military. Indeed, he had previously made the unusual (for a senior military officer) suggestion that the General Staff Academy should be transformed into an Academy of National Security and Defense. Its purpose would be similar to the American War Colleges: to train military officers and civilian officials together, to give them an opportunity to interact while studying national security matters.

Second, Rodionov was also outspoken in his support for a professional cadre of non-commissioned officers (NCOs). He pointed to the Western experience, where long-serving, professional NCOs carried considerable prestige and played a major role in training, disciplining, and leading soldiers. He had long believed that Moscow would never have a first-rate, professional Army until it introduced NCOs. The idea of making conscripts NCOs at a time when junior officers were both untrained and overworked was a recipe for disaster. It was the main cause of the notorious *dedovshchina* hazing policy.

Third, Rodionov was convinced that the number of Army units and personnel had to be brought into balance. It made no sense to have large numbers of units that were only half manned or less. Besides, Russia could not hope to support such large units given budgetary realities. A smaller military, but one with high-tech weapons, would be far more lethal. As he explained, "It is essential to increase the number of fully manned, combat-ready large units by sharply reducing the number of military formations of reduced strength."[3] In the meantime, he also convinced Yeltsin to wait five years before implementing his plan to move to an all-volunteer army starting in the year 2000. While no one seriously believed that this change would occur even then, it at least gave the military much-needed bureaucratic breathing space.

Fourth, according to one Russian source, Rodionov was also viewed as a man with high moral standards and—something rare for Russian soldiers of his day—a man who believed in God.[4] There had been considerable talk about the importance of Russia having a civilian defense minister. Indeed, several national security specialists, such as Andrei Kokoshin from the Institute for the Study of the USA and Canada, had been rumored as candidates for the job. Not surprisingly, senior military officers were opposed, and Yeltsin did not want to alienate them. So he reached a compromise, one that he hoped would satisfy both the civilians who wanted a civilian defense minister and the senior officers who wanted to keep a career officer in the position. On December 11, Rodionov retired from the Army to become Russia's first "civilian" defense minister.

Rodionov had been thinking about military reform for several years as head of the General Staff Academy, and he had some ideas on how to implement his proposals. His approach contrasted sharply with Grachev's simplistic ideas. Rodionov's approach was much more intellectual, and his ideas were more straightforward and better thought-out. To begin with, he saw a difference between the concepts of military reform and reforming the armed forces. According to Rodionov, "Military reform is the process of bringing the entire defense activity of the state into conformity with the new political, economic and social changes in society." In this sense, he was talking about changing the societal sub-structure, to use the Marxist phrase. Responsibility for changes of this nature lay with the country's political authorities, because not only are military assets involved, but the economy, society, and the rest of the polity as well. The second aspect, reform of the armed forces, is subordinate to military reform; it is a part of the superstructure, to again apply the Marxist terminology. While political direction was critical, planning and making the key changes was the responsibility of the defense ministry. It meant a fundamental modification in military affairs, and that meant a change in military doctrine, the document that controls almost all aspects of military affairs.[5] In Rodionov's mind the best way to proceed was to have a unified policymaking body, and, toward that end, he recommended the creation of a Defense Council. "This new body was given a mandate to gather information from all the actors involved, and to draw proposals concerning the future tasks of the Armed Forces, as well as the other troops."[6]

Another area where Rodionov broke new ground was his call on the Russian military to prepare for "low-density" conflicts, such as the First Chechen War. He also opposed the idea that the country could be defended by either nuclear weapons or a professional military. "The first blow could be devastating. The task was to absorb the first blow, to make it possible for the country to move from peacetime conditions to wartime conditions. For this reason the main task for [the] military organization of society was the presence of ready reserves."[7] This is why he saw military reform as part of a much-larger process involving the whole of society. Despite its intellectual sophistication, and its common-sense appeal, Rodionov's approach had a major problem. It carried a large price tag, and the military was experiencing a severe financial crisis. When Rodionov took over, the military's debts accounted for almost 30 percent of its operating budget.[8] Indeed, the military had witnessed several occasions when civilian suppliers had turned off the power because of unpaid debts.

Yeltsin agreed to Rodionov's suggestion to create a Defense Council. In fact, he welcomed it, because he saw it as a counter to the Security Council headed by Lebed. The new Defense Council was created on July 25, 1996, but it was to be headed by a civilian, Yuri Baturin, Yeltsin's assistant for national security affairs. Rodionov would spend almost all of his ten months as defense minister arguing with Baturin, who was tasked with overseeing military reform. Rodionov considered Baturin illiterate when it came to military issues. He knew nothing about the military, yet here he was making proposals on how to reform it. The battle went on until February 1997, when Rodionov accused Baturin of "conducting a misinformation campaign about the state of affairs in the armed forces." He went so far as to demand that Baturin be dismissed.[9] Rodionov was convinced that the military had to be cut back, and he recognized that it would be extremely expensive to do so. Officers who were let go had to be paid a separation allowance, and then there was the cost of housing for them since officers who retired or were involuntarily demobilized had to be provided with housing. All of these expenses were in addition to the cost of structural modifications and new weapons purchases, not to mention operations and maintenance costs. How could officers who had served twenty or twenty-five years be let go without a separation allowance? It would be morally wrong. Suggesting that military reform could be carried out without spending money was nonsense. In fact, it was worse than that. As Rodionov put it, "When I am told that reform can be implemented without financing, without money, this is pure demagogy."[10]

Baturin, on the other hand, saw it as his duty to convince the military to cut back on spending, given the country's fiscal problems. He argued that Russia had 85 percent of the Soviet Army but only 60 percent of the USSR's GNP.[11] At one point, he argued that the budget should be cut by up to 30 percent.[12] Through most of 1997 (until Rodionov was dismissed), there was a new Cold War between the head of the Defense Council and the Defense Minister. Much to Rodionov's chagrin, Yeltsin tended to side with Baturin when it came to debates over how much to spend on the military. Baturin would continue to argue with the military over how much money it was to spend until he was replaced by First Deputy Defense Minister Andrei Kokoshin the following August.[13]

LEBED LEAVES THE ADMINISTRATION

While obviously disappointed by Yeltsin's decision to create the Defense Council, Lebed attempted to save his position by jumping into the Chechen situation. The Chechen rebels attacked Russian forces in Grozny in an effort to embarrass Yeltsin at a time when he was about to be inaugurated for a second term as president. On August 10 Yeltsin appointed Lebed to be Moscow's representative in Chechnya. The general proceeded to do the seemingly impossible. He met with the Chechens and, on August 31, signed a peace settlement, a power-sharing agreement with Aslan Maskhadov. The agreement "covered withdrawal of federal troops; deferred the definition of Chechnya's status for five years; and called for a unified commission to supervise implementation of the agreement."[14] Lebed commented on the conflict, noting, "There are no victors in this war."[15] Not surprisingly, given the unpopularity of the war in Russia, the agreement made Lebed an instant hero.

Predictably, Yeltsin took exception and ordered Lebed to avoid the public spotlight. But Lebed marched to a different drummer. He had an enormous ego and refused. He continued to fight with General Anatoly Kulikov from the Interior Ministry as he tried to wrest control of that institution. However, he overestimated his political strength.[16] The war between the two generals created an impossible situation. "When generals fight each other," Yeltsin commented, "civilians as well as law and order can suffer."[17] Lebed was getting too assertive and too powerful. Yeltsin wanted to pick his own successor as president, and he was not about to permit this upstart general to take over the country. But Lebed continued to do as he pleased. He even went so far as to call a press conference in which he claimed, "The armed forces were on the verge of mutiny and that national security was threatened by new nuclear accidents and other disasters."[18] He then blasted the chaotic decision-making process in the Yeltsin administration. Yeltsin felt threatened and saw no need to put up with this very assertive general any longer. As a result, on October 17, Yeltsin fired Lebed. The general ceased to be an important voice in Russian national security affairs. Furthermore, given Lebed's ouster, Yeltsin saw no need for the Defense Council, and it was eliminated the following March.

RODIONOV TRIES TO PUT THE MILITARY BACK TOGETHER

Despite his close ties to Lebed, Rodionov continued to serve as defense minister, with General Viktor Samsonov as chief of the General Staff. He was determined to place primary emphasis on combined-arms operations. This meant less attention to the airborne forces, an action that even Lebed (an airborne officer) opposed. However, there were systemic problems facing Rodionov and Samsonov. To begin with, they, like other military leaders, expected civilian control, but for that to be effective, the political leadership had to give clear and concise directions about what it wanted the high command to do. But as long as Yeltsin remained as unpredictable both in terms of his health (no one could be certain when he was in charge and when he was permitting things to drift) and his political views, how could the generals rebuild the military? Instability was a *sine qua non* in the Yeltsin administration. The eternal economic problem also was a complication. In the past, the generals had always complained that the key problem was money. It cost money to modernize weapons, to hold training exercises, etc., but part of the problem was that the generals had not adjusted to the new situation. They were still trying to keep the Russian Army configured like the old multimillion-man-strong Soviet Army, ready to repulse an invasion by NATO.

In May 1996 Yeltsin ordered the Security Council to draft a new National Security Concept. A draft was completed in May 1997 and seemed to provide the basis for the military reform that Rodionov was seeking. The preamble reads:

The Concept of the Russian Federation's National Security is a political document, which reflects a total combination of official adopted views as regards specific goals and the appropriate state strategy aimed at ensuring individual, public, and state security against political, economic, social, military, man-made, environmental, information, and other internal and external threats (with due account taken of available resources and possibilities). The concept formulates the most important state-policy guidelines and principles, constituting a foundation for the elaboration of concrete programmes and organizational documents in the field of ensuring the Russian Federation's national security.[19]

The problem with the remainder of the statement, however, was its vagueness. The military was looking for specific guidance; instead, it was given ambiguous and fine-sounding language. Meanwhile, Rodionov set out to make some structural changes, modifications that would enable the Army to defend the periphery of the country, a very difficult task because troops had not been deployed in a way that would defend Russia when the USSR broke up. Whole areas were left undefended because they had been far away from the periphery of the country. Faced with the need to come up with a better and more reasonable approach, Rodionov began by cutting the military from 1.5 million troops to 1.2 million. This meant downsizing both ground and airborne forces, an action that met considerable opposition inside the military. In a testimony to the condition of the Russian military, Rodionov wanted to set up at least one combat-ready division in each military district out of available forces. "In the Moscow District, for example, a new division, the 3rd Motor Rifle Division, has been created since 1997 from elements of two under-strength divisions which were originally part of the Western Group of Forces."[20] The military is like other bureaucracies and those generals affected by the changes were not happy, and they made their displeasure known both inside and outside of the Army. For example, the commander-in-chief of the Ground Forces, General Vladimir Semenov, was critical of Rodionov's cuts. "As a person versed in these affairs I know that an early reduction of the armed forces to this figure (1.2 million men) will lead to the collapse of reforms."[21] Unfortunately for Rodionov, Yeltsin once again refused to give him the support he needed to implement this restructuring plan.

In the meantime, the military was well aware that the interior troops were getting the lion's share of the budget and that they had grown even larger than the Army. For example, in 1996, General Makhmut Garayev estimated the interior forces were at 2 million troops compared with about 1.5 million troops in the Army.[22] While the Army wanted to avoid again being put in a position where it had to use force against the civilian population, the two organizations were highly competitive and resented each other's slice of the budgetary pie.

Then Yeltsin appeared to agree on the funding issue. He understood the country's economic problems, but he knew he would have to allocate the military a larger budget if he was going to solve its many problems. In October, he ordered Prime Minister Viktor Chernomyrdin to set up a special commission to look into armed forces financing. In particular, he wanted the commission to come up with an approach for dealing with the constant back-pay problems. Some officers were forced to wait four or five months for their money, an almost impossible situation for individuals whose only income was their government paycheck. Meanwhile, Rodionov continued to harp on the need to do something. He went so far as to suggest that he could lose control of the military if salaries were not addressed.[23] Then in 1997 Rodionov claimed that Russia's missiles and nuclear systems were in danger unless greater funding was available. Yeltsin ordered a slight increase in the budget—from $42.1 billion to $45.9 billion—but it was well below what Rodionov believed necessary to rebuild the military.[24]

Rodionov's position had been seriously weakened when Lebed, his primary supporter, was fired. There was no one left to defend him, and Yeltsin was not about to put up any longer with another assertive general. As a result, in May 1997, Yeltsin humiliated and fired him and Samsonov on national TV. He blamed them for the Army's failure to reform. As he explained in a televised session of the Defense Council: "I am not simply dissatisfied. I am indignant over the state of reforms in the army and the general state of the armed forces . . . The soldier is losing weight while the general is getting fatter."[25] While it was fair to note that military reform had not succeeded, the biggest problem was the president, who had failed to provide Rodionov with the backing he needed to do his job. Yeltsin was particularly perturbed by Rodionov and Samsonov's willingness to stand up for the Army in areas such as funding. As such he considered them dispensable. Yeltsin was president and Rodionov and Samsonov were to carry out his policies regardless of whether or not they hurt the military.

THE CASE OF GENERAL LEV ROKHLIN

Lieutenant General Lev Rokhlin, a veteran of the Afghan war, was a hero for his action in taking Grozny in the First Chechen War despite his deep and sincere misgivings about the conflict. He saw it as a national tragedy—and he objected strongly to the position it put him and his troops in. He gained even greater public respect by his refusal to accept any medals or awards. He even turned down the Hero of Russia medal that Yeltsin tried to give him. In his mind, he was a soldier doing his duty, nothing more.

Given Rokhlin's national popularity, a number of political parties tried to convince him to run for a seat in the Duma. He initially associated himself with the Our Home Is Russia party and later with the Communists, but was really a man above party membership. For example, in 1995 he was a member of Our Home is Russia, but he ran for a seat as an independent and won. He was appointed chairman of the Duma's Defense and Security Committee. Rokhlin was, to use Barylski's words, "The very embodiment of the military's anger and disappointment with Chechnya and of its stoic ability to maintain discipline and loyalty to the State and Russia."[26] He had one purpose in mind: to improve the situation inside the military. When asked about the influence the Defense and Security Committee would have on military affairs he replied, "All of us should be united by a desire to help the Armed Forces solve their problems."[27] At the same time, like many military professionals, he had a hard time adapting to the world of legislative politics, the give-and-take and compromising that is a part of life in the Duma. That sort of bargaining was foreign to someone who had spent the majority of his life giving and following orders. Discussion was not part of the process nor was ambiguity. You received an order and carried it out. Because of his apolitical nature, neither Yeltsin nor Grachev saw Rokhlin as a threat. In the meantime, the Ministry of Defense quickly focused on him as the man best able to represent its interests in the Duma. True to form, Rokhlin ran the committee like it was a military organization.

Given his no-nonsense approach and his respect for the military and its procedures, Rokhlin reacted very negatively to Yeltsin's decision to fire Rodionov, whom he saw as an honest and sincere officer trying to improve the military's situation. He was even more incensed when Yeltsin cut the 1997 budget by 20 percent. "This amount would not even cover the cost of six months of the salaries and benefits mandated by Russian law."[28] In his mind, the Russian Army was no longer capable of carrying out its duties because of Yeltsin's inept policies. In December 1996 Rokhlin made a speech in which he criticized the country's political leadership for failing to understand the need for military reform and failing to provide the necessary financial guarantees.[29] He even wrote a letter to Yeltsin accusing him of "destroying" the military. On another occasion, he remarked, "If this happened to the army of a well-to-do country, there would have been a military coup long ago."[30] He went so far as to suggest to military personnel that they hold officer's assemblies, pass resolutions, and send them to the authorities. Then, shortly after Rodionov was fired, Rokhlin further alienated Yeltsin by sending out 900 copies of a letter he wrote to top military officers protesting the government's failure to properly fund the armed forces.

In view of his strong negative feelings toward the administration, it is not surprising that Rokhlin took Yeltsin on. For example, on July 9, 1997, Rokhlin founded a new organization: the All-Russia Movement for Support of the Army. The group's stated purpose was to defend the Army and its members from Yeltsin's arbitrary actions. Rodionov joined Rokhlin and blasted the Yeltsin administration for its failure to support the Army. Two months later, Rokhlin was calling on Yeltsin to resign. Traditionally, the military went out of its way to remain apolitical. However, given the stance of Rokhlin's organization— even though a large part of its membership was *retired* military officers—many observers thought that the armed forces were coming perilously close to direct involvement in the political process. But the organization did not represent the military as a whole and the new defense minister immediately denounced Rokhlin.[31] This was about as close as the military came to moving against Yeltsin. Nevertheless, they were fed up with him and his policies.[32]

In the end, Rokhlin's efforts were unsuccessful. He was not able to galvanize military opposition in a politically meaningful fashion. The military—and its officers—were too diverse a group to unite behind any single political party or movement. Then a year later, on July 3, 1998, Rokhlin was mysteriously found shot to death—presumably by his wife—at their dacha near Moscow.

IGOR SERGEYEV BECOMES DEFENSE MINISTER

On May 22, 1997, Army General Igor Sergeyev was appointed to replace Rodionov as the next defense minister. Sergeyev was very different from his predecessors. Instead of coming from the airborne or ground forces, Sergeyev was from the Strategic Rocket Forces. He was an unknown in Russia, not a surprise after the problems Yeltsin had with Lebed. The president wanted someone who would not steal his limelight. Furthermore, Yeltsin was convinced that a missile officer would place greater emphasis on nuclear forces, which are much cheaper to build and maintain than conventional forces. If nothing else, the appointment would keep the Army from constantly coming to him for more and more money at a time when there was no money.

Colonel General Anatoly Kvashnin was appointed acting chief of the General Staff on May 23, 1997. Kvashnin's most notable accomplishment to date was that he had commanded Russian troops in Chechnya from December 1994 to February 1995, the months when Russian casualties were at their highest. He was an extremely ambitious officer, one who was prepared to take advantage of the 1996 Law on Defense to oppose Sergeyev when it suited him. Indeed, he would continue to be a major obstacle to military reform under President Vladimir Putin as well.[33]

Meanwhile, Yeltsin demanded that the military learn to live with less money. One of the first things he did was to inform Sergeyev that he planned to cut military expenditures from 5 percent of Gross Domestic Product (GDP) down to 3.5 percent.[34] For his part, Sergeyev was very blunt in pointing out to the officer corps the problems facing the Army:

> We are faced with a simple choice. Either we stick to unjustified numbers, numerous overgrown administrative structures—they are absolutely useless because they have no-one under their command—understaffed troops, defective equipment, pitiful military order—such as we have had for more than three years now—or we cut our numerical strength and structural organization and instead make it possible to transfer some of the funds previously earmarked for the armed forces to research and design work aimed at creating breakthrough technologies. This should enable us to lay down the foundation for the serial production of new arms and equipment. As you understand perfectly well, in the 21st century one's strength will be determined not by numbers but by flexibility and speed.[35]

In July 1997 Yeltsin signed the decree On Priority Measures to Reform the Armed Forces of the Russian Federation and Improve Their Structure. Its purpose was to provide the military with a document that would serve as the basis of a military reform program, the sort of thing that Rodionov had pleaded for. In fact, the structural changes contained in this plan, which Sergeyev supported, were very similar to those proposed by Rodionov. It was split into three phases: From 1997 until 2001 the military would be reduced to 1.2 million; from 1999 to 2001 the services would be combined into the Air and Space Forces, the Ground Forces, and the Navy. Finally, from 2001 to 2005 the three services would be combined into Air-Space Forces, Air Defense Forces, and Operational Forces, including ground and naval elements. In fact, the Space

Forces were absorbed into the Strategic Rocket Forces (becoming the Strategic Deterrence Forces) and the Air Defense Forces lost their anti-air units, as they became part of the Air Force. In essence, this meant that there was now a single system of command and control over all nuclear weapons.

From Sergeyev's standpoint, he had no alternative but to make major cuts. The country faced a basic fiscal problem: no money. But where to make the cuts? Sergeyev believed that the decrease had to come out of the ground forces. As Frank Umbach put it, "Sergeyev, the Foreign Ministry, and many well known civilian experts justified their favoritism for Russia's RVSN [Strategic Rocket Forces] on the grounds that under all circumstances Russia must maintain nuclear parity with the U.S. and NATO, and portrayed U.S. nuclear strategic forces as the most dangerous threat to Russian national security."[36]

Toward this end, he eliminated the Ground Forces high command. This decision was almost inconceivable—the Ground Forces had long been seen as the premier service in the Russian Armed Forces. His action was deeply resented by the Army's largest branch. "Its functions were distributed among a dozen or more General Staff directorates, and the senior ground forces officer was now just head of the General Staff's main directorate of the ground forces. In theory this implied that the ground forces were no longer an independent branch of the armed services ranking with the air force or navy."[37] To add insult to injury, the ground forces were told to repair the damage to their forces as a result of the war in Chechnya out of their budget, even though there was no money appropriated for that purpose. What money there was would be spent on developing and expanding the nuclear forces. Indeed, as long as Sergeyev was defense minister there would be no money for the procurement or maintenance of conventional weapons.

Sergeyev also cut positions at the Ministry of Defense. Only absolutely critical positions remained, while others were either eliminated or transferred to the field. The armed forces could not afford to have an army of bureaucrats sitting at desks drawing salaries when they were not indispensable. He also decided to cut the number of generals from 1,700 to 1,298.[38] That may not sound like much, but in a military that was as top-heavy as the Russian military, this cut would have a significant impact on the personnel structure. Next the number of military districts was also reduced from eight to six (as of January 1, 1999, the Siberian and Trans-Baikal districts would be merged, and in 2001 the Volga and Urals districts would be combined).

Equally important, Sergeyev decided to do something about the chain-of-command problems the military had faced both before but especially during the First Chechen War. Accordingly, Military Districts were given the status of Operational-Strategic Commands. That meant that the military district commander was responsible for all the forces in his area of responsibility (and that included Interior Ministry troops). As Brunius put it, "On the shoulders of the district commander was placed the responsibility and the authority to estimate the military-political condition, and to accomplish missions within his zone of responsibility."[39] Considerable command authority had now been shifted to the field, at the Military-District level, where the commander would be in charge of all security organizations. He would be responsible for training and equipping the units under his command. Permanent-readiness units were also introduced, which were supposed to be at least 80 percent manned. This concept would play a major role in Putin's efforts to reform the Army. Finally, personnel strength was cut by a further 500,000 down to 1.2 million. Yeltsin issued decrees in July implementing these reforms and they became law.[40]

In operationalizing his nuclear-weapons approach, Sergeyev decided to place all such systems under a single command. He also backed production of a new missile, the Topol-M SS–27, and a new missile for the Navy, missiles that he hoped would be put in series production. The logic of Sergeyev's position was that the military was being relieved of the need to worry about internal threats, a task that was being assigned to Interior Ministry troops. The problem, of course, was that this left Russia without any meaningful capability to respond to conventional threats regardless of their nature. As Walter Parchomenko noted with regard to Sergeyev's emphasis on nuclear weapons:

> Sergeyev's plan also embraces nuclear reform. He is actively aware that there is little money to pursue key reform goals, notably a professional army and major procurement of nuclear weapons, for at least several years. Consequently, Sergeyev believes greater reliance on nuclear deterrence in military strategy is essential, and the highest priority should be given to programs aimed at developing Russia's strategic nuclear forces, which account for less than 20 percent of the defense budget. Given Russia's grossly inadequate defense budget, this means virtually no conventional defense procurement is possible for the next few years in order to make the nuclear shield reliable.[41]

Regardless of its military value, Sergeyev's approach must have sounded like music to Yeltsin's ears. Finally, a defense minister who understood the need for the military to get by on a minimal budget! However fiscally rational

that approach may have been, it ran up against the politics of military bureaucracy; in fact, Sergeyev would be heavily criticized for his policy by others
in uniform. His plan, as Baev pointed out, put Sergeyev (and Yeltsin) in direct
conflict with the chief of the General Staff, Kvashnin, and his preference for
conventional warfare.[42] Kvashnin was a ground-forces officer and technically
he did not work for the defense minister. He reported directly to the president. Kvashnin was determined to rebuild conventional forces, and he intended to resist strongly any attempt to keep money away from them. Tsypkin
aptly summarized the differences of approach between Sergeyev and Kvashnin when he commented:

> If we go beyond personalities, the Sergeyev–Kvashnin conflict represents
> a clash between those in favor of radical reform and those opposed to it.
> The latter continue to adhere to a somewhat attenuated form of Soviet
> military doctrine; those opponents of reform think that the West is a real
> threat to Russia and that it must be deterred by a combination of strategic
> nuclear forces and sizeable conventional forces. The former believe that
> the threat from the West or from China is unlikely to arise in the immedi-
> ate and mid-term future as long as Russia maintains its nuclear arsenal.
> They believe that this allows for a breathing space, during which money
> could be saved by reducing conventional forces to the minimum neces-
> sary for prevailing in local conflicts.[43]

Given the conflict that was inevitable between Sergeyev and Kvashnin, why
didn't Yeltsin remove Kvashnin at this point? There are two explanations.
First, having Kvashnin as chief of the General Staff permitted him to "divide
and conquer" by keeping the defense minister and chief of the General Staff
at each other's throats. Second, Yeltsin probably did not want to take on the
military bureaucracy at a time when the defense minister was actually doing
what he wanted.

In the meantime, Sergeyev and Yeltsin told the military that officers salaries'
would be raised, indeed Sergeyev's plan called for the doubling of salaries and
benefits while "per-capita spending on new military equipment would triple
by the year 2001."[44] With a smaller, better-qualified, and better-trained officer
corps, and with new, ultra-modern weapons, Sergeyev believed the Russian
military would become increasingly competitive. While regrettable, the old
cadre of officers would need to be retired to make way for a new generation of
young, better-educated individuals. Furthermore, Yeltsin argued that many

support systems would have to be privatized. Sergeyev also tried to ingratiate himself with the officer corps by claiming that he had "defended our positions" in dealing with Yeltsin.[45]

Officials announced that the defense budget would be raised in 1998 by increasing the ratio allocated to defense from 3.5 percent to 4 percent. Following his typical political approach to dealing with problems, Yeltsin decided to visit a number of military installations to announce publicly the wonderful things he was going to do for the troops, namely increase their salaries. Then in December 1997 Sergeyev claimed that considerable progress had been achieved in the reform program. He argued optimistically that transformation was moving in the right direction to "a small, fully capable rational structure and number of personnel."[46] However, as often happened in Yeltsin's Russia, the country's military leader was overly optimistic. Baev pointed out two major problems with Sergeyev's plan. "First, strategic 'muscle' was of no use in a world of growing unconventional security challenges. Second, and more serious, Sergeyev did not have enough time or perhaps courage to advance the second part of the plan: downsizing and modernizing Russia's conventional forces, which would have necessarily involved a head-on confrontation with the General Staff."[47]

In fact, most of the country's top generals were opposed to Sergeyev's approach. Few thought it would lead anywhere. As one officer put it, "The five-year military 'reform' has not yielded anything good for the country and society, the state, and the Armed Forces . . . Military reform is replaced by endless conversations about it."[48] The generals were tied to conventional forces; indeed, most of them had spent most of their lives in the ground forces or airborne troops. The idea of placing all bets on nuclear forces bothered them. What if Russia were faced with a conventional threat? It is one thing to threaten nuclear retaliation, but that could be like hitting a fly with a baseball bat, "overkill," to use the military term.

The military also had to decide how to fight terrorism.[49] The First Chechen War had demonstrated that the Kremlin was not in a position to fight against terrorism effectively. The collapse of the USSR had destroyed the country's counter-terrorism capability. Steps had to be taken to get the various security organizations working together. Accordingly on November 6, 1998, a Federal Antiterrorist Commission was created. It was headed by the prime minister and included organizations such as the Ministry of Internal Affairs, the Federal Security Service, and the Ministry of Defense. In most cases, the Ministry of Internal Affairs would be in charge of an operation, unless it required military force.

This changed the role of the military in several ways. First, it blurred the distinction between peace and war. In the event of a terrorist attack, the high command could not count on the issuance of a declaration of war, thereby giving it the opportunity to convert to a wartime footing. In addition, the distinction between military combat and security operations was blurred. This increased Yeltsin's power, because it meant that he did not have to declare a state of emergency in order to deploy security forces without legislative approval.[50] It was up to him to define terrorism.

THE AUGUST 1998 ECONOMIC CRISIS

In early 1998 world oil prices collapsed. This had an immediate impact on Russia, because it hurt the inflow of hard currency into the country, and the Russian economy was heavily dependent on the export of oil. By May the country was experiencing a financial crisis. Stock prices dropped 10 percent on May 20, 1998. "Between October 1997 and July 1998, the Russian market lost more than 60 percent of its value."[51] The country's economy was on the verge of collapse. The International Monetary Fund (IMF) provided Moscow with a loan to tide it over, but only after major pressure from the United States. By July there were even rumors of a possible coup attempt. Social unrest increased as the Russian government was increasingly unable to pay salaries. The IMF loan did not solve the problem, and the situation grew increasingly worse. Then on August 10, Russian stocks again dropped precipitously. Finally on August 17, the "government announced a dramatically new approach to currency policy. The main ingredients of this approach were a ruble exchange rate fluctuating with the new limits of the 'currency corridor.'"[52] The result was a 50 percent devaluation of the ruble. The country's economy was in shambles.

Yeltsin fired Prime Minister Sergei Kiriyenko, and for several weeks there was no government in Moscow. During that period, there were rumors flying around Moscow suggesting that the military might be planning a coup similar to what had occurred under Gorbachev in 1991. Some even feared that the situation could deteriorate into a confrontation such as took place in October 1993. Indeed, there was a report indicating that Yeltsin might have seriously thought about using force at one point. According to Aleksandr Golts, Yeltsin considered using the military to dissolve the Duma. It was at that point that Andrei Kokoshin, then secretary of the Security Council, reportedly sent Yeltsin a memorandum "stating that the ministry of defense and internal ministry troops would not obey an order to use force to carry out Yeltsin's political plans." Golts believes that notice forced Yeltsin to abandon such plans.[53]

The military budget had already been in serious trouble as early as 1996. The shortfall in that year—the part of the budget promised but not paid—was R25,000 billion. It was so bad that the average officer was due about R10,000 in back pay.[54] In January 1997 Defense Minister Rodionov had even begged private banks to bail out the military, a request that must have hurt the high command's pride. In 1997, the shortfall was R34.4 billion.[55] To make matters worse, because of the military's starvation budget, there was less and less money for purchasing new weapons. As Alexei Arbatov pointed out, the budgets from 1997 to 1999 allocated up to 70 percent for maintenance, while cutting personnel by 30 percent. This left almost nothing for research and development. Funds allocated to them "were barely sufficient for modernization of the minimal strategic forces."[56]

The most immediate impact of the 1998 economic crisis was that it undercut any serious effort to implement Sergeyev's military reform plan. While it is impossible to compare this military budget with those of preceding years, given the devaluation of the ruble, one source has compared the percentage of GDP allocated to the military and, based on that data, it is clear that there was a drop. Where 2.97 percent of GDP was allocated to the military in 1998, the following year it was down to 2.34 percent and only up to 2.63 percent by 2000.[57] Needless to say, any idea of a rational, carefully constructed plan went out the window. The military was already underfunded, and then it was faced with a further drop in its budget. Sergeyev probably put it best just prior to the collapse when he noted, "To draw up a budget like Mozambique but demand forces like the United States is not entirely logical." Given the problems he was facing in getting even part of what the military was allocated when the overall budget was decreasing, the idea of obtaining a budget like Mozambique's probably looked good by the end of 1998, since the military only received 55 percent of what it was promised that year.[58]

Sergeyev spoke out again publicly in 1999 concerning the military's economic mess. On September 28 he stated that the situation in Russia was so bad that the Army could not expect to "increase spending to the point needed to reequip the military until 2006."[59] Taylor summed up just how hard the military had been hit under Yeltsin: "Russian defense spending declined from 142 billion dollars in 1992 to four billion in 1999, a ninety-eight percent decrease!"[60] Or, as Parchomenko observed, the current defense budget "provides six times less than the minimally needed funding for adequate combat training."[61] It was clear that under these circumstances any thought of military reform was out the window for the foreseeable future.

KOSOVO

Before discussing the details of the Kosovo operation, some background is needed. When NATO agreed to send peacekeepers to Bosnia in 1997, U.S. President Bill Clinton strongly believed that it would strengthen matters if the Russians were involved as part of the Implementation Force (IFOR). There was a problem, however, and that was that Moscow did not want to be part of a NATO-led coalition for political reasons. On October 23, Clinton met with Yeltsin and convinced him to send two battalions of Russian soldiers, about 2,000 troops, who were placed *not* under NATO control, but under an American commander, General George Joulwan.[62]

While primarily populated by ethnic Albanians, Kosovo is sacred to Serbs because it contains some of Serbia's most important and treasured historical sites and religious shrines. Furthermore, hatred between Albanians and Serbs has simmered for centuries. The Serbs were determined to keep Kosovo a part of Serbia, while the majority Albanians had long-wanted autonomy—if not independence. By 1997 the Albanian Kosovo Liberation Army (KLA) had 15,000 to 20,000 troops under arms and was getting weapons from a variety of sources. The KLA then began what amounted to a guerilla war, attacking Serbian police stations and other buildings and individuals they believed supported the Belgrade government.

The Russians had long supported the Serbs, first, because they had a long historical association and, second, because Serbian and Russian are both Slavic languages and the Orthodox Church predominates in both cultures. Furthermore, Moscow had long been perturbed at NATO's anti-Belgrade policies because the Kremlin had supported the Serbs in dealing with Bosnian Muslims and Croats as well as the Albanian population in Kosovo. Moscow, and especially many of Russia's top military leaders, believed that it was time for the Kremlin to stand up to NATO. In May 1998 Serbian leader Slobodan Milosevic began to retaliate against the Albanians. Russia needed to get involved.

Officers like Kvashnin saw this as a perfect opportunity to undermine Defense Minister Sergeyev and his emphasis on nuclear weapons. Such weapons were useless for exerting Russian influence vis-à-vis NATO in Kosovo. Russia appeared impotent to the entire world. While the evidence is unclear, Taylor argued that Kvashnin consulted Yeltsin in advance on what to do, while Sergeyev was left out of the loop. In any case, on June 11–12, 1999, Russian troops moved from Bosnia to the Slatina Airport at Pristina, the capital of Kosovo, in order to preempt the planned arrival of NATO's Kosovo Force (KFOR) troops. NATO was outraged. General Wesley Clark, the U.S. commander, reportedly ordered General Mike Jackson, the commander on the scene, to dispatch helicopters to take control of the airport before the Russians arrived. However, Jackson refused.[63] The Russian troops were almost to the airport and removing them at that point could have led to major confrontation between the Russian paratroopers and NATO forces, something no one wanted.

Regardless of whether Yeltsin knew what was planned or if he was misled by Kvashnin, the simple fact was that the Kosovo operation demonstrated the impotence of Sergeyev's military policy. Emphasizing nuclear weapons might save money, but it was useless when it came to conventional warfare. This was a point that would be made even clearer in September 1999, when the Russian Army was faced with the need to use force against Chechnya again.

THE ATTACK ON DAGESTAN

From 1996 to mid-1999, the situation in Chechnya deteriorated. The Chechen government that took over after the Russians left was never able to build a viable nation-state. "Chechnya descended into anarchy and became one of the most dangerous places in the world. It was estimated that as many as 1,300 people lost their lives in Chechnya between 1997 and 1999 and many thousands more fled the republic."[64] Kidnapping became a way of life. Even worse, as Dmitry Trenin pointed out, after Chechen President Dzhokhar Dudayev was killed by a Russian missile in 1996, Chechnya was "consistently unable to reach a consensus choosing a new national leader who enjoyed unquestionable authority and could represent Chechen society as a whole."[65] Aslan Maskhadov, a former Soviet general and a man seen by most observers to be moderate, tried to gain control of the republic. At the same time, there was pressure for a more radical, Islamic-based government and society. In other words, as Paul Murphy argued, there was a strong movement toward the creation of Wahhabism, especially in parts of Chechnya and Dagestan, the Russian republic that borders Chechnya to the southeast.[66] In 1997 one of the key Chechen leaders invited a famous fundamentalist imam, Bagauddin Mohammed, to come to Chechnya. Then in 1999 this imam, together with his followers, resettled in Chechnya.

Furthermore, by late 1998 and 1999, as Trenin and Malashenko pointed out, the key motivating factor in Chechnya was no longer political or economic reform, but the radical Shamil Basayev and those who supported him convinced the "Congress of the Peoples of Chechnya and Dagestan" to institutionalize the idea of the unification of Chechnya and Dagestan into a single Islamic imamate (a theocratic state).[67] Indeed, by mid-1999 the moderates appeared to have lost control of the Islamic movement.

In August 1999 Chechen extremists, led by Shamil Basayev and Emir al Khattab, an Arab mercenary, invaded Dagestan. Basayev claimed that he crossed into Dagestan because "many Dagestani political parties and movements are fighting for Dagestan's freedom nowadays. Some of them have asked me to take up the command of the Mujahideen United Armed Forces of Dagestan."[68] His troops first moved toward a number of villages inhabited by friendly Wahhabists, who he hoped (in vain, as it turned out) would inspire other Dagastanis to rise up and support him and his forces. Estimates on the number of Basayev's troops ranged between 300 and 2,000.[69] The action by the radical Chechens was a direct challenge to Moscow and to Yeltsin's authority. To quote Murphy, "Thus Basayev and Khattab not only precipitated an act of war on Russia by invading Dagestan, but their new Islamic organization officially and publicly declared war on both Dagestan and Russia."[70] The Kremlin had to respond; Basayev and Khattab were threatening Russia's territorial integrity. If Moscow stood by and did nothing, another republic, especially one with a Muslim population, might follow suit.

On August 10, Yeltsin put newly appointed Prime Minister Vladimir Putin in charge of the crisis, and ordered him to "impose order and discipline."[71] Putin sent Interior Ministry troops to Dagestan, where they, together with local security forces and some military units, engaged the Chechens. As Blandy argued, if nothing else, it was an acknowledgment of "the grave seriousness of the situation."[72] Fighting lasted for three weeks. It involved "Russian heavy aerial bombing, rocket attacks from Russian helicopter gunships, and artillery assaults to dislodge Basayev and Khattab from Dagestan. Conventional weapons did little good. It was the use of devastating fuel air explosives . . . that did the trick."[73] According to Blandy, August 16 was the turning point, at least in southwestern Dagestan, "where it was becoming obvious that the Chechens and Islamist extremists were not making the necessary progress."[74] The most important development from a purely military standpoint came on August 17, when control over military operations was transferred from the Ministry of Interior to the Ministry of Defense. On that day, Kvashnin announced that Colonel General Viktor Kazantsev, who was in command of the North Caucasus Military District, would be in command of all Russian troops in the region. The problem, however, was that command flip-flopped. For example, on August 27 it was given back to the Interior Ministry. That soon turned out to be a major mistake, so on September 4 it was given back to the Ministry of Defense.

Eventually, Russian troops were able to restore Russian authority over Dagestan while forcing the rebels back into Chechnya. Indeed, on August 23 Basayev told his troops to retreat to Chechnya. "On August 25 Russian military aircraft attacked the Chechen villages of Vedeno and Urus Martan, where rebel forces retreating from Dagestan had fled."[75] According to one source, the Army suffered forty-seven dead and 180 wounded, with twelve dead and twenty Interior Ministry troops wounded.

According to official Russian sources, it was at this point that the Chechens decided to take their battle to Moscow. For example, on August 31 a bomb exploded in Moscow's underground Manezh mall, killing one and injuring forty-five. Then on September 4 a bomb exploded at military housing in Buinaksk. Sixty-four people were killed and 174 wounded. Then two apartment houses in Moscow were attacked, one on September 9, the other on September 13. The first explosion killed ninety-four and wounded more than 200, while the second killed 124. A bomb at another apartment bloc was defused the next day, and on September 16 a truck bomb blew the facade off an apartment house in the city of Volgodonsk, killing eighteen people and wounding 342.[76]

Just who was responsible for these bombings remains unclear. Former Russian oligarch Boris Berezovsky claimed that it was planned and carried out by the Federal Security Service (FSB), without Putin's knowledge. Others argue that responsibility for the bombings has not been determined, although Murphy points to the fact that on September 15 the Islamic Liberation Army of Dagestan claimed responsibility. But was this part of Basayev's group? Moscow has long claimed that it was, and Murphy concludes, "The evidence that Khattab was responsible for the apartment building bombings in Moscow is clear."[77] Regardless of who did it, the bottom line was that these bombings had a cataclysmic impact on the Russian populace. There were calls, even demands, that the Kremlin do something about the situation in Chechnya. As Shevtsova pointed out, "In November and December 1999, between 61 and 70 percent of those polled approved of the operation in Chechnya."[78]

LEARNING FROM THE FIRST CHECHEN WAR

While the Russian high command can be legitimately criticized for its failure to recognize that the end of the Cold War had radically changed the nature of military power, it would be wrong to suggest that they did not learn some lessons from the First Chechen War. According to Oliker, Russian analysts noted three major weaknesses in the first Chechen campaign.[79] First, there was the failure of Russian forces to encircle effectively Grozny, which enabled the Chechens to re-supply their forces and evacuate their wounded. Second, the various forces failed to work together. This was especially true of forces from the Ministry of Defense and the Ministry of the Interior. Finally, there was a recognition that the Chechens had won the propaganda war during the first campaign.

Training changed to emphasize joint operations. As noted above, the joint-command structure changed so that the commander of a military district was in charge (and responsible for) of all of the forces in the district, whatever their affiliation. The importance of having tanks, artillery, and infantry work to-gether was also emphasized. The Ministry of Defense did not plan to go into war again with infantry that did not know how to work with tanks, or artillery that did not know how to support infantry. The Ministry also decided that it would win the propaganda war next time, although as events would demon-strate, it did not do a very good job preparing for that eventuality. The biggest problems that faced the Ministry of Defense, and issues that it did not effec-tively address, were the importance of learning how to fight in an urban envi-ronment and how to conduct mountain warfare. Urban fighting was very dif-ferent from the old idea of smashing through a static obstacle, especially if the goal was to leave the city standing. Learning how to fight in either environ-ment was difficult, and the Russian Army was hampered by its reliance on con-scripts and the lack of money to pay for training. Officers would complain again about the ineptitude of soldiers as a result of poor or no training.

Given the problems they faced in finding money to train soldiers, and the lack of concern for collateral damage, the high command decided it would avoid a repeat of the situation by simply obliterating Grozny. That way they avoided casualties. Furthermore, while the Kremlin did a better job in the sec-ond war in bringing units to Chechnya there was still a problem with cohesive, structured units. All too often soldiers did not know even the name of the in-dividual next to them until they were well on their way to battle. Furthermore, many of the conscripts were not trained in how to use equipment, a situation that often led to equipment breaking down.

Yet training was not totally absent. The generals understood very well that it was the key to success in battle. However, given their lack of financial resources, there were serious limitations on what they could do. That was why the primary focus was on relatively small command-staff exercises between March 1997 and July 1999. According to one source, they carried out at least fifteen of them.

In addition to a lack of training for the troops, one of the biggest problems facing the Russian Army as it prepared for Chechnya II was personnel. In the First Chechen War, the military suffered from a lack of direction. True, they were fighting Chechen bandits, but what was the purpose of the operation other than to get rid of the bad guys? How could troops be made to understand why some people hated Russia so much that they were prepared to die for an independent Chechnya? In the past, it had been easy to call the Chechens crooks, but now foreign fighters had joined them to fight for their religious beliefs. There were still no political officers around in the Russian Army to explain to the average soldier why they went to war.

On the plus side, the high command understood this time what it was up against. Logistics were handled much better, and the troops were better prepared for battle. Coordination had improved as had intelligence collection and analysis. General Eduard Vorobyev, who resigned rather than lead troops in the First Chechen War, summed up the difference between the two wars when he commented that the situation was much improved from the standpoint of the Russian soldier who had to fight it:

> During the summer the fighters had initiated combat operations on the territory of Dagestan. But then, having received a repulse, they departed back to the territory of Chechnya. Federal troops quite simply had to respond to the challenge of the terrorists. Secondly, the preparation and training of Federal troops was much better. The tactics being used testified to the fact that the military command had refrained from frontal or "storming" assaults. According to him [Vorobyev], it has been evident in the main that the Federal operation rested on the principle of avoiding direct troop contact and close quarter battle, but played to their strengths by destruction of the illegal bandit formations by direct and indirect "fire for effect" from self-propelled and towed tube artillery, multi-launch rocket systems such as Grad and Uragan, other missile attacks using some form of Scud and strikes by federal aviation. Then and only then, after that form of "preparation," were troops used.[80]

Nevertheless, serious problems remained. For example, coordination and cooperation between the Ministry of Defense and Ministry of Interior forces remained strained. There would be instances "where Internal Troops, lacking military expertise, failed to reconnoiter routes effectively and where, too, Ministry of Defense subunits were slow to respond to the plight of Internal Troops who had been ambushed."[81] Another area where the Russian military would turn out to be severely behind the times was in understanding the psychological aspects of attacking the local population in Chechnya, specifically the idea of "winning the hearts and minds" of the local populace. Such a concept had not been part of Russian military thinking in the past, indeed, the entire concept sounded strange to many Russian officers.[82] Despite their experience in Afghanistan and the First Chechen War, Russians did not factor in concepts such as counterinsurgency warfare. As a consequence, throughout the Second Chechen War, the Russian Army (and interior troops) would often turn out to be their own worst enemy.

PRIME MINISTER PUTIN AND CHECHNYA

While he lacked formal authority over the armed forces, Vladimir Putin made good use of Yeltsin's decision to put him in charge of Russian actions in that region. On August 9, 1999, he moved from being head of the FSB to become acting prime minister. At that time Yeltsin also announced that he wanted Putin to succeed him as president. Putin was confirmed as prime minister on August 16. It was Putin who declared on September 15 that the individuals who had blown up the apartments in Moscow were Chechens and demanded that the Chechens hand over these individuals. It was also Putin who would accept personal responsibility for Chechnya, a comment that would be of considerable importance to the military, which had not completely overcome the Tbilisi Syndrome. Here was a politician who did not shirk responsibility for what he ordered the military to do.[83] While the military appreciated his support, Shevtsova correctly noted that it also helped solidify his political position in Moscow: "After the military attack on Chechnya began, Putin no longer needed to continue the difficult struggle for power. All he had to do was point to the enemy, who were Chechens, naturally. War lifted him to the peak of the political Olympus."[84] And Putin would play up his role in the Chechen affairs. As Golts observed, he flew down to Grozny in a jet fighter, which, if nothing else, emphasized his connection to the war.[85] He also promised to crush the

Chechen "scum" and to bring back law and order to Russia, comments that appealed to the Russian people. "He was uncompromising in his determination to exterminate what he saw as a terrorist nest in Chechnya, stating in September that Russian forces would *'be following terrorists everywhere. If we catch them in a toilet, then we will bury them in their own crap'.*"[86] Equally important—for Putin—his able handling of the early stages of the Second Chechen War increased his standing in public opinion polls. "From two percent in late August 1999, his support stood at 25 percent at the end of October . . . Russian Public TV showed a poll on 20 November, which put support for Putin at 41 percent, with [Communist]Gennady Zyuganov in second place at 15 percent. One poll in mid-December put Putin's support at 46 percent, with Zyuganov as his closest challenger at 17 percent."[87]

This raises the question of whether the Second Chechen War was simply a vehicle to help Putin win popularity so that he would be in a good position to succeed Yeltsin. Certainly Smith's comment about the presidential election of 2000 was accurate: "Putin's success in the presidential elections are due almost entirely to the Russian population's support for the Russian military operation in Chechnya."[88] While there may be some truth in such an argument, the bottom line was that he was doing what the Russian people wanted. A survey taken in November 1999 asked the question, "Do you think the Chechens are now getting what they deserve?" The response favored the prime minister: "34 percent said definitely, 27 percent said probably, with 14 percent saying probably not, and 7 percent definitely not."[89] The key factor was that the Kremlin had no choice but to respond when the Chechens moved into Dagestan. Furthermore, it was obvious even after the Chechens were thrown out of Dagestan that Chechnya was quickly sinking into chaos with the religious fundamentalists taking control. Regardless of who was in authority, Moscow likely would have been forced to move against the Chechens in one form or another, in order to maintain its status as a great power. Regardless of why Putin supported the war so strongly, his backing was considered critical by one observer who explained:

Another factor, perhaps the most important one, for the success of the invasion was the resolve and direction demonstrated by the political leadership in Moscow, namely Vladimir Putin as acting Prime Minister. Putin's authorization of the use of fuel-air explosives in Tando in Dagestan was one example of his determined, positive and *no-nonsense* response to this crisis.[90]

Besides, there were reports that the military leadership was only too happy to oblige. They had been embarrassed by their defeat in Chechnya I and were looking for an excuse to win back the Army's honor.[91]

One key difference between the First and Second Chechen Wars was that in the first, civilians constantly intervened, telling the generals how to fight the war. In the second, the politicians stayed out. They left fighting the war to the military: "While Defense Minister Igor Sergeyev . . . was quite unenthusiastic about the whole enterprise, the Chief of the General Staff Anatoly Kvashnin gathered a group of combat generals (Konstantin Pulikovsky, Gennady Troshev, Viktor Kazantsev, Vladimir Shamanov) driven hard by the desire to take revenge for the humiliating defeat in 1996."[92]

THE SECOND CHECHEN WAR—EARLY STAGE

On September 20 General Valery Manilov, the first deputy chief of the General Staff, commented that the Army might have to enter Chechnya; the next day Russia's border with Chechnya was sealed. By September 29, sources in the Defense Ministry were stating that preparations were under way for a military operation against Chechnya.[93] By September 31, the high command had begun to prepare troops to carry out ground operations in Chechnya. On October 1, the Army moved into Chechnya. By October 9, Russian troops were making good progress.

Operationally, the Russian high command broke the attack on Chechnya into two phases. The first involved seizing territory north of the Terek River, an operation that does not appear to have encountered major opposition. This "easy going" on flat open land in turn "created overconfidence within the General Staff, reinforcing their delusions about the weak disposition of rebel forces."[94] The second phase was aimed at occupying the republic's major cities. To ensure that the Army could meet any level of resistance, the high command also sent in massive numbers of troops: up to 100,000 (compared with 30,000–40,000 in the First Chechen War). Of all the cities the Russians intended to occupy, once again the most important was the capital, Grozny. Given indications that the Chechens would fight to defend the city, Russian officers decided to pull back and permit artillery and air power to blast the small rebel units. In addition to the use of these strikes, the Army put together well-trained sniper units that not only took out designated targets, but also provided valuable intelligence.

The attack on Grozny began on December 25, 1999, after the towns of Gudermes and Argun had fallen. Grozny was not captured until February 8 and, in the process, the Russian Army turned it into a slaughterhouse. According to one estimate, "up to 80 percent of the city's high-rise buildings and 50 percent of its homes [were] destroyed." It was what Felgenhauer called "a zone of utter destruction."[95] A former MiG pilot, who was serving as a reporter in Chechnya, provided the best commentary I have seen when he described Russian tactics:

> "You take up positions as far away as possible," Zhilin said, "and shell the hell out of them. You use jets, attack helicopters, artillery—whatever has lead and metal and flies. You hit them day and night without pause. You send in men only once you've leveled everything." The onslaught was calculated to lose as few Russian soldiers as possible, while killing as many Chechens, armed or not, as possible. "Costly in terms of hardware," Zhilin called the plan, "but effective."[96]

The result of Moscow's devastating use of force led one well-known military correspondent to comment, "This strategy of victory by bombardment has inevitably led to massive war crimes . . . The use of such mass-destruction weapons as aerosol [fuel] munitions and ballistic missiles against civilian targets was undoubtedly authorized by Moscow and may implicate President Putin personally, as well as his military chiefs, in war crimes."[97] There is no question that the Russians went far beyond what would be normally considered sufficient in such an operation. Note, for example, the comments of two Russian officers: "On average in the conduct of combat operations to kill one Mojhakhed (*boyevik*) in Afghanistan required up to 6,000 bullets and 55 shells, in Chechnya more than 7,000 bullets and 70 rounds from regimental artillery."[98] Given this overwhelming use of force, the total disregard for collateral damage, and reports of widespread human rights violations, it is not surprising that while the Russian Army was successful in capturing the republic's key cities, it also succeeded in radicalizing many otherwise supportive parts of the population.[99] The remaining Chechen fighters moved to the mountains in the south, determined to continue the war.

THE IMPACT OF YELTSIN'S POLICY ON INTERNAL MILITARY AFFAIRS

It is hard to believe that at a time when the Russian military was being called upon to deal with a situation as volatile as Chechnya, Yeltsin would continue to cut the budget. Not only was it being cut, but the military seldom received what it was promised. While part of this was understandable, given the financial crisis of August 1998, it still reflected the economic policies followed by Yeltsin and his regime. From the standpoint of the generals and admirals, it was up to the politicians to manage the economy. Yet this administration clearly had no idea how to do so. Meanwhile, the lack of funds, in particular, had a devastating impact on the internal life of the Russian Army.

As has long been the case with the Russian military, its heart was its officer corps. And the situation among officers continued to deteriorate. In 1997 "80 percent of those surveyed are 'totally dissatisfied' with their low material status, and with delayed wages for the last three years." Furthermore, about 75 percent were convinced that "the state no longer cares about the armed forces," and they "no longer have faith in the reforms and transformations."[100] To make matters worse, junior officers continued to leave as fast as possible, creating a situation in which "only 30 percent of the officer cadre are regular officers, the rest are reservists called up for two years' service after graduating from civilian universities."[101] Officers could not support their families. By 1999 it was reported that a lieutenant made R354 a month, and a lieutenant colonel R2,135, while the poverty line for a family of three was R2,600–4,600, depending on where the individual lived.[102] Often their pay was two to three months late. This is one of the fundamental reasons why officers accounted for almost 60 percent of suicides. "In October 1998 . . . a major and a lieutenant colonel committed suicide in Moscow. An investigation revealed that their families were starving and both officers knew that if they committed suicide their families would get their death benefits. Their monthly pension would be paid to their families when it was due, in contrast to the delays faced by those on active duty."[103]

Under these circumstances, it is not surprising that almost all of the newly commissioned lieutenants wanted to resign as soon as they were commissioned. In 1998 alone, 20,000 officers under the age of thirty resigned.[104] In some instances, the situation was just as bad for those who wanted to remain in the military. In 1998, for example, General Anatoli Kornukov, who was commander of the newly combined air force and air defense forces, commented on the inability of the air force to utilize graduates of its officers' schools. "We had 415 pilots, and 363 of them were dismissed. This is painful, we feel bad about it. But our aim was not to lose first-class pilots who are 25–30 years old."[105]

In 1999 another Chechen War was on the horizon, and many in the military had a good idea it was coming, yet the situation within the military continued worsen. Educational institutions were at a point where they accepted anyone just to fill their ranks, while only 52 percent of officers "thought positively of continuing their military careers, 25 percent were ready to leave the service at any moment, and 23 percent articulated no position on the matter."[106] The reasons for their dissatisfaction were obvious. First, housing. In 1997 126,000 men, "one of every four professionals who have linked their lives with the army, have no roofs over their heads."[107] The next year, the number of those needing improved housing was 140,000, while 90,000 had no housing at all.[108] In 1999, with another Chechen War coming, Moscow reported that there were 92,400 homeless officers; by January 2000 that number had increased to 93,600.[109]

The situation was even worse for conscripts. Who would want to serve in a military when the majority of the population looked down on it? For example, a survey conducted in 1998 and 1999 by RIA-Novosti found that 56 percent of respondents had a negative attitude toward the military, while only 21 percent (1988) and 19 percent (1999) were positive.[110] As a result, the Army's trials and tribulations with the draft continued.

In 1997 2.2 million Russian men were subject to call up. Of that number 1.5 million had deferments, 225,000 had medical problems, and 71,000 were in jail, leaving 437,000 available for service. Of that number 50,000 evaded military service and 12,000 went AWOL.[111] The quality of recruits continued to go down. Furthermore, in 1999 the syphilis rate among draftees increased 1,000 percent over the 1992 level. Alcoholism, drug abuse, and inhalant abuse increased 100 percent and pleurisy related to tuberculosis had increased 50 percent among men of draft age.[112] Furthermore, in 1998 its was reported that 40 percent had not attended school or held a job two years prior to reporting. "One in twenty had a police record."[113] In 1999 a new problem came to the fore: 57.6 percent had a limitation on where they could serve.[114] What this meant was that 57.6 percent of those actually drafted were not qualified for elite units like the Naval Infantry, airborne units, the submarine service, or some infantry units.

Once a young man joined the Army, he continued to face the problem of *dedovshchina*. During the first nine months of 1997, more than 1,400 servicemen were abused by brutal hazing.[115] The reasons for the hazing sometimes reached the bizarre. For example, "In May 1998, a young soldier was buried in the southern city of Budennovsk. He was beaten to death because he refused to mend an older conscript's soccer shoe . . . During the first eleven months of 1998, 57 soldiers died, and 2,735 were injured from hazing."[116] That same report continued, "In the first 11 months of 1999 300 soldiers committed suicide—many because of their inability to put up with hazing."[117] And the problem was increasing—by 50 percent in 1998.[118] The brutality was not limited to recruit-on-recruit. There was also a serious problem with inebriated officers who would beat recruits. In fact, the armed forces spoke out very clearly on the matter, noting:

> The most negative, the most significant characteristic of today's officer or general-knight is his careful relations with his subordinates. Never in circumstances, never by orders should he himself permit a decrease in respect for soldiers, which, unfortunately, in the most recent time has become widely dispersed. In such circumstances, the commander should very seriously look at his own vocation, highly valuing his rank as a general or officer in order to work to eliminate the low regard for subordinates.[119]

The problem was that, regardless of how important close ties with the troops were, officers did not have enough time to spend with the troops. The political officers were gone, and the educational and psychological officers did not fill the gap. Regular officers did not have the time to spend at the unit level dealing with soldiers, and they could not be in the barracks at night to stop *dedovshchina*.

As mentioned earlier, the armed forces were to embrace contract soldiers to take care of the problem. Unfortunately, the situation did not improve. In January and February of 1997, for example, while 2,755 men were accepted as *kontraktniks*, 5,942 quit.[120] Furthermore, while the Kremlin could boast of having 230,000 *kontraktniks* on active duty, of this number, 115,000 were women—primarily the spouses of military officers who were trying to make ends meet and they were primarily in staff positions.[121] The male conscripts were not of the best quality. Lieutenant General Vladislav Putilin probably said it best when he observed that, given the dangerous conditions and low pay faced by many contract soldiers, a person who volunteered for such service "would either be one of the long-term unemployed or someone who has already poisoned his mind with alcohol."[122]

Crime and corruption remained major problems. By the end of 1997, twenty-one Russian generals were under investigation for corruption.[123] Then in May 1999 Russian law-enforcement officials discovered several schemes that were just the tip of an iceberg. "Russian intelligence officers seized large amounts of weapons and explosives that soldiers from the Russian Navy's Pacific Fleet were trying to sell on the black market."[124] Discipline also appeared to be collapsing. In 1997, for example, the chief prosecutor noted that fifty soldiers were shot that year by their fellow servicemen. And these were only the number of soldiers who were on guard duty. It did not include soldiers shot while not on guard duty. Then in May 1998, four soldiers in the Far Eastern Military District shot and killed their commanding officer. Even more alarming was the spate of shootings at nuclear weapons facilities. The situation became so serious that on October 20, 1998, President Yeltsin ordered an inspection of troops at a nuclear weapons production facility.[125]

Meanwhile, crime increased. For example, during the first eleven months of 1998 crimes in the military rose from 10,000 in 1997 to 10,500.[126] To emphasize just how serious the problem was, from 1979 to 1999 twenty soldiers were tossed out of the army for psychological reasons—soldiers who had access to nuclear weapons.[127] The situation was so bad that members of the Duma described it "as alarming and in need of emergency measures."[128]

Combat Readiness

It is hard to imagine how low the combat readiness of the Russian military was during this period. By the latter part of 1996, General Rodionov reported, "Russia had no units capable of being rapidly deployed in action." Why? According to journalist Anatol Lieven, because they were out digging potatoes and cabbages.[129]

Despite the First Chechen War, combat readiness continued to decline in 1997. Sergeyev reportedly repeated Rodionov's 1996 comment—i.e., that "not a single unit was combat ready except for the nuclear forces and some paratroopers."[130] The Army's financial situation deteriorated to the point that almost all government meteorological stations stopped passing critical weather information to the military, and then-Prime Minister Chernomyrdin had to sign an order forcing power stations to keep supplying military installations with power even if they had not paid their electrical bills.

In 1998 Sergeyev reported that "53 percent of aircraft and 40 percent of the anti-aircraft systems, helicopters, armored equipment, and artillery were in need of repair."[131] The situation in the Navy was even worse. More than 70 percent of its ships were in need of major overhauls.[132] In the opinion of a number of experts testifying before the Duma in 1998, the Kremlin had a military "currently incapable of conducting strategic operations or speedily carrying out a major redeployment of troops."[133] Duma Security Committee Chairman

Viktor Ilyukhin went so far as to say that Russia's armed forces could no longer serve as a guarantor of Russian security.[134] In December, Sergeyev painted an even bleaker picture. According to the defense minister:

> About one-third of the armed forces' military hardware is not combat-ready and that some 60 percent of the country's strategic missile systems have been in service for twice their service life. Some 70 percent of the ships in Russia's navy require repair . . . while in the air force about two-thirds of all aircraft are incapable of flying. This year . . . the armed forces had not received a "single nuclear submarine, tank, combat plane, helicopter, or piece of artillery."[135]

The military's problems grew worse. In July 1999 Sergeyev told an audience at the Air Defense University in Tver that it would be at least 2005 before the Army received any new weapons. In the meantime, the Army would have to make do with what it had.[136] Qualified pilots were still being sent to infantry, armor, artillery, or communication units because there were no planes for them to fly.

Given the complete mess the Russian military found itself in, it is a miracle that the Army did as well as it did in the Second Chechen War. Arguably, it was only through the massive use of force—including in some cases weapons from World War II—that the Army was able to conquer most of the republic, including its major cities, but not the mountains. If the Army had to rely on the soldier carrying a rifle (*kontraktniki* or conscripts) to take Grozny or other hard targets (without first destroying it), Moscow could have faced a replay of Chechnya I. The lack of training, equipment, weapons, experienced cadres, all undermined combat readiness. Moscow's continuing failure to develop a NCO corps did not make the situation any easier. Problems with *dedovshchina* were evident even in Chechnya. "The brutal hazing for which the Russians are infamous continued even on the front lines. One young Grozny veteran survived several battles unscathed, only to land in the hospital with a broken jaw bestowed on him by his 'comrades.'"[137]

MILITARY CULTURE

Yeltsin continued to disrespect the uniformed military, as his handling of Rodionov demonstrated. Rodionov was typical of most Russian generals in that he believed that a military reform plan must be comprehensive and involve all aspects of the Russian polity. The idea of reforming the military in a vacuum made no sense to him. However, in this instance, military culture clashed openly with Yeltsin's undisciplined approach to dealing with problems. Rather than trying to find a broad approach to reform, Yeltsin wanted a "quick fix" and was unpredictable in his choices. But political leadership was critical if a comprehensive military reform plan was to become reality, especially given the country's serious economic problems. Telling Rodionov to introduce military reform without supporting him—indeed, while actually cutting the budget—was an insult to the high command. The situation was not much better for Sergeyev. A new military reform plan was introduced in 1997, only to be quickly followed by Yeltsin's announcement that he was cutting the military budget. Sergeyev would try to take the money from the ground forces and move it to nuclear weapons, but that only led to intensified inter-service conflict. The 1998 economic crisis further undermined military readiness and made any serious talk of military reform almost irrelevant. Yeltsin would constantly tell the military that he was prepared to come up with more money, but he just as regularly failed to deliver. How did the president plan to fight a conventional conflict if the ground forces were not ready to go to war? That was not Yeltsin's concern.

Yeltsin also showed a distinct lack of respect for Rodionov and the military when he placed Yuri Baturin in an co-equal position in designing doctrine. Baturin knew little about the military and Yeltsin was aware of it. Many generals resented Andrei Kokoshin's appointment as deputy defense minister in the Ministry of Defense, but they respected his in-depth knowledge of military matters. Yeltsin was warned repeatedly about the declining status of the military, yet he did little to deal with it. One of his worst acts occurred when he publicly disgraced Rodionov and Samsonov by relieving them of command on live television, an action that alienated important military officials such as Lev Rokhlin. [138]

On the positive side, the military, and especially Kvashnin, appreciated Yeltsin's willingness to let Russian paratroopers rush to seize the airport at Pristina in 1999. It gave them a nationalistic shot in the arm. The high command also appreciated the "free hand" Yeltsin gave them in conducting the Second Chechen War. Having said that, entering Chechnya with untrained troops, with old weapons and equipment, was not the generals' idea of how to fight a war. Nevertheless, the old Russian idea of using brute force cut down Russian Army casualties (although it killed a very large number of civilians, both Russian and Chechen, in the process).

While Yeltsin played no part in it, the high command showed that it was capable of learning from its mistakes, namely, its horrible performance in

Chechnya I. Logistics, intelligence, tactics, and joint operations were vastly improved—although there was still room for improvement in all four areas.

The biggest problem with Yeltsin's tenure in office, however, resulted from the accumulation of his almost ten years of neglect of military affairs. The high command was not blameless, to be sure. Many generals were still tied to the Cold War, refusing to make the kinds of psychological changes needed to deal with the new world. They refused, for example, to come to grips with the issue of NCOs or *dedovshchina*. There were attempts to deal with the chaos inside the military. Certainly Rodionov tried, even if his reform plan was too heavily tied to the world of the Cold War. Sergeyev also tried, but he was constantly undermined by Yeltsin.

Then came Vladimir Putin. When he took over as Acting President on January 1, 2000, following Yeltsin's surprise resignation on New Year's Eve, he inherited a military in chaos. Any plans for military reform had been pushed aside, while the high command focused on the Second War in Chechnya. The situation in the Army was not only in far worse shape than it was when Yeltsin took over, it was so bad that the new president would be forced to start from square one in rebuilding it.

CONCLUSION

In her book, *Putin's Russia,* Lilia Shevtsova commented that what Russia needed in the 1990s was a "leader of a special type, a politician with an enormous amount of charisma." As far as Yeltsin was concerned, she maintained that he should have been retired after 1996. Prior to that time he succeeded in destroying communism as a viable political force in Russia along with all other potential political forces in Russia. After that, the situation changed. The task was not so much to destroy the old as it was to create stability while building something new. Yeltsin was not the leader to build the new Russia, "both because he was not up to it and because he did not understand what he should do next and did not know how to change it."[139]

One might also add that Yeltsin's leadership style was too chaotic, too unpredictable, too focused on keeping himself in power to deal effectively with the country's deep-seated problems. There is little doubt that Moscow's military leadership would have agreed with Shevtsova. When it came to leadership, the generals found Yeltsin seriously lacking. They may not have liked the direction he would have taken the military and they would have probably fought him behind the scenes. After all, getting these very conservative, traditional generals (e.g., Kvashnin) to think military problems through anew would not have been easy. However, Russian officers believed they had a right to expect the president to show leadership. Instead of a president who was prepared to work with them in reforming the military, they were forced to deal with a man who did not understand their problems, who showed very little interest in—or respect for—them. And when Yeltsin resigned, he left the generals with a military that was badly broken. They were happy to see him go.

CHAPTER SIX
PUTIN, THE GENERALS, AND STABILIZING THE MILITARY, JANUARY 2000–JANUARY 2006

> Every year—and I would like to stress it—we increase the
> Defense Ministry budget by 15–20 percent.
> *Vladimir Putin*

From the perspective of the generals, Vladimir Putin contrasts sharply with Boris Yeltsin. Following the chaos and unpredictability of the Yeltsin period, Putin worked hard to reintroduce stability and predictability into the military. He has not been completely successful. Problems are everywhere—personnel, weapons, equipment, Chechnya—the list goes on and on. Nevertheless, by 2006 the situation in the armed forces was more structured and stable than it had been under Yeltsin. As a result of Putin's efforts, a new chain of command has been introduced, while the outlines of the future Russian armed forces are beginning to emerge. How formidable that military force will be is open to question. The important point, however, is that it is more likely to occur under Putin than it would have been had Yeltsin remained in office.

PUTIN'S LEADERSHIP STYLE

Putin's leadership style could not be more different from Yeltsin's.[1] As Sakwa noted,[2] Putin made a fundamental decision when he came to power: Russia had endured enough instability and revolution. Since 1992 the country had undergone revolutionary, and in many cases chaotic, change. He decided that what Russia needed above all was stability and "orderly change." Toward that end, the Putin Kremlin worked to avoid the arbitrariness and unpredictability that had characterized Yeltsin's tenure in office.

Putin also decided to give Russian society greater stability and he believed that structures should play a bigger role. Decisions should not be made on the spur of the moment. Rather, they should be thought out and, probably because he had spent most of his life in a bureaucracy, staffed out to that organization so that military officers had a chance to accommodate themselves to the changes he introduced. His approach was to keep pushing and pushing, expecting the bureaucracy to implement his reforms.

Putin also recognized the importance of Russian political culture. He understood, for example, that Russia had more a subject than a participatory political culture. Russians wanted a strong leader and feared anarchy and chaos, which many citizens associated with the West and its talk of democracy. Coming from the KGB, Putin also understood something about military culture. There were differences between the two organizations to be sure, but there were also a number of similarities, most notably, their bureaucratic hierarchical structure and the premium they assigned to direction and obedience in carrying out orders. This was one of the main reasons he selected a number of his leadership cadre from the security services and the military, and he tended to avoid direct interference in internal military matters unless he believed the generals were standing in the way of needed change. He was prepared to intervene, but only if it was absolutely necessary.

Putin has also been nonideological. He has been suspicious of precooked solutions, whether they came from politicians or bureaucrats. In this regard, he was flexible and open to suggestions. His primary criterion for determining which approach to use for solving a problem was simple: which one worked, which one actually helped solve the problem. If an approach from the left would be most effective, fine; but he was just as ready to look at an approach from the right if it would do a better job.

Putin has not been a long-range planner. Observers who expected him to be the kind of leader who carefully thought problems through and then designed long-term solutions were disappointed. Rather, Putin has always been a problem solver. Just like in the KGB, he goes from one problem to another. Putin has also believed strongly in centralized control. This was evident not only in his determination to build up the security and military forces, but in his strengthening of the state apparatus by creating seven superpresidential administrative districts, by gaining control of the upper house of parliament, and by a number of other actions aimed at enabling the Kremlin to recreate the centralized control that Yeltsin had destroyed.[3]

Finally, Putin has always been cautious. He is not the kind of leader who is prepared to "break glass" in an effort to make dynamic changes in a very short period of time. He has been a gradualist, not a revolutionary. In Aesop's tale Putin would be the turtle, not the hare. He has not been the kind of leader who introduced numerous, radical changes all at once.

Perhaps the most appropriate phrase to describe Putin's approach for dealing with problems in the military is "muddling through." His approach has been to encourage a number of small steps, some of which have had a major impact on the military, others of which were of less importance. The end result was a major step toward structural change.

Putin's bureaucratic approach was evident shortly after he was elected president in March 2000. He set up commissions to look at problems within the Army. The proposals, which dealt with the period up to 2010, were approved by the Security Council. They included a broad range of issues such as: improving the management of the military, increasing combat readiness, restructuring the defense-industrial complex, upgrading the status of servicemen, increasing financial assistance to the military, as well as upgrading command and control.[4] What was notable about Putin's approach was how much it contrasted with Yeltsin's. Putin preferred to look at specific problems. There would not be a master plan full of broad, ambiguous, nice-sounding phrases but little content.

Finally, while Putin has been cautious, he has not been afraid to make decisions and to see to it that they are implemented. This is something that both the minister of defense and chief of the General Staff would learn, as would the generals who opposed a professional army. Once Putin made a decision, he expected it to be implemented.

SERGEYEV VERSUS KVASHNIN

It is hard to imagine two more different individuals than Marshal Igor Sergeyev and General Anatoly Kvashnin. Sergeyev, a missile officer, spent his life working to develop the country's strategic deterrent, while Kvashnin was an infantry officer who briefly commanded Russian troops in Chechnya. Sergeyev was considered by many to be diplomatic and soft-spoken. Kvashnin, on the other hand, could be abrasive, outspoken, and disrespectful when it suited him. Despite Kvashnin's personality, it would be reasonable to assume that their relationship would have been formally correct. After all, Sergeyev was the country's defense minister, while Kvashnin was chief of the General Staff. But because of Yeltsin's actions, both officers reported directly to the president. As a result, Kvashnin, who was responsible for implementing Sergeyev's decisions, continually fought with him. Sergeyev wanted to continue the policy outlined in Chapter 5 of primary reliance on strategic missile forces. He did not think that conventional forces were unimportant, but he was convinced that putting Moscow's limited financial resources into strategic weapons would enable the country to deter an outside attack.[5]

Kvashnin, however, believed Sergeyev was being shortsighted at best. He wanted to eliminate the Strategic Rocket Forces. Kvashnin believed that, given the unlikelihood of a nuclear conflict, the Kremlin was wasting time and money putting all of its assets into nuclear weapons. Instead, he argued that it should redirect part of the money to conventional forces. Moscow could not leave the control of internal disturbances or the war against terrorism to the interior troops. And, what if a country along Russia's long border should become a problem? What did Moscow intend to do—launch nuclear weapons? Only strong, mobile, modern, and flexible conventional forces could handle such a job. Therefore, the Kremlin should maintain and even increase its conventional forces.[6]

The two men each represented different schools of thought in the Russian military. Frank Umbach emphasized this point when he observed that this argument was really a continuation of a long-standing difference of opinion between traditionalists and realists:

> A "traditionalist" school of thought who saw Russia's military potential as the guarantor of its international great power status and directed its policies against any foreign policy losses or deterioration of Russian military power in general and of its Strategic Nuclear Forces in particular; and a more "realist" school of thought who favored aligning Russia's future with contemporary economic and political realities inside and outside Russia. Its continuation at the highest level inside the Russian high command led to a split of the military elite.[7]

The problem was that the military was out of control—or at least deeply split.

THE NEW MILITARY DOCTRINE

In April 2000 Putin signed a new military doctrine into law that superceded the 1993 Doctrine Statement. There were a number of important items in the new law. First, the role of the president was stressed and strengthened. He was given considerable responsibility for the organization and training of the military. The obvious implication was that Putin intended to work toward more centralized control over the military. How vigorously he intended to move toward improving the armed forces was another question. Second, and of particular importance for the battle between Sergeyev and Kvashnin, the role of the Defense Ministry was described as to coordinate "the activities of the executive federal structures that are involved with defense." In addition, the Ministry of Defense was responsible for "working out concepts for the construction and development of other troops." Thus Sergeyev, not Kvashnin, was designated to create blueprints to develop the other services. This suggests that Kvashnin, who had long wanted the General Staff in charge of such things, lost this bureaucratic battle.[8] The document, however, confirmed that the General Staff still exerted operational control and was responsible for operations, planning, mobilization and command, control, communications, and intelligence for the Army. This left Kvashnin a strong bureaucratic position.

Sergeyev won a partial victory with the inclusion of a statement that if there were a large-scale war using only conventional weapons there would be a high probability of it "escalating into a nuclear war with catastrophic consequences for civilization and the basic elements of human life and existence."[9] Thus even though the document called for "highly maneuverable forces" and mentioned the importance of peacekeeping forces and counterterrorist forces, the bottom line was that a serious conventional war ran the risk of escalating, thereby making Moscow's nuclear deterrent critical. Then, when Sergeyev was scheduled to retire, Putin extended his tour of duty as defense minister for another year, until May 10, 2001. While this extension could have been aimed at checking Kvashnin, more likely, given his gradualistic approach to such things, Putin merely wanted to avoid instability in the high command at a time when he was new to the office of president. In June Putin appointed Kvashnin to become a permanent member of the Security Council, when it was normal for only the defense minister to hold such membership.

While the Kremlin had adopted a new doctrine, it was a "transition" document. Putin had inherited a mess, and the document was aimed at giving the Kremlin more authority without laying out any "plan" on what to do on the ground.[10] Similarly, one of the main problems with the doctrine was that it did not seriously look at the issue of small wars, which was rather surprising, given the ongoing conflict in Chechnya. Baev perceptively commented, "Traditional military conservatism could easily be identified as a source of inattentiveness and even negligence, and it was reinforced by the lack of any engagement into this 'marginal' issue of such influential branches of the armed forces as the navy, and, particularly, the SRF."[11]

PUTIN ENTERS THE DEBATE

The war between Sergeyev and Kvashnin was far from over. On July 12 there was a meeting of the military collegium of the Defense Ministry. At that meeting, Kvashnin argued in favor of disbanding the Strategic Rocket Forces (SRF). For example, he reportedly stated that the number of intercontinental ballistic missile (ICBM) divisions should be cut from the existing nineteen to only two. Furthermore, he reportedly wanted to cut the number of ICBMs from 756 to only 150 by 2003, to cut back production of the Topol-M SS-27 long-range missile, and downgrade the SRF to a command (*rod*). The SRF's share of the budget would be cut from 18 to 15 percent. The money saved would be given to the Ground Forces.[12] The meeting failed to reach a decision, but it was clear that things were not going Sergeyev's way. He responded in an interview on July 14 in which he bluntly called Kvashnin's plan "criminal stupidity and an attack on Russia's national interests." The next day, Putin ordered both generals to "silence their debate and come up with realistic policy proposals."[13] Meanwhile, by the beginning of August 2000, ten of Sergeyev's supporters had been removed from the military high command.

Kvashnin repeated his criticism of the SRF's preferential treatment at a Security Council meeting on August 11. What was different about this meeting was that Putin was present, and he realized that he would have to do something to break the logjam between Sergeyev and Kvashnin. He began by expressing his frustration over the situation in the military. For example, Putin stated, "When pilots do not fly and sailors do not got to sea, can it be said that everything is right and proper in the structure of the Armed Forces today?" He then made it clear that he was well aware of the war going on between the General Staff and the Defense Ministry, noting, "I have been rather tolerant of the debates in the defense ministry and society as a whole . . . now is the time to bring the matter to its rightful conclusion."[14] The meeting adopted a Plan for Armed Forces Development to 2005. Sergeyev put a good face on matters when he remarked, "The discussions are over and the Supreme Commander-in-Chief has passed the decision. It is well-grounded and substantiated within the framework of the country's economic possibilities. Not a single booster rocket will be dismantled before it serves its full operational life."[15] In fact, the plan was more favorable to the kind of military that Kvashnin wanted. As he remarked, "Our main objective is the harmonious development of all Services of the Armed Forces."[16] "Harmonious development" were code words for treating the ground forces more equally. No longer would the SRF receive special treatment. After all, most of its missiles were reaching the end of their service life, and, unless Moscow was prepared to pour massive amounts of money into the Topol-M, the SRF would inevitably become less and less relevant. The meeting also decided to release a total of 365,000 soldiers and more than 100,000 civilians working for the military. More important to Kvashnin, Sergeyev's 1997 decision to get rid of the Ground Forces as a separate service was reversed. The Space Troops were also folded into the Strategic Rocket Forces. Furthermore, Kvashnin got his way and the SRF was downgraded to a command. Needless to say, Sergeyev was upset. According to Golts this schematic was not really a plan, rather it "simply strengthened the victory of in bureaucratic channels of the 'combat arms generals' over the 'missile' generals." [17]

Then on August 12, Putin was publicly humiliated by the Navy's inept handling of the sinking of the submarine *Kursk,* the pride of the Russian Fleet, which killed 118 sailors. Putin, the country, and the military were deeply embarrassed, not only because of the sinking, but also by the admirals' refusal to accept foreign assistance as well as by their constant lies that the *Kursk* was sunk by a foreign submarine. The truth was that a faulty practice torpedo on the submarine, one that should have been removed from service, had exploded. The prosecutor general blasted the Navy for "a general 'sloppiness' in the way that the Russian Northern Fleet command had organized the August 2000 naval exercise in which the *Kursk* was lost, and of a similar disrespect for discipline and proper procedure in the actions of the submarine's own crew."[18] Sergeyev offered Putin his resignation over the tragedy, but the president refused it.

However, the *Kursk* incident taught Putin, first, that he had to do a better job himself in showing his concern for the victims of such tragedies, and, second, that it was critical for the Russian armed forces not to lie about what happened in the future. This was a major change. Previously Putin had avoided getting deeply involved in military matters. He did not want to upset the apple cart, because he needed the troops to fight the war in Chechnya. However, these events convinced Putin that he had to act. As he put it in an interview on August 25, 2000, "Our Armed Forces should accord with demands on the one hand, and the possibilities of the state on the other. The army should be compact, but modern, and well paid."[19] Change was on the way.

According to Steven Main, it was clear that Putin had decided to direct his attention to conventional rather than nuclear forces, a point he emphasized at a meeting with the high command in November 2000. As Putin put it:

> The Army and the Navy must be ready in all strategic directions to neutralize and repulse any army conflict and aggression. And one important task—the creation and stationing of groups of permanent readiness units in the South-Western and Central Asian strategic directions. Here the state of the general-purpose forces is of primary importance. Such forces must have the latest technology.[20]

Putin's reference to permanent-readiness units was one that military professionals would hear frequently during the next six years.

The Security Council met again on November 9, 2000. It was a critical meeting for the future of the Army, as the agenda was based on the work of the commissions that Putin had set up on May 27 and August 17. Their findings were presented to the Security Council and dealt with the development of the military up to 2010. They included a broad range of issues, such as improving management, raising combat readiness, improving the defense industrial complex, upgrading the status of servicemen, increasing financial assistance to the military, and improving command and control.[21] Putin acknowledged the importance of nuclear weapons, but he also mentioned the need to "see other challenges."[22] It was clear that his primary concern was improving the Army's conventional capabilities. The plan adopted by the meeting foresaw a two-stage process. Phase one covered 2001 to 2005 and would focus primarily on personnel. Some 470,000 military personnel and 130,000 civilians would be eliminated. By 2005 the total size of all of the Kremlin's security services (including the military) would be reduced by 19.7 percent. Putin confirmed that the Army would be cut by 365,000 troops while Sergeyev's beloved SRF would lose 60,000 personnel by 2005.[23] The second phase focused on providing the military with the kind of logistical support it needed. Greater emphasis would be placed on personnel issues, such as improving infrastructure and salaries. On January 15, 2001, Putin approved this plan.

The key point in comparing Putin's approach with the various reform plans put forth during Yeltsin's tenure was that Putin's plan read more like a general approach for dealing with a variety of problems. There was no grand, glitzy, master plan. Instead, like the bureaucratic problem-solver he is, Putin focused on specific problems and attempted to deal with them systematically.

SERGEYEV IS REPLACED BY IVANOV

On March 28, 2001, despite reports that Sergeyev had asked to serve for another year, the Kremlin announced that the defense minister had stepped down as to become a presidential adviser.[24] He was replaced by Sergei Ivanov, up to that time head of the Security Council and one of Putin's closest confidants. The two had served together in the KGB, and Putin decided that Ivanov, a former KGB general, and a man who had been intimately involved in the Security Council's efforts to come up with a reform plan, understood the military and was the one to bring order into the armed forces. His task would not be an easy one, although as head of the Security Council he had been intimately involved in drafting the plan signed by Putin in January. Putin also took the unprecedented step of appointing a woman—and a civilian—Lyubov Kudelina, a deputy minister of defense. She came from the Finance Ministry and was given the task of making sense out of the financial chaos at Defense.

Why was Sergeyev fired? A number of reasons come to mind. First, Kvashnin's arguments made sense. The Cold War was over, and the United States had no intention of attacking Russia. Therefore, a minimal nuclear shield would be enough to protect Russia against any rogue country that might decide to attack. Second, Kvashnin had successfully used the seizure of the Pristina airport by Russian paratroops to emphasize the value of conventional forces. Nuclear weapons would have been useless in that operation. Then there was the war in Chechnya, which had clearly demonstrated the inadequacies of Russia's conventional troops. There was a tremendous need for new weapons and equipment, not to mention a new personnel policy. Finally, the fighting between Sergeyev and Kvashnin had almost paralyzed the military. When Kvashnin did not agree with what Sergeyev said or ordered him to do, he ignored him. As a result, little was accomplished.

When Ivanov was first appointed, there was hope that he would quickly take charge and reform the armed forces. Observers believed that his close ties to Putin would enable him to make major changes : "Ivanov can make decisions and can make things happen. He can implement the reforms the military badly needs and actually create a smaller, more capable professional army. Ivanov, fully supported by the Kremlin, can bypass Russia's corrupt and ineffective bureaucracy. He can suppress dissent among the generals."[25] Or as Moscow-based defense analyst Francoise Deauce noted:

He is someone who is outside the armed forces, who has a lot of authority
... notably from his [earlier] posts inside the security services ... and so
maybe he can impose decisions on the army that it might see as going
against its interests. In other words, he may be capable of fighting the corporation of the military institutions that until now was largely responsible for breaking successive attempts at military reforms since 1991.[26]

Despite these optimistic comments, Ivanov faced a very difficult situation.
To begin with, he was an outsider. True, he was a former general from the security services and a friend of the president, but he was up against a general
who did not take orders from anyone. Kvashnin also had the right to go directly to the president when it suited him—over the defense minister's head.
To make matters worse, Kvashnin had just won a major bureaucratic victory,
and it would not be easy to convince him to play second fiddle to Ivanov.

The one thing that was clear, given his close ties to Putin, was that Ivanov
would follow an evolutionary approach to military reform. He emphasized
this point by making it clear that he had no intention of being a "revolutionary" when it came to stabilizing and modernizing the military.[27] He fully
understood how desperate and difficult the situation was in the armed forces,
but he also knew that Putin would never support a policy aimed at solving the
military's problems overnight. Any changes would be gradual.[28] They would
focus on streamlining and reorganizing the army. There would be a reduction
of personnel and movement toward a professional army. Ivanov's task was to
implement these changes, changes that Putin had approved, and the latter
made it clear that Ivanov would be key in any reform plan. As Putin put it, "He
was the head of the group which worked out the main parameters of reform."[29] Furthermore, if there was any doubt about Ivanov's intentions, he removed them in May when he observed, "Today, the discussions are over . . .
The armed forces reform plans have been approved by the president, it's time
to implement the approved decisions."[30]

Meanwhile, on March 24, 2001, Putin had signed Decree No. 337, On Supporting the Plan for Conversion and Development of the RF Armed Forces
and Improving Their Structure. The decree broke the Strategic Rocket Forces
into two commands(*rodi*): the Strategic Missile Troops and the Space Troops.
In addition to the merging of two military districts discussed above, the
Ground Troops were given back their independent command (to replace the
Main Directorate of the Ground Troops in the General Staff). Finally, the decree set the size of the Russian military at one million as of January 1, 2006.[31]

In a certain sense, there was a similarity between Putin and Rodionov. Both men refused to look at military reform as an isolated event. Both men understood that the military was a part of society, and that what happened in the military was a reflection of Russian society as a whole; social, economic, political, and cultural factors all play an important role. In other words, whatever happened in the military had to be seen against the backdrop of Russian society as a whole. But a grand plan? As time would show, Putin would accept an interrelated framework for military reform, but only after considerable bureaucratic battles and compromises had produced something that made sense as a way to bring the Russian military into the twenty-first century.

On May 11, 2001, a commission Putin had formed presented him with proposals for dealing with the social problems faced by military personnel. Based on this report, Putin placed a priority on reforming the pay and allowances systems, as well as achieving pension reform and improving housing and medical services. Then on October 17, Putin chaired a session of the Security Council that focused on the military-industrial complex. It led to increased attention on the need to reform the military-industrial complex from the old Soviet model to a new, more competitive one. In addition, Putin announced that the military would be getting more money. "Deputy Minister Alexei Kudrin, who was present at the meeting, said that an additional 4 billion rubles would be found for the army this year, and that funding for military procurement would be upped by some 27 billion in the year 2002."[32] Finally, on November 27, 2001, Putin chaired another Security Council meeting focused on the question of mobilization readiness. He was also instrumental in ensuring that another 34.6 billion rubles were allocated for pay and allowances, and he worked on repaying the Ministry of Defense's outstanding debts.[33]

Given his proclivity to work within the bureaucracy, it is not surprising that Putin waited for the military to provide him with a proposal for changing its form of technical support. The plan was delivered on November 1. He received other suggestions as well. He approved the plan on November 16. He simultaneously ordered the high command to "come up with a reform plan that would see through a transition to a fully professional military by 2010."[34] Toward that end, the leadership proposed an experiment with one or two units in order to "determine more precisely the nature and scope of measures and the outlays necessary for converting them to the contract method of manning with servicemen."[35]

The generals had several reactions. They agreed that a volunteer, professional military was in many ways preferable to what they had when it came to combat. Yet there were many generals who wanted to keep the old system, which provided free labor to help build dachas for officers. The conscripts could always be loaned out to civilian enterprises with a hefty profit for the officer concerned. Then there were those who believed that military service was critical for socializing young men. It taught them how to love their country and obey orders, attributes they believed were critical for Russia's future.

In the meantime, there were 157,000 contract personnel in the Army by January 2002. Unfortunately, 40 percent of them were women, mainly officers' wives and daughters. While one could understand the need for officers' families to find employment, given their husbands' and fathers' low salaries, and while many officers considered the women more reliable because of the lower incidence of alcoholism, this high percentage of women represented a problem for the military. "As a rule, the men serve in Chechnya, Tajikistan, and other hot spots, while contract servicemen are paid more than the average 1,500 rubles a month."[36] That meant that, from a combat point of view, only 94,200 of the total cadre of *kontraktniks* were eligible for combat. The women earned the same salaries as other *kontraktnikis,* but they did not have to serve in combat. The situation was even worse three months later, when there were only 132,000 *kontraktnikis*. The military claimed that salaries were the problem. How could the military expect to attract top-quality personnel when the soldiers were only making around $100 a month?

Meanwhile, in February 2002 the General Staff offered a blueprint for moving the military toward contract service. It was finally submitted to Putin in July 2002. The Defense Ministry was not the only organization to offer a plan for reforming the military, however. The Union of Right Forces political party, under the leadership of Boris Nemtsov, also had its own version that would transform the army into a professional military almost immediately. Pay would be increased significantly to attract contract soldiers. At the same time, conscripts would serve only six months, and instead of working in the fields and building dachas for generals, they would be trained as specialists and then sent to the reserves. Indeed, supporters of this approach even worked out numbers for the transition.[37]

KVASHNIN IS FIRED AND THE GENERAL STAFF IS NEUTERED

By the end of 2003, it was clear that the constant conflict between Kvashnin and Ivanov was out of hand. The existing Law on Defense stated that the

Defense Ministry exercised command and control, while the General Staff was "the main organ for operational control of the Armed Forces." This gave the two structures equal status, except that everything that the Ministry of Defense wanted the troops to do had to go through the General Staff.[38] As a result, Kvashnin was able to modify or ignore those orders he opposed. But in January, with Putin's support, Ivanov suggested that the General Staff needed to be overhauled. In particular, he argued that the General Staff should stop its involvement in operational matters.[39]

Ivanov prevailed. On June 14, the Duma changed Article 13 of the Law on Defense to mention only the Defense Ministry: "Oversight for the Armed Forces of the Russian Federation is carried out by the defense minister via the Defense Ministry."[40] Furthermore, Article 15, which had listed the main functions of the General Staff, was declared null and void. In essence, this meant that the chief of the General Staff now worked for the Defense Minister.

Henceforth, the General Staff would stay out of operational matters. As Ivanov explained, "In the view of the supreme commander [Putin], it is important that the General Staff focus more on future wars and the prospective development of the armed forces, and not be involved in routine affairs."[41] Putin then fired Kvashnin after seven years on the job. The pretext for his firing was raids by Islamic militants against military posts and villages in Ingushetia, which killed nearly 100 people, due in large part to the fact that it took the Army twelve hours to respond.

While many in the military appreciated Kvashnin's effectiveness in advocating a greater role for conventional forces, his incompetence, arrogance, and brash way of dealing with subordinates had alienated many of them. According to military analyst Pavel Felgenhauer: "When officers, both retired and still serving, speak of Kvashnin, they recall his total incompetence, bad manners, berating of commanders in front of subordinates, and so on. There is also much talk in the ranks about rampant corruption at the top of the defense establishment."[42] Kvashnin's replacement, Yuri Baluyevski, would turn out to be a very different kind of person. He was modest, better qualified, and more ready to oversee the development of the armed forces.

Putin had made his choice. The chief of the General Staff had lost his right to appeal directly to the commander-in-chief. In the future, Ivanov would be responsible for actions taken by the Army. He now had the authority—and the responsibility—to make decisions, a point Ivanov emphasized. "There is one immutable constant in military organization: the principle of one-man command and one-man control. Armed forces remain what they are only for as long as this principle prevails and a rigid vertical command structure is ensured."[43] It would be up to Ivanov to lead the Russian military into Putin's second term, and he would need to be assertive and creative to tackle the Army's many problems, particularly when it came to professionalizing the military.

PROFESSIONALIZING THE MILITARY

Recognizing the bureaucratic problems he faced in dealing with the military, but convinced that he had to keep pushing the generals and admirals if he hoped to get anything done, Putin put his support behind an "experiment." The idea was to take the 76th Airborne Division (7,000 soldiers) at Pskov and to use it to show the generals that a professional military was both possible and effective. The experiment began on September 1, 2002. It was to last a year, and then the government would evaluate it. The contracts these soldiers signed made it clear that the *kontraktniki* were expected to serve in difficult and dangerous combat areas such as Chechnya. In addition, the individual *kontraktniki* had a right to housing—a new benefit for enlisted personnel in the Russia Army. One author warned that the basic salary for a soldier would have to be increased to 4,000 rubles a month if the Army hoped to attract enough *kontraktnikis*.[44]

In order to make the experiment a success, the government would also have to improve infrastructure. Past experience with *kontraktnikis* had indicated that they would not join or stay in the military if they were expected to live in the same kind of barracks as conscripts. As General Andrei Nikolayev, the chairman of the Defense Committee of the Duma, noted, "You cannot drive contract servicemen into dilapidated barracks."[45] In addition, they expected things like schools, stores, and social services for themselves and their families. Consequently, each *kontraktniki* was promised individual quarters.

The generals were unhappy with the experiment and went out of their way to sabotage it.[46] First they emphasized the extraordinary cost of a *kontraktniki*. They argued that a conscript cost 17,900 rubles a year, while a professional soldier cost 32,000. In short, a professional army costs twice as much as a conscript military.[47] Then Kvashnin visited the Pskov division on September 28, 2002, and made the stunning announcement, "No one intended to give apartments to the soldiers."[48] He followed that up with a statement to the effect, "The complex would be built without a kindergarten and school and that not all of those expecting flats would get them (of the originally slated eight apartment blocks, only five would be finally built). Following Kvashnin's announcement, some forty NCOs immediately handed in their resignations."[49] The General Staff also criticized the 76th division airborne command and gave it poor inspection grades. The high command then made these confidential grades public.

While the media focused on the generals who opposed the Pskov experiment, a second battle was being fought behind the scenes. Kvashnin and Airborne Commander General Georgi Shpak had long been at loggerheads. Kvashnin wanted to get rid of the airborne forces as an independent unit, while Shpak wanted to maintain the airborne force's separate status. Consequently, Kvashnin's criticism of the 76th was aimed as much at Shpak and the airborne forces as it was at the experiment with professionalism. As one source put it:

> Kvashnin, who heads a special commission evaluating the combat readiness of the country's airborne forces, told airborne forces commander Colonel General Georgy Shpak that he rates the readiness of Shpak's forces as "mediocre," *Izvestiya* reported. Kvashnin has long had an antagonistic relationship with Shpak and has proposed abolishing the airborne forces and creating instead a highly mobile rapid-reaction force capable of combating terrorism.[50]

In the end, Shpak lost the battle and, partly as a result of Kvashnin's criticism of the airborne units, he was forced to retire in September 2003.

The major challenge facing those who wanted the experiment to succeed was how to make military service more attractive. According to Thornton, in setting up the experiment at Pskov, Shpak had divided the process into several parts. First, he wanted to man the 104th regiment and make it combat ready. Within three months, the percentage of *kontraktnikis* was up to 77 percent (1,500 officers and men). The following June the unit was declared ready for combat and sent to Chechnya. Next in line was the 234th regiment, as well as the division's operations and supply sections. It turned out to be very difficult to find enough volunteers to man this regiment. In fact, it was not until December 2003 that it had enough manpower to send it to Chechnya.[51]

In the meantime, there were problems with the kind of individuals who signed up to be *kontraktnikis*. Felgenhauer referred to Pskov as "a criminal zone with marauding drunken *kontraktniki*."[52] Ivanov personally expressed dissatisfaction with discipline in the unit. "Last year there were forty-one deaths in this part of the Armed Forces; and in the first half of this year, there have already been thirty-two deaths among the paratroops due to various accidents."[53] Clearly, something had to be done.

In response to problems at Pskov, the Union of Right Forces suggested that the pay (then 3,000 rubles a month) for soldiers should be raised to 4,000–4,500 rubles a month. They also recommended that officer pay should be increased by 40–50 percent.[54] They further proposed that soldiers who signed a contract should be given free tuition if they decided to continue their education when they finished their service, and that conscription should be immediately ended.

Putin was well aware of problems at Pskov and in the military in general. Yet at a November 26 meeting, he stated that he had a "generally positive" outlook on the changes under way in the military, a clear sign that he expected further movement toward a professional military. However, in an effort to delay the transformation to a professional military, the generals tried to drag the process out by making it go through three stages. The first, like the Pskov division, was to end in 2004. The second, was to cover a period of seven years. The goal was to have 50–60 percent of soldiers and sergeants serving on contract. The third stage was left undefined: "It is planned that all armed forces will be manned with 'contractees' during the third stage."[55] Putin was not happy with the generals. After all, the second stage would end after he left office. The proposed timetable seemed to confirm the critics who believed the generals merely sought to wait Putin out. Regardless of the 76th's problems, it took a year and four months to man the 76th Division fully with *kontraktnikis*. When he visited the unit in December 2003, Ivanov proclaimed the experiment a success. He also mentioned that Moscow understood that it would have to do more about housing and after-hours recreation, and he emphasized that he knew this would continue to be a problem for some time to come.[56] The second part of the experiment took place in 2004. According to General Alexander Belousov, "In 2003 the 76th Airborne Division at Pskov was switched to the contract principle of manning. In 2004 it was the 42nd Motorized Rifle Division, stationed in the North Caucasus."[57]

PERMANENT-READINESS UNITS

While there had been problems with the airborne unit at Pskov and the 42nd Division, it the Putin administration believed that this was only way to transform the military. Their idea was to set up a two-tier system. After 2008, there would be approximately 144,000 volunteers serving in permanent-readiness units (e.g., airborne, infantry, naval infantry) while conscripts would serve for one year. Only professionals would serve in combat except in the most serious situations, while the recruits would be stationed in noncombat areas, leave the military, and join the reserve after completing their service.

Among the problems facing the Ministry of Defense as it pushed toward the creation of these units were creature comforts:

In 2005 the task is to convert forty Defense Ministry units and subunits at once. In fact, this is where the difficulties have developed. We were allocated money to build hostels and mess halls and modernize firing ranges (79.5 billion rubles), but the social and cultural sphere was forgotten. After all, a contract serviceman is not a soldier on compulsory service. At 1800 hours, if he has no official duties, he is free, like an officer. And what is he to do? A fit 25 year-old cannot simply lie around the barracks looking at the ceiling.[58]

Pay was also a problem. A survey conducted in 2004 indicated that the vast majority of candidates who might consider joining a professional army expected to get at least 10,000–12,000 rubles a month. However, the salary of a private who was on contract was still only 4,600.[59] The Putin administration addressed this issue by focusing on those serving in combat in Chechnya. By 2004 the salary for a *kontraktniki* in Chechnya was up to 15,000 rubles, and this improved their quality somewhat. However, problems with recruitment remained.[60] As General Baluyevski explained, "Despite the additional payments . . . it is mostly citizens, who as a rule have not established themselves in civilian careers, who apply for contract service, as well as residents from areas with poor economies and from the countryside, while many still consider the current reward for military work associated with life to be inadequate."[61] Furthermore, according to Belousov, nearly 70 percent of those who sign up to be contract soldiers are conscripts extending their military service. "Incidentally, the fact that the main bulk [of contract soldiers] are yesterday's drafted personnel is a problem. At the moment, our contract soldier is the same old compulsory-service soldier, remaining at the same level in terms of his education and training, but very expensive."[62] Instead, the military wanted to recruit highly qualified, educated personnel to staff these units.

Despite these problems, the Putin administration remains committed to creating a professional military. Putin called it a priority task, and General

Baluyevski made it clear that the General Staff had carefully planned out the transition:

> I should like to remind you that the federal target programme was set for 4 years. In 2004, one formation of the Russian armed forces was transferred to contract manning. In 2005, there will be over 30 such formations and units, and in 2006, 20 formations and units of the Russian armed services will change over to contract manning. It 2007, there will be another 11 formations and military units.[63]

In an effort to recruit more and better-qualified *kontraktnikis,* the military launched an advertising campaign. It played up improved pay and living conditions (arguing that pay had been raised to around 7,000 rubles a month), that meals were free and that new barracks had been built.[64] In addition, the 2005 budget set aside 3 billion rubles for combat training for *kontraktnikis* and materials for units manned by volunteers. Furthermore, by 2005, the pay for a private in Chechnya had increased again. It was now up to 190,000–200,000 rubles a year (or about 16,000 rubles a month).[65] Furthermore, permanent-readiness units were given priority when it came to placing officers who had graduated from military educational institutions.

The Putin administration has registered some successes. In 2005 Ivanov announced that close to 16,000 individuals had been selected to be privates and sergeants during 2004, which enabled the government to complete the manning of the 42nd Motorized Division in Chechnya and to build housing for the unit.[66] Still, serious problems remain, and it appears that the government recognizes that it must "create acceptable conditions for service and life. Make it worth their while with various benefits."[67] The 2006 draft budget addressed this issue: "Funds allocated to the special federal program 'Transition to the All-Volunteer Force in 2004' will amount to 22.3 billion Russian rubles ($789 million) next year, which is 15 percent more than the 2005 budget (19.7 billion rubles [$697 million]) and two-fold as much as the 2004 budget 9.6 billion rubles ($340 million)."[68]

How successful this program will be in recruiting the kind of quality professionals the Kremlin wants is open to question. Problems with the quality of *kontraknikis* remain. In January 2006, the military announced that the 98th Airborne Division had failed to fill 500 positions "for privates and NCOs." As a result, instead of going over to a fully professional unit, it was "allowed to retain one conscript battalion."[69] However, the Putin administration is committed to dealing with them to the degree that the budget will permit.[70]

WEAPONS AND THE BUDGET

If he hoped to build the military to the level required to modernize and stabilize it, much less pay the troops, Putin had to tackle the budget. He began by reversing Yeltsin's starvation budgets, but he did not go as far as the high command wanted. The generals had argued that 3.5 percent of GNP should be allocated to the military, in accord with a 1998 presidential decree by Yeltsin. While Putin was not prepared to go that far, the military budget has increased substantially under Putin, as shown in Table 6.1. In addition, Ivanov stated in 2005 that defense spending will increase from 20–25 percent a year, "remaining at 2.5 percent to 2.7 percent of GDP.[71]

The infusion of money under Putin has helped stabilize the situation. The major problem has been inflation, which has tended to wipe out budgetary increases. As one member of the Duma, a retired general, pointed out with regard to the budget for 2006, "The matter is that the government and the Finance Ministry particularly have forgotten about inflation and the steady growth of prices on fuel, energy, services, goods and defense products."[72] As a result, the military has a long way to go before it will be capable of defending the country.

Russian weapons were outdated. New weapons accounted for only 15–20 percent of the Russian armed forces, while the corresponding figure for NATO was 60–70 percent. "There has been no mass production of new technology such as the KA-32 helicopter, T-90 tank, close-battle-radar location stations, and closed communications radio stations for the Russian Army."[73] General Baluyevski, chief of the General Staff's Operations Department at that time, underlined the seriousness of the problem in 2001 when he noted that arms procurement accounted for only 6 percent of total defense expenditures, compared to a "minimum of 20 percent in NATO countries. The greater share of Russia's defense budget goes to wages, food, uniforms, and so on (these items account for 25–27 percent of the defense budget in NATO countries)."[74] Russia was five-to-twelve years behind the United States in the production of weapons.[75]

To deal with the situation, in January 2002 the Putin administration adopted a State Program for Armaments for the Period up to 2010, which increased spending on arms and research. "Klebanov said the procurement plan tops last year's expenditure by nearly 40 percent . . . The 40 percent figure corresponds to remarks made last year [2001] by Finance Minister Alexei Kudrin, who said the 2002 procurement budget would likely increase by 27–79 billion rubles (from $850 million to $2.5 billion)."[76]

Table 6.1. Russian Defense Budget, 1999–2006

Year	1999	2000	2001	2002	2003	2004	2005	2006 est.
% of GNP	2.34	2.63	2.66	2.60	2.65	2.691	2.82	2.74
Billions of rubles	109.03	146.0	218.9	284.185	344.06	411.57	471.8	498.769

Note: It is extremely difficult to provide accurate budgetary figures given the changing value of the ruble and the different figures provided by different sources. The one point on which all sources agree is that the budget increased significantly under Putin. For example, in 2000 the budget was 146 billion rubles. In 2005 it was 471 billion rubles thanks in large part to the strengthened economy and tax collection procedures. See Stephen J. Blank, "The General Crisis in the Russian Military," *Journal of Slavic Military Studies* 16, 2 (June, 2003): 7 and "Army Losing Battle with Oligarchs," gazeta.ru (March 28, 2005) in WNC (March 29, 2005). By 2006 it was expected to be 498.76 billion rubles. "Draft 2006 Budget Shows Increased Spending on Defense," Interfax (August 17, 2005) in WNC (August 19, 2005).

Despite this budgetary increase, Ilya Klebanov, the minister of science, industry, and technology, reported, "In-depth modernization of combat aircraft, ships, nonstrategic missiles, precision weapons systems, and other military hardware on the existing basis will make it possible to carry out work also in the sphere of (long-term) research and development."[77] This meant that it would be a long time—2110 according to the commander of ground troops—before new weapons and equipment would be available.[78] In the meantime, what money there was for weapons and equipment would be used to modernize existing systems. There was a tremendous need for modernization. For example, Lieutenant General Sergei Solntsev, who was in charge of flight safety for the Russian Air Force, commented in 2002 that over half of Russia's airbases were in need of complete refurbishment, while another report on the Air Force commented, "The share of up-to-date aircraft of the fourth generation amounts to less than 45 percent of the aircraft fleet. The share of operational aircraft in general has fallen to 60 percent. Only a little over 30 percent of airfields are ready for operation. The personnel's annual flying hours do not exceed 20 to 25 percent of the required number."[79] By 2002 the military budget had tripled, from 109 billion rubles to 284 billion rubles.[80] While this might sound significant, it really only meant that the situation had at least begun to stabilize. The military had a long way to go before it would be combat ready in any meaningful sense of the term.

In 2002 the long, exceedingly slow process of rebuilding began. The Air Force was scheduled to receive twenty modernized Su–27 general-purpose planes in 2003, after obtaining twelve modernized planes in 2002.[81] In addition, army aviation received fifteen new helicopter gunships.[82] It was clear that the Putin administration was trying to turn things around. "In 2001 the total value of the state weapons order was 53 billion rubles; this goal was met fully.

In 2002 the state weapons order increased to 80 billion rubles and this target was also met. In the current year the weapons order was planned at 119.8 billion rubles; only 112 billion rubles were actually allocated."[83] The point is that progress was being made, even though it was very limited and very uneven. The administration simply did not have an unlimited supply of cash to spend on weapons.

The year 2003 brought more of the same. In March the deputy commander of the Air Force, Yuri Grishin, complained that the Air Force would "have to fly planes that are twenty to forty years old."[84] Another source echoed this concern, noting, "Some 80 percent of Russia's military-industrial complex is obsolete . . . the average years of service for the machinery of the complex is thirty, as compared with 7–8 years in the developed nations of Europe."[85]

In 2004, some new weapons began to appear, albeit in extremely small numbers. For example, in July the Army announced that it had obtained fourteen T-90S tanks, and it hoped to get another twenty to thirty tanks in 2005.[86] However, the next year Ivanov announced that the Army would get only eighteen.[87] Similarly, the Army received between thirty and forty BTR-80 armored personnel carriers. The Air Force announced that during 2005 it would purchase one Tu-160 strategic bomber and repair a second one. It planned "to modernize seven Su–27 fighters, purchase four Topol-M strategic missiles, two Iskander tactical missile systems . . . one warship and one diesel submarine."[88]

The 2006 draft budget included 225 billion rubles for weapons acquisition. This is a growth of one billion rubles over the proceeding year. This will permit the military to acquire seven Topol-M missiles and seventeen tanks, while seventeen Su–27 fighters will be modernized.[89] At the same time, the Army's main strike helicopter, the Mi–28N, will begin to enter service.[90] These new purchases represent a drop in the bucket, however. As one critic argued, "We need to buy 140–150 planes, 60 helicopters, 200 tanks, 250 artillery weapons annually, but next year we will buy mere single pieces of equipment."[91] This critic's frustration is well founded. However, it is worth noting that instead of waiting until 2010, as had been anticipated when Putin came to power, his administration has begun to bring new systems on line earlier, albeit in limited quantities.

In addition to hiring Kudelina to oversee the budget, the Putin administration took a number of structural actions in an effort to improve efficiency in purchasing weapons and equipment. First, a single-purchasing-agent system was set up. According to Ivanov, when he took over as defense minister there were fifty-two entities inside the Defense Ministry that had the power to purchase military equipment and weapons and to order research and development. The number was first cut to twenty and then to only one.[92] However, major problems remained. For example, from 2001 to 2004 there was a 160–170 billion ruble shortfall, because the state budget is drawn up annually. Almost all major weapons systems take anywhere from three to ten years to develop. As a consequence, each weapon system is reviewed annually, and a decision may be made to stop production, even before it has reached the testing stage. Viktor Litovkin argued that federal budgets should be drawn up for at least three years—and perhaps even longer—thereby building some predictability into the system.[93]

Putin's idea was to systematically rebuild the country's military in ten years. The success of this ambitious plan will depend on how the economy does and how persistent Putin is in pushing his modernization agenda.[94] There is no question that the country is capable of producing high-quality weapons, as indicated by the willingness of the Chinese and the Indians to outfit their militaries by purchasing almost exclusively Russian weapons.

DEALING WITH PAY AND HOUSING

Problems in rebuilding the Russian Army were even more obvious when it came to salaries for officers and housing. At one point Putin promised an increase in officers' salaries effective January 1, 2002. The raises were soon put off until mid-2003. Then an increase in wages for the rank and file was moved from 2003 to 2004.[95] In the meantime, officers' pay remained abysmal.

The problem, however, was that even if the government were able to give officers a raise, it was simultaneously taking away benefits, such as requiring soldiers to pay income taxes as well as lose other discounts. One hot-button issue was free travel on public transport for soldiers. Local authorities wanted to abolish the benefit, because it cost money to maintain local transportation systems. In cities with a large military presence, municipalities were not being reimbursed for military personnel who used public transportation. "Their privileges are torpedoing the possibility of developing public transport and updating the bus and trolley bus fleet."[96] To make matters worse, the inflation rate was 18 percent, which meant that whatever raises they received were quickly eaten up. There was talk of indexing pay, but like everything else, it seemed to be just that—talk. The average officer's pay was only around $100.[97] Indeed, according to figures from 2002, "43 percent of officers lived under the poverty line, defined by a monthly wage of at least $59."[98]

This effort to take away the military's special privileges would soon become a major problem, as the government botched the entire process. First, the Putin administration decided to add a monthly payment of 50–120 percent to a serviceman's salary to compensate him or her for the cost of mass transportation. "The average sum will total 700 rubles. These payments will range from 350 rubles to 1,500 rubles, given the level of development and conditions in the regions."[99] Meanwhile, there were rumors that servicemen's pay would not be increased in 2004 and 2005, even though 34 percent still had an income that was below the subsistence rate for a family.[100] Faced with these continuing problems, officers, especially junior ones, continued to leave in droves. In 2003, a report noted that "up to 50 percent of the graduates of military schools leave military service a year after graduating."[101]

Pay was not the only problem. In 2001, 92,000 officers in Moscow still did not have apartments and another 45,000 did not have any housing at all.[102] The next year the situation was not much better: 168,000 servicemen needed housing while another 60,000 officers and warrant officers would have to be resettled because some military installations were to be closed and others were too isolated.[103] Problems with housing and pay were taking their toll. In 2002, for example, a General Staff study showed: "Every tenth medium-rank officer position is vacant and among petty officers, every third. In the last few months over 100 officers lecturing in the Ground Forces Academy have asked for dismissal from military service, and if this trend continues, the academy will have to close in six months. About 70 percent of the officers who resigned last year were 30 or younger."[104]

By 2005 complaints were rampant. One source argued that poor pay was a threat to the military's very "existence," noting that plans for indexing salaries in 2004 were left "unfulfilled." In addition, the increase in the price index between 2003 and the end of 2005 was expected to be around 25 percent.[105] The salary situation was continuing to have a negative impact on the country's officers: "85 percent of officers of the Russian Armed Forces assess negatively the enforcement of the law on replacing benefits with cash payments."[106] The situation among officers was so serious that some of them took the almost-unprecedented step of openly protesting. For example, a letter adopted at one unit's officers' assembly and sent to Putin read:

The deprivation of servicemen and their families of the lost social benefits was not bolstered by a significant rise (by a factor of 3–4, at a minimum) of their pay and allowances has created critical social tension and is contributing to the outflow from the army of skilled regulars. Thirty-five officers, including 13 pilots, 3 maintenance technicians, and 19 ground-service engineers, left the service early in 2004 alone. The officer shortfall runs to 192, of warrant officers to 62, and of contract servicemen to 20.[107]

The Putin administration took such expressions of concern seriously. The reason that many officers lived below the poverty line, according to the director of the Armed Forces Sociology Center, was that it was very difficult for wives of officers to find work because they were stationed at remote garrisons.[108] The regime's response was another promise to raise salaries. The chairman of the Duma Defense Committee claimed that the wages of "lieutenants at the position of platoon commander will be 7,485 rubles ($270) a month, while the minimum wage in Russia for a family of two parents and one child is 7,594 rubles ($274) a month." When monthly bonuses were added in, the individual officer would be above the poverty line, but barely.[109] The regime even announced that the pay of enlisted servicemen would be raised by 100 rubles from 200 rubles a month to 300 rubles and, beginning September 2005, pay would go to 400 rubles a month.[110] It was not enough to get rich on, but better than the $2–$3 a conscript was paid in the Soviet Army. In addition, soldiers (and officers) who were wounded in military service would get an additional 1,000 rubles per month beginning January 1, 2006.[111] Finally, it was announced that military pay (including veterans benefits) would be increased 15 percent beginning January 1, 2006, and Putin announced in November 2005 that during the course of the next three years military salaries would be raised by 67 percent.[112]

Meanwhile, the Putin administration came up with a plan to deal with the eternal housing shortage. At the end of 2002 Ivanov announced that the government would be "radically transforming the system of providing housing to servicemen."[113] Service personnel were divided into three categories. The first consisted those who had been discharged and who must be provided with housing in accordance with state commitments. The second category dealt with those who joined the military after 1998. They must be provided with official housing. Finally, there were those who joined the military after 2003. This group would be covered by the new plan, a mortgage savings system. Toward this end, the Duma passed a law on August 5, 2004, On the Accumulation and Mortgage Credit System for the Provision of Housing to Military Service Members, and Putin signed it on August 8, 2004. The law went into effect on January 1, 2005. According to this plan, the serviceman would make deposits into a personal savings account, and the Army would put in 37,000 rubles ($1,300) per year "Later on the sum will be revised on an annual basis taking into account the rate of inflation."[114] After three years the individual could take the money out and, together with a loan from a bank, buy an apartment. The Russian military then created a new structure, the Federal Directorate for the Mortgage System for the Provision of Housing for Servicemen, to implement this program.

> Then the money the state has promised apartment-less servicemen will start flowing in a generous stream for a beginning into the intermediary office that is intended to "serve" them . . . The cost of the issue is tens, and later will be hundreds, of billions of rubles . . . R1.3 billion will be spent to implement the new mortgage housing program in 2005. In 2006, the figure is planned to triple (R3.3 billion). And by 2010 the total figure for all mortgage accounts for servicemen will be in the hundreds of billions of rubles.[115]

This still did not completely solve the housing problem. The high command faced cutbacks and the obvious problem of building and finding enough housing for those who joined prior to 2003. For example, in February 2005, Ivanov commented that there were "85,000 soldiers living in "communal housing facilities; 49,000 are renting housing; and 1,300 families are taking shelter in offices and barracks of military units."[116]

It soon became obvious that there were problems with the new housing system. On November 28, 2005, Putin criticized the system arguing, "The average price of housing is 29,000 rubles per one square meter of floor space, while we assume it's 11,000 rubles. And we wish you good luck. Why are we pulling the people's leg?"[117] He subsequently ordered the government to allocate an additional 15 billion rubles to housing programs.[118]

The Putin administration finally received some good news in a March 2005 report. According to this study, more than half of all officers had adopted a wait-and-see attitude when it came to staying in the military.[119] They were watching to see what the Kremlin would do and how the housing certificates would work. They needed to know if the savings program would keep up with inflation, or would it just be another broken Kremlin promise. But despite the Kremlin's efforts, officers are continuing to leave. Ivanov complained in November 2005 that "over 12,000 officers have retired early from the armed forces.[120] The best that can be said is that the Putin administration appeared to be trying to come up with a plan to deal with pay and housing issues.

CRIME, CORRUPTION, AND *DEDOVSHCHINA*

Putin had to deal with three enormous problems: crime, corruption, and *de-dovshchina*. All three were out of control when he took over.

Crime and Corruption

Crime and corruption plagued all levels of the armed forces. At the end of December 2000, the military prosecutor opened cases against a number of senior Strategic Rocket Forces officers in Arkhangelsk Region.[121] There were also problems with Russian peacekeepers in Yugoslavia. Because of issues with drugs, crime, and corruption, 286 troops had been sent back to Russia in 2001.[122] In 2002 proceedings were initiated against the commander of the Leningrad Naval Base, a vice admiral, while another report indicated that crimes were up by 9 percent in the northwest.[123] The situation did not improve. Embezzlement and theft of equipment was common. The situation had deteriorated to the point that it was impossible to calculate just how serious the problem was:

> No one has ever been able to put a figure on the scale of theft in the Russian armed forces overall. Rations are sold while soldiers go hungry. Arms and ammunition disappear, perhaps to hunters, gangsters or terrorists, but no one knows. Fuel, spare parts, and vehicles can be bought. Recently, in Mulino, home of a permanent-readiness motor rifle regiment, tanks ran out of fuel on the ranges because it was being sold by the tanker-loader to local businesses. A motor rifle regimental commander sold all his unit's lorries [trucks], becoming briefly, a millionaire.[124]

Similar reports continued in 2003. Senior officers were convicted of corruption, including General Georgii Olenik, the Ministry of Defense's chief financial officer, while the theft of weapons and equipment continued.[125] Russian Air Force planes were even used to smuggle caviar. "We confiscated 5.5 tons of red caviar, 160 kg of black caviar, and 0.5 tons of sturgeon fish from on board a Russian Air Force Tu-154 aircraft that was on the point of taking off for Moscow. Representatives of the military were unable to explain where this consignment came from."[126] Crimes even went so far to include letting conscripts stand out in subzero weather in summer clothes, while their officers were inside drinking. Later 100 of the conscripts were taken to a hospital and treated for pneumonia.[127] In 2005 about 5,000 officers, among them five generals, were convicted by Russian military courts.[128] Examples abound, but the bottom line is that by the beginning of 2006, crime and corruption in the armed forces appeared to be out of control.

Hazing

If the situation regarding crime and corruption is a sad commentary on the situation in the Russian military, incidents of *dedovshchina* (hazing) were even worse than under Yeltsin, and it had devastating effects on recruiting. The military continued to face major problems in recruiting young men, because potential conscripts had heard the horror stories from the barracks. By the end of 2000 the military was once again rounding up young men on the streets of Moscow and sending them off to the Army.[129] And even then the military was often unsuccessful in finding qualified recruits. Looking at the fall draft 2001, a poll conducted among recruits from Siberia reported:

> Twenty percent of the draftees have primary education, and only 1.8 percent higher education. Every fourth conscript has grown up in a family without a father and 1 percent are orphans. Forty-three percent had studied and 37 percent had worked before army service. Eleven percent frankly confessed to alcohol addiction being their worst habit. Up to 4 percent of respondents used drugs and 11 percent already had police records for various reasons.[130]

Given the poor quality of draftees, and the continuing lack of NCOs, it was not surprising that "barrack room fagging and bullying is endemic."[131] Recognizing the danger that *dedovshchina* presented, the high command began posting morale officers to units, but to little avail. " 'The older soldiers educate young troops,' says the young lieutenant, who identifies himself only as Dmitry. 'This is the way the army is built. We mustn't break established rules.'" Then to give an idea of how he understands the concept of discipline, he produced a "72-centimeter, hard-nosed baton he uses to punish unruly soldiers. He refers to it as an 'educator.'"[132] The situation undermined combat readiness, especially when it led to malnourishment among the troops; senior soldiers took food from more junior ones. Abuse did not stop there. According to the main military prosecutor, in 2002 some 800 servicemen from security agencies were killed by other soldiers. Not surprisingly, the fear of violence in the barracks had a direct impact, especially on the desertion rate. In 2002, 4,200 soldiers fled.[133] In attempting to explain the reason for bullying, Russian military spokesmen continually pointed to the low quality of those drafted; i.e., it was society's fault. There was a strong feeling that if the quality of recruits improved the situation would improve. But the situation was not getting better, and one of the main reasons was the decision by the Duma to get rid of the guardhouse.

Prior to July 2002, commanders had the option of sending unruly or disobedient soldiers to the guardhouse for up to ten days. However, the Duma decided to close these military jails so that Russia would look better in the eyes of the European Union. Instead, the move further undermined discipline. It put officers in a very difficult situation. The only way they could enforce discipline was with their own fists. However, officers who beat up enlisted personnel ran the risk of being arrested. In 2003, for example, "Almost a battalion of officers [was] sentenced for violence with a general at the head and half of them behind bars."[134]

Meanwhile, the demographic situation continued to deteriorate. The General Staff's own figures from 2002 showed that, as a result of the declining birth rate, whereas there were 380,000 young men eligible for the draft in 2001, there would only be 100,000–120,000 in 2011.[135] Health problems were also beginning to be a matter of concern. By 2004 one out of every three recruits had problems that were sufficiently serious to keep them out of the more strenuous military branches. "Fifty-four percent of young soldiers are unfit for service in classified units, the VDV (airborne troops), the navy, and the border and missile troops based on medical testimony."[136] This meant first that the overall percentage of those who were eligible to be drafted was down to 9.5 percent of the draft contingent. However, even among those who were drafted, there were many who had limited educations or drug or disciplinary problems. As a consequence, more than half could not serve in difficult physical conditions. The military even had to send some recruits to medical units where they could be fed and nourished before they could serve even in positions with minimal physical demands.

A firestorm broke out in January 2006 following revelations that on New Year's Eve a soldier stationed at the Chelyabinsk Tank Military Academy was brutally beaten for three hours by the *deds* and a few officers. He was refused medical treatment as the unit tried to cover-up what had happened. Four days later he found his way to a civilian hospital, where doctors discovered that gangrene had already spread into his legs. As a result, the physicians were forced to amputate his legs, the tip of the little finger on one of his hands, as well as his reproductive organs.[137]

Faced with public outrage, Putin and Ivanov demanded action and punishment for those guilty. The country's senior military prosecutor, Alexander Savenkov, took over the case, while the commander of the academy, Major General Viktor Sidorov, was fired, thrown out of the Army, and had charges filed against him. Charges were also brought against twelve other servicemen, including two officers, while Putin demanded that the military introduce new "educational measures" to improve relations in the military, along with new measures to "toughen the penalty for army commanders who conceal information about accidents or crimes, including hazing."[138] While the outrage expressed by Putin, Ivanov, and Baluyevski was appropriate, the real question is what new steps will be taken to eliminate this scourge from the Army.

Based on its past actions, the high command seems to believe that cutting the length of conscription to one year, beginning 2008, will help break the *dedovshchina* process. If recruits only served for one year versus two, there would only be two age groups serving at any one time. The second group would not have been in the military long enough to pick up the habits of the *deds*. The high command also hoped that a new law that made military training in schools obligatory would help improve the quality of conscripts.[139]

Improving the Quality of Recruits

Ivanov and others also launched a number of test balloons in an effort to increase both the number and quality of recruits. First, the Army fought hard against the idea of alternative service, a battle that it lost. However, the military did succeed in attaching restrictions that make alternative service very unattractive, except for individuals with a very strong moral commitment to avoiding military service.

Second, there was the question of deferments, which numbered up to twenty-five categories. There were suggestions that the number should be cut back, but given public opposition, at first the military backed down. Ivanov also tried to reduce the number of conscripts who avoided actual military duties and turned his attention to college-level military training.

Prior to 2005 Russia had 229 universities offering ROTC courses. Ivanov noted, "There are more military departments [at universities] in the Russian Federation than there were in the Soviet Union."[140] Yet, only 10 percent of the 170,000 students who take these courses actually end up serving in the armed forces. For practical purposes, ROTC was a way to avoid military service; it produced "paper lieutenants." Ivanov ordered schools to drop their courses, so that only thirty to thirty-five universities would offer "approved" military training after 2009. Anyone enrolled in 2005 would be permitted to finish their schooling, but effective 2005 no new students would be enrolled, except at universities selected by the military. Students who signed up for ROTC would have their education paid for by the military and receive military training while at the university. They would agree to serve at least three years as an officer upon graduation. The Kremlin hoped that these individuals, unlike the "reserve" officers who graduated from one of the 229 universities, would have both the training and motivation to serve as small-unit officers and hopefully be able to have an impact on problems such as *dedovshchina*. Students who did not take ROTC would be part of the regular draft pool once they finished their university studies. This meant that in 2008 the military will go to a one-year draft.[141] This included both those individuals who did not take ROTC as well as those who did not go to university.

In an effort to deal with problems like *dedovshchina,* the military also has begun to consider the use of chaplains. The position of a human rights ombudsman was also created.[142] Traditionally, the military has shied away from chaplains, likely a hangover from the Soviet period. In fact, one military psychologist tried to convince his commander that a Baptist minister he knew might be able to convince some of the soldiers to moderate their behavior, but the idea was dismissed.[143] Then in November 2003, the head of the Armed Forces' Education Department, Colonel General Nikolai Reznik, solemnly declared that the military would not be using chaplains.[144]

By 2005, however, there had been a major change of opinion about chaplains. On January 5, Ivanov met with the Patriarch of Moscow to thank him for the Orthodox Church's spiritual support of the army, while the military's prosecutor general called on the military to make use of the Orthodox Church in the Army's effort to fight crime. Finally, on June 10, General Nikolai Pankov, who is in charge of personnel and educational issues in the Army, stated, "We will actively work with all traditional religions." The biggest hindrance to recreating the Imperial chaplaincy is how to handle the wide variety of religions in Russia. Pankov noted, for example, "Up to 50–60 percent of soldiers and sergeants in subunits are Muslims."[145] Following the 2006 hazing incident in Chelyabinsk, chief military prosecutor Savenkov intensified his call for the introduction of chaplains. "There may be different attitudes to the chaplain service, but 'it has proved effective,' as seen from the experience of foreign armies."[146]

The military also moved to reestablish the guardhouse to give junior officers a nonviolent way to deal with especially difficult soldiers. According to one report, during the three years without guardhouses, "A significant growth (by almost a third) has been seen in instances of assault and battery (*rukoprikladstvo*) of commanders. Both the representatives of civilian society and the military declare with one voice that, seeing the (commanders') impotence, barracks hooligans simply threw aside all restraint, and drunkenness and *dedovshchina* flourished."[147] A bill reestablishing the guardhouse was introduced in the Duma in September 2005.[148]

Will the Putin administration's plan work? There were rumors that NCOs from professional units would be used to train conscripts (and live in the barracks), thereby ensuring that *dedovshchina* was halted. Reintroducing the guardhouse and closer cooperation with the Orthodox Church might help improve discipline and ethics. If salaries improve over time, and if the military prosecutor follows up by sending soldiers guilty of crime and corruption to jail, the problem might resolve itself over time. The brutal hazing incident in Chelyabinsk in 2006 might force the military to take *dedovshchina* seriously and not cover it up as has happened in the past. However, it is still too early to tell.

THE WAR ON TERRORISM

The September 11, 2001, terrorist attacks on New York City and Washington, D.C., functioned as a wake-up call to most world leaders, including Putin. He clearly realized that what took place in the United States could happen in Moscow. For Russia, terrorism was no longer limited to Chechnya. Putin was the first world leader to call U.S. President George W. Bush, and he quickly joined the global "war on terrorism." He immediately offered assistance to the United States for its war against the Taliban in Afghanistan, despite opposition from the General Staff. Kvashnin, among others, initially declared, "Russia has not considered and is not planning to consider participation in a military operation against Afghanistan." He also reminded the Central Asian states of "their relevant bilateral and other obligations" to Russia.[149]

By September 24, Putin had heard enough military opposition to close cooperation between the Russian and American militaries. Before leaving for a visit to the United States, Putin stopped at the Defense Ministry and made it clear that he expected cooperation from the armed forces. He agreed to step-up support for opposition forces inside Afghanistan, and he gave "tacit approval for the United States to use former Soviet bases in Central

Asia."[150] That same day Defense Minister Ivanov, in a major reversal of his previous negative position, said that the United States could use military facilities in Tajikistan to launch strikes on neighboring Afghanistan, "if the need arises."[151] Access to these facilities was especially important to Washington, because of concern over the volatility of fundamentalist Muslim groups in Pakistan, its other major staging area. Then Presidents Nursultan Nazarbayev of Kazakhstan and Askar Akayev of Kyrgyzstan said that they were willing to provide the antiterrorist alliance with the use of their airspace and military bases. By December 1, some 500 U.S. troops were deployed at the Karshi-Khanabad Air Base in Uzbekistan, and the United States had signed agreements granting it landing rights in Tajikistan and Kyrgyzstan.

While Putin may have thought the war in Chechnya was over, the Chechens did not. For example, terrorists struck Moscow on October 23, 2002, as Chechen rebels seized a Moscow theater taking 800 people hostage. Putin refused to negotiate with them and instead ordered the special services to seize the building. Commandos pumped a toxic gas into the theater that killed the Chechens, but also inadvertently caused the deaths of 120 hostages and made close to 600 others extremely ill. Putin's response to the theater attack was immediate.

Putin also gave the armed forces a new objective: "to fight terrorism at the global level."[152] The General Staff was confused and had no idea what he had in mind. "The top brass in the General Staff are at a loss," reported *Novaya gazeta,* "because the new tasks set by the supreme commander-in-chief greatly differ from the current strategy of the Russian Armed Forces."[153] After all, with the exception of Chechnya, Russia's generals had been focused on fighting external enemies. A few days later, Ivanov gave an interview to *Izvestiya* in which he declared, "War has been declared on Russia, a war without frontiers, borders, or visible enemies." He reiterated a statement he had made to the effect that Moscow must be in a position to strike those who carry out—or finance—such undertakings. He emphasized, "Russia reserves the right to use precision-guided weapons to strike training bases or other objects related to international terrorism."[154] On November 26, Putin met with senior military officers and bluntly declared: "The state needs already today, not tomorrow, the armed forces that are able to guarantee the country's safety."[155]

To Putin, this meant closer cooperation between the military and law-enforcement organs. He said that the army should "cooperate more effectively with the law-enforcement bodies and with other military structures."[156] Indeed, if there were any questions in the military's mind, Putin removed them the next day, when he stated that the military's main task was to fight terrorism.

That did not mean that they were relieved of other tasks; the high command still had to carry out traditional military functions such as deterring an attack by external enemies.[157] However, for the foreseeable future, the fight against terrorism would be the military's "main task."[158] Kvashnin responded in December by ordering "commanders of all military units and garrisons to submit contingency plans for the prevention of terrorist attacks."[159] At the same time, General Nikolai Kormiltsev, the commander of ground forces, stated that combat training programs would have to be reoriented toward the fight against terrorism. As examples, Kormiltsev noted, "practice raids on highland areas and ones with dense vegetation and [to] learn how to break out of encirclement and an ambush." In addition, the general noted the importance of protecting strategic facilities, i.e., nuclear power plants, hydro-electric stations, chemical plants, and munitions depots.[160]

Increasingly, decision makers like Ivanov began to speak of Russia facing a new kind of threat. The danger of military aggression from the United States or NATO or any other nonterrorist Western source had significantly declined. As he noted at a meeting of the Academy of Military Sciences in Moscow on January 18, 2003, "After September 11, 2001, and [the October 23–26 hostage drama in Moscow], it has become completely clear that the Cold War has been replaced by a new type of war, the war against international terrorism."[161] He tried to push his ideas to become the basis for a new military doctrine (the Ivanov Doctrine), but it did not become official.[162]

Meanwhile, there was talk of the Ministry setting up antiterror units, while work was progressing on a new law, On Combating Terrorism. Then, on September 1, 2004, a grammar school in Beslan, North Ossetia, was seized by terrorists, who held approximately 1,000 parents, teachers, and students hostage for three days. This traumatic event had a deep impact not only on Putin, Moscow, the military, and Russia, but the rest of the world was well. At least 339 people were killed, most of them young children.

Putin responded immediately. First, he initiated a major overhaul of Moscow's centralized political structure by announcing that governors of the country's eighty-nine regions would no longer be elected by popular vote, but he would appoint them, subject to approval by the local legislature.[163] As he had in the past, Putin decided that the best way to deal with what he perceived to be local incompetence was to centralize matters, to transfer authority to Moscow. He also moved to gain greater control over elections to the Duma, the lower house of parliament. He maintained that these changes were necessary to put the country in a position to fight terrorism effectively.

For his part, Baluyevski announced that the Army reserved the right to make preemptive strikes against terrorist bases, regardless of where they were located. "That does not mean that we are going to deliver nuclear strikes. The use of military force against terrorism is a last resort."[164] In October Ivanov noted that Moscow was planning to equip special forces with special equipment so that they would be better able to fight terrorism.[165] Meanwhile, the Duma overwhelmingly voted for a new counterterrorism law that gave Putin the power to declare states of emergency and to restrict free speech and the media during terrorist threats or attacks. Polls shows that 84 percent of the population favored these types of action.[166]

In February 2005, the Duma revised the law On Defense to permit the Army to take part in counterterrorism actions involving the use of military force. The action was taken at Putin's request, in an effort to clarify the procedure for using the military in situations such as Beslan, as well as the use of the armed forces outside of Russia's boundaries. The real question, of course, was what impact this legal change would have on military operations.

While traditionally the high command first put doctrinal statements on paper and then followed them up with tactical and operational plans, this time the military appears to be approaching the task of fighting terrorism by working with two other organizations—the Interior Ministry and the FSB—to carry out training exercises. For example, in September 2005 an exercise was conducted in the Far East involving all three organizations. "Under fire support from Mi–24 fighting helicopters and artillery, a scenario of a mock battle was staged . . . In combination with the military operation, which the Defense Ministry regiment was tasked to conduct, issues of coordination and joint actions with border troops and the Interior Ministry were rehearsed."[167] This was one of several training exercises involving other ministries. While details are lacking, it appears that the military hopes to work out procedures for fighting terrorism by working with the other agencies on the ground. In any case, the War in Chechnya will have a major impact on the kind of procedures the military adopts to fight this new kind of war.

Meanwhile, in early 2006 there were rumors that Baluyevski had come up with a plan for a significant reconfiguration of the Army. According to reports, this plan calls for a complete separation of the Ministry of Defense and the military, with the Ministry becoming a "civilian institution exercising control over troops, conducting personnel policy, and supplying troops." Morale will also be a primary Ministry concern. "The General Staff will command the troops."[168]

Such reorganization would also lead to a major modification of the traditional branches of the military. As Stephen Blank noted:

> Under the new plan, all of the six existing military districts would be abolished and replaced by regional directorates for the West, South, and East . . . In that configuration there would be no reason to maintain the high commands of various services and commands of branches like the Strategic Missile Forces, Space Forces, and Airborne Forces. Similarly, the four fleets and the Caspian Flotilla would also be folded in these directorates. Thousands of command positions would correspondingly be abolished.[169]

Such a reorganization would create a military better able to carry out "counter-terrorist operations and for rapid power projection to hot spots on Russia's peripheries."[170]

THE MILITARY AND CHECHNYA

Ivanov and the generals have also stabilized the military's involvement in Chechnya. Instead of the chaotic, open-ended commitment that characterized military involvement in the First Chechen War, and to a lesser extent the second one, beginning in 2003 the Ministry began to try to bring some order into the Army's participation in Chechnya.

First, the high command gradually transferred responsibility for operations in Chechnya to the Interior Ministry. Thus in September 2003 Lieutenant General Valeri Baranov from the Ministry of the Interior took command of all large-scale operations in the republic. Then in May 2005 the Interior Ministry began to take over command of all nineteen military commandant offices in Chechnya. Furthermore, the number of Ministry of Defense troops serving in that republic was reduced until there were only 30,000 Army troops *permanently* stationed there, primarily with the 42nd Motorized Infantry Division, although there were a few other small units. (There are about 50,000 from the Interior Ministry and the Federal Security Service.)[171] All of the airborne divisions had been withdrawn by December 2004, although some airborne troops remain attached to the 42nd. Furthermore, on March 15 the Ministry of Defense claimed that it was no longer sending conscripts to Chechnya; the 42nd was entirely staffed by the much better-paid volunteers.[172]

This is not to suggest that Army troops are not fighting and dying in Chechnya. They are, but with the reduction of military forces, the numbers are decreasing. For example, General Belousov noted, "Whereas a total of 499 died in Chechnya in 2002 and 480 in 2003, in 2004 this figure was around 150." Belousov argued that the reduction in numbers was partly due to the absence of conscripts, which he also maintained "has raised the quality of military personnel."[173] These changes indicate that the high command succeeded in convincing the Kremlin that the War in Chechnya is primarily an internal security matter, one in which the Army could help, and probably improve its ability to carry out unconventional warfare operations. But the bottom line is that the generals have convinced the Kremlin to limit the army's involvement in this never-ending and resource-draining war in the Caucasus. Meanwhile, problems remains among both army and interior force troops. For example, soldiers continue to complain about poor food and inferior equipment and weapons.[174] Disciplinary problems also continue, but given the way Russians report such things, it is impossible to determine whether such incidents involve Ministry of Defense or Interior Ministry troops.

PUTIN'S IMPACT ON THE MILITARY

While it is still too early to measure Putin's overall impact on the military, it is clear that the Russian Army finds itself in a different situation than it did when he came to power in 2000. He has brought stability and predictability and this is beginning to show up in a variety of areas, despite serious problems that still need to be solved.

Combat Readiness

Despite Putin and Ivanov's efforts to stabilize the situation inside the military, the Army continues to face problems with combat readiness. On the plus side, training has improved. For example, pilot flying time has reportedly increased. "While three or four years ago, pilots spent 20 to 22 hours in the air a month due to the shortage of funds to buy fuel, now they fly 50–70 and in some units 100 hours."[175] However, there is still a long way to go. As Colonel General Alexander Skorodumov, head of Moscow's Armed Forces Combat Training Directorate, noted in 2004, "The results of the combat training do not meet requirements of the modern battlefield, and that in fact troops are not ready to face existing and future threats."[176] Skorodumov was also not optimistic about 2005, commenting, "Only 115 million Russian rubles ($4 million) have been allocated for combat training in 2005, which is three times less than required to train the force thoroughly."[177] Still, even with the many problems it faced, the Kremlin was working to increase the money available for training. In 2005 Belousov commented:

> In 2005, R115.4 [billion] has been allocated for military training in Russia's armed forces, not including the cost of materials and equipment for the troops. This amount is 25 percent of the R459.9 [billion] requested this year . . . Compared with last year there has been a significant increase in funding for operational and military training for the troops. In particular, in 2004, R95.4 [billion] was allocated for this, which was 26 percent of the requested amount of R370.7 [billion]. "In light of this definite increase in funding for operational and military training, in 2005 the number of field exercises for troops and sea exercises will increase and flight crews will have more professional training will increase."[178]

Training exercises for reservists were also becoming more common.[179]

Still major problems remained. At a conference in December 2004 Skorodumov commented, in Ivanov's presence, "Only 15 percent of the command and staff exercises conducted in the current year were graded as 'good,' and the rest were 'satisfactory' or 'unsatisfactory.'"[180] One of the major reasons for this dismal performance was the lack of training exercises in the past. The Army was now full of regimental commanders who had never trained troops at the platoon or company level. This meant that the officer teaching a regimental commander how to conduct operations did not know what he was talking about. As Skorodumov put it, "That is to say, this means nothing other than that the ignoramus is teaching the ignoramus."[181]

Nevertheless, the frequency of training exercises has increased significantly. For example in August 2005 Russian forces engaged in four exercises that all began on the same day.[182] Sixty battalion-level tactical exercises were carried out in September, and the military held its first logistical exercise in six years.[183] In addition in November 2005, it was announced that a new training concept had been worked out, which will last ten months (instead of the current six-month cycle) in order to better facilitate training for the permanent-readiness units.[184] While Russia may lag far behind the rest of the world when it comes to exercises, this marks a major step forward in comparison with what took place under Yeltsin.

MILITARY CULTURE

Putin has had a significant impact on military culture. First, and most important, he introduced a sense of order and predictability. The military is not happy with the idea that it will not obtain weapons until 2008–2010, but at least it now has a better idea of what will take place so it can plan. The same is true of areas like Chechnya. Unless something unforeseen happens, the military's contribution will remain at around 30,000 professional troops. Putin also took the lead in pushing the *kontraktniki*/conscript program, despite its many problems and opposition from many of the generals and admirals. Furthermore, the high command knows that by 2008 the military will be shifting to a new structure, made up of two kinds of troops. *Kontraktniki* will be used for the permanent-readiness units, while conscripts will serve as a reserve after their one year of service. From the military's standpoint, this is a welcome change. Progress in these areas will not suit all the generals and admirals, but at least now there is some rationality in the process. The big question is whether Putin and Ivanov can force the military to stop covering up things like crime and *dedovshchina*. They are clearly making an effort to do so, but it remains to be seen how successful they will be.

Putin's the biggest impact on military culture came when he fundamentally changed the nature of the relationship between the high command and the defense ministry. Putin saw at first hand the kind of chaos that Yeltsin's "divide and conquer" approach to dealing with the military had created. It was destroying any effort to impose order and predictability in the military, so Putin acted. Kvashnin was fired, and it was made very clear to his successor, Baluyevski, that he worked for Ivanov. Putin said he believed in civilian control, and now Moscow had exactly that. Putin also made it clear that he wanted the General Staff out of operational matters, something that Baluyevski understood. There are no doubt some officers who are unhappy at Putin's assertion of civilian control over the General Staff. But at least Putin has given the military a rational chain of command. The chances of the General Staff opposing Ivanov or Putin or of outwardly undermining the president's orders will become more difficult.

Putin's gradualistic approach to dealing with the military also fits in with conservative Russian military culture. It gave the armed forces time to gradually adapt to the changes he introduced. Instead of immediately firing Sergeyev or immediately subordinating the General Staff to the Ministry of Defense, Putin moved in an incremental fashion. The military would have preferred a more planned approach, one that would have accorded more with Russian military culture. However, given the chaotic situation they were in at the beginning of 2000, they appreciated the fact that he was at least moving in the right direction.

On several occasions, Putin pushed the military hard, such as in the aftermath of the attack on the grammar school at Beslan. Given the tendency of the Russian high command to live in the past, to continue to see the world in Cold War terms long after that world had disappeared, Putin's forceful approach was needed. Many of the generals (e.g., Kvashnin) were upset by his approach, but as events unfolded, it became increasingly clear that Putin was right: Moscow needed to focus more on unconventional or substate conflict.

CONCLUSION

From the high command's standpoint, Putin has been a very different kind of president than either Gorbachev or Yeltsin. His goal has been to stabilize the system while at the same time working to rebuild it, and that included the armed forces. He has been a much more decisive leader than Yeltsin, and he has been more interested in the military than was Gorbachev. Thus, when *compared* with these two individuals, Putin has been a far better president—at least in the eyes of the generals and admirals. It is also worth noting that while Yeltsin may have used the money for other purposes, Putin has had the benefit of a windfall of petrorubles, money that enabled him to increase the military budget.

Many of the generals, such as Kvashnin and Sergeyev, disagreed with Putin on a variety of issues, including the direction he was taking the armed forces. However, they appreciated the fact that they had a strong arm at the helm, a man who was committed to bringing about change in the military.

Putin did not by any means solve the military's myriad problems. Indeed, the military continues to be faced with so many problems that there are serious questions about the eventual outcome of Putin's military reform. However, the important point from the generals' standpoint is that Putin dealt with the military in a serious fashion. He and Ivanov made mistakes, such as how the monetization program was implemented, and he was not able to give them the funds they believed they needed for arms, salaries, and training. He also did little to deal with problems like crime, corruption, and *dedovshchina*, apparently believing that time, the structural changes to be introduced in 2008, and a more affluent Russia would help resolve them. Whether or not that will happen remains an open question.

CHAPTER SEVEN

CONCLUSION: PRESIDENTIAL LEADERSHIP AND THE RUSSIAN MILITARY

Fighting bureaucracy in Russia is a very difficult undertaking.
Vladimir Putin

The role of presidential leadership has a critically important impact on the military in a collapsing or transitional state like the USSR and Russia, especially if that state is beset with instability and heading into a politically unknown world. If the president uses his or her power to provide a highly structured organization like the Soviet/Russian armed forces with clear guidance and attention while respecting military culture, *the military will have a better chance of surviving the transition intact, cohesive, and subordinate to civil authority.* This is true even if it is forced to undergo major—even fundamental—changes, such as downsizing from five million troops to slightly over one million, with a new doctrine and new organizational structure. This is particularly true if a once generously funded Army suddenly finds its budget slashed. From the military's standpoint, any downsizing or change in its budget, size, organization, and personnel should take place in a predictable, systematic, and stable fashion.

Generals and admirals want to be able to predict the armed forces' future, not only for selfish personal reasons, but because they have been trained to live that way. The need for advance knowledge goes to the heart of military culture: structure, order, stability, predictability. When that is missing, or when the president does not take the actions necessary to provide the military with that kind of an environment, organizational chaos will result, as the Russian experience confirms. Chaos means that, if the military is called upon to go into combat, then soldiers, sailors, Marines, and air force personnel will die unnecessarily because they do not have the weapons, equipment, leadership, or training to carry out the mission. Indeed, as Chechnya I demonstrated, the troops may not even know what the mission is. In short, the military could end up paying a heavy price if the president does not pay it sufficient attention.

Unfortunately for the Soviet/Russian military, only one of its three presidents since 1985 has supported it. The first two, Mikhail Gorbachev and Boris Yeltsin, were either not interested in the Army, lied to it repeatedly, made numerous unfulfilled promises, or failed to provide it with even minimal economic and political support. Only the third and current president, Vladimir Putin, has made an effort to come to grips with the Army's multifaceted and serious problems. Putin's problem, however, was that by the time he assumed the office of president, the problems in the military were so deep and the organization in such chaos that putting it together again made Humpty Dumpty's situation seem mild in comparison.

Let us now turned to a brief discussion of the three presidents and their relationship to the high command.

MIKHAIL GORBACHEV, 1985–1991

Gorbachev took a number of actions that alienated him from the USSR's generals and admirals. When he came to office, he gave the impression that he had a "plan" to reinvigorate the country's stagnant economy. The generals and admirals knew only too well that something had to be done; after all, they were falling further and further behind the Americans in the area of high technology. They believed they finally had someone who would reverse the decades of economic decay.

While it could be argued that Gorbachev was naive or that he had no alternative but to introduce policies like acceleration, democratization, glasnost, or even perestroika, the generals initially believed these policies would make a positive difference. But it soon became obvious to them that Gorbachev was not a leader; in fact, he had no idea what he was doing. From their perspective, he was destroying the system they had sworn to protect and defend. Then there were the effects of policies like *demokratizatsiya* and glasnost. Not only were they disrupting Soviet society, they were destroying the chain of command that is fundamental to a hierarchical organization like the military. Gorbachev's broad concept, democracy in the military, would not eliminate poor management and corruption. The generals did not believe that destroying the Army's command and control system would solve the problems. In fact, they shared a completely opposite view. They advocated giving the centralized system more authority to deal with such problems or perhaps firing staff who were incompetent or guilty of corruption. They were favorable to Defense Minister Dmitry Yazov's evaluation system, which would have officers reviewed more frequently. But they did not want to throw the baby out with the bathwater.

When it came to Gorbachev's decisions to cut back—and then publicize—the military budget, the generals were astounded. It meant the end of the culture of secrecy in which the Soviet military had operated. Still, as much as they opposed Gorbachev's decision to reduce the budget, they were far more upset about his efforts to dictate strategy. Who was this man who had never worn a uniform to tell the generals how they were to organize and structure a military? And his orders were confusing at best; what did terms like "sufficiency" mean? If the military was not supposed to count weapons systems, then what did Gorbachev mean when he moved to "qualitative measures"? How does one quantify qualitative factors? Their culture demanded that military experts be the specialists in the use of military force, weapons design, and doctrines. Gorbachev and those supporting him in building this new doctrine were civilians.

Gorbachev's decision to blame the military for using force against civilians in Tbilisi, Baku, and Vilnius, instead of accepting personal responsibility for sending the troops in, also rankled the country's military leaders. A military leader is supposed to take responsibility for his or her actions. While no Soviet officer wanted to be put in the position of using force against his own people, they expected the politicians, and certainly the president, to accept responsibility for ordering them into such action. Worse still, they were blamed for wounding and killing innocent civilians in Vilnius when the Army had not even been involved. It was Interior Ministry soldiers who attacked the radio station and killed civilians.

The Soviet military had a long tradition of staying out of the political process. The military implemented national security policy decisions. They did not make the decisions, although generals and admirals were prepared to provide the leader with their views if asked. Soon, however, it became apparent that the Soviet regime was about to collapse and a group of conservatives stepped forward to reverse the process in August 1991. With the exception of Yazov and a few others, the military refused to become involved. Generals like Shaposhnikov, Gromov, Lebed, and Grachev were infected by the Tbilisi Syndrome. They did not trust Gorbachev, and they did not want to be blamed for the deaths of civilians again. In addition, there was the long Soviet military tradition of noninvolvement in civilian affairs, especially if it meant the use of force against ordinary citizens.

Finally, the generals did not believe Gorbachev cared about them or the Army. They believed that he ignored them. At minimum he sat by while the military experienced tremendous internal problems. Officers were being tossed out of the Army, and internal problems like crime, corruption, *dedovshchina,* the draft, too few junior officers, desertion, and aging weapons systems were all getting worse. Most Soviet officers understood the difficulties that Gorbachev faced, and they knew that there were bound to be major cutbacks. Money would have to be spent elsewhere, and as Marshal Akhromeyev showed by bringing his deputies with him to the United States, professional soldiers would have to learn how to operate in a new political and economic environment. But they expected Gorbachev to work with them, to provide guidance, and to listen to what they had to say. Instead, they lost the stability and predictability on which the high command depended.

On the positive side, Gorbachev made no effort to force the generals to accept institutions like Western-style NCOs or to permit greater initiative from lower ranks. He was not interested in those issues, nor did he care whether they based their strategy on a mass army. He was just interested in cutting the military budget, not in working out a meaningful alternative strategy.

BORIS YELTSIN, 1991–1999

Boris Yeltsin entered the scene while the generals were struggling with Gorbachev, and Yeltsin initially looked like a much better leader. Unlike Gorbachev, he went out of his way to court them. He told them how much he respected them and appreciated their contribution to Russia's defense. He also made a series of promises aimed at calming their concerns over the difficulties the Army was experiencing. He made clear, for example, that Russia would support the military regardless of where it was deployed. His acts of courage during the August 1991 coup attempt also impressed them. As a result, the generals were pleased to see him emerge as Russia's leader.

Their enchantment with Yeltsin was to be short-lived, however. They soon found out that he had little or no intention of showing them the kind of leadership they had expected. His only interest was to keep them on his side politically. Toward that end, when picking a defense minister, he turned to Pavel Grachev, a man that almost everyone in the military agreed was not up to the task. It was one thing to command a regiment but another to head the Ministry of Defense. However, Yeltsin wanted a weak military and a weak Army leader and that is what he got. He had no interest in the generals' input when it came to choosing Russia's first defense minister, and in their minds, it was one of the blunders of the century.

Yeltsin's confrontation with the parliament in 1993 upset the high command. They had just endured the use of force in Tbilisi, Baku, and Vilnius and had avoided that possibility during the 1991 coup attempt. Now the president was heading for a battle with parliament, and the generals wanted no part of the "action." However, Yeltsin again resorted to flattery, building up the Army and the critical role it played, and promising the generals more money. Then when Yeltsin ordered the generals to attack, they appreciated the fact that this time they had a president who was prepared to issue an order in writing, even if he was not happy about doing it.

Military reform under Yeltsin was a joke. It was led by Grachev, a man who was only interested in his beloved airborne forces, while Yeltsin was completely uninterested and provided little or no leadership. His only concern was to give the appearance that something was being done. In the meantime, the internal problems that had begun to come to the surface under Gorbachev worsened. The Army was collapsing from within. Yeltsin's impulsiveness only exacerbated the situation. He cut the length of service for conscripts without consulting the generals, and the change threw the entire draft process upside down. He was even worse than Gorbachev when it came to disrespecting them. Furthermore, he cut and cut and cut the military budget. There was no way the high command could reasonably predict where the military was headed and make plans accordingly.

The Army was in a mess going into the First Chechen War, and Yeltsin knew it. The generals advised against attacking Chechnya, but Yeltsin was completely uninterested. Instead, he ordered the Army into action without giving the generals time to get organized. Units were in chaos—soldiers sitting next to each other had never see each other before or exercised together. The same was true of officers, most of whom were fresh out of civilian university training programs. The end result was a ragtag group of GIs, few of whom knew what they were doing or why they were being sent to Chechnya. Numerous officers and generals revolted. The deputy commander of Ground Forces, who was ordered to command the operation, refused—and he was joined by 557 others. The Army finally went along with Yeltsin's order, but its performance was abysmal, not surprising given its lack of training, equipment, weapons, and just about everything else. Most of the officers involved never forgave Yeltsin for his insistence on moving in December 1994 instead of giving them time to prepare something as complex as a military operation. They felt the same way about Grachev for going along and supporting Yeltsin. When it was clear that the operation had cost far too many lives, instead of accepting personal responsibility,

Yeltsin blamed the military. Once again a president had sent them into action against their own people, and then blamed them for his mistakes.

To make matters more difficult, but to ensure that Yeltsin had total control over the armed forces, he split authority between the General Staff and the Ministry of Defense. The move undermined the chain of command and created bureaucratic chaos. Yeltsin then pushed the Army toward greater reliance on professionals, the *kontraktniki*, but he refused to provide the military with the money necessary to fully realize the plan. As a result, and since many of the generals were not enamored with the idea anyway, nothing significant occurred. Yeltsin's failure to support the military caused a further decline in combat readiness.

The last half of Yeltsin's presidency was not much better. Rodionov came into office as defense minister with a plan to restructure and revitalize the military, but Yeltsin was not about to put up with a strong-willed general, especially one who wanted money to implement his plan. So Yeltsin fired Rodionov just as he had Lebed, another strong military personality. Indeed, Yeltsin not only fired him, he showed his complete lack of respect for the military by criticizing both Rodionov and the chief of the General Staff publicly. Then he appointed Sergeyev because of his background in the Strategic Rocket Forces, and because he did not expect Defense Minister Sergeyev to be as demanding when it came to the military budget. After all, nuclear weapons were a lot cheaper than conventional forces.

Yeltsin's appointment of Sergeyev failed to bring order to the military. When he also appointed the assertive Kvashnin to be chief of the General Staff, the two generals were soon at each other's throats. After all, Yeltsin's earlier decision to bifurcate authority between the Ministry and the General Staff meant that Kvashnin ignored Sergeyev, while Sergeyev tried to cut Kvashnin's conventional forces. It was bureaucratic deadlock, a recipe for inaction, and just what Yeltsin wanted. He could have easily placed the General Staff under the Ministry of Defense, which would have gone a long way toward solving the problem. But he was more interested setting one against the other to maximize his control over both entities.

Yeltsin also continued his policy of promising the military the moon, while cutting their budget. Then came the August 1998 economic crisis, an event that the military believed was the result of his inept economic policies. The military itself did a better job of fighting the Second Chechen War, although their "scorched earth" policy and failure to worry about "winning the hearts and minds" of the populace meant that they made more enemies than they would have if they had shown some restraint.

About the only areas where Yeltsin acted in a manner that pleased the high command was his lack of interest in things like the role of NCOs or his failure to force them to come to grips with the end of the world of mass armies. Most senior Russian generals did not want to face the fact that the world had changed, and Yeltsin made no attempt to deal with the issue. He wanted a doctrine that gave the impression that things were improving, not one that actually dealt with the new world of terrorism and substate conflict.

It is difficult to convey just how bad the situation inside the Russian military was when Yeltsin left the scene. *Dedovshchina* was rampant, crime was out of control, officers were leaving the Army in droves, equipment and weapons were falling apart, the draft was a joke, the *kontraktniki* process was not working, and combat readiness was at an all-time low. The question was no longer whether a ship or plane or tank could carry out its mission, it was whether or not it could even get underway, fly, or move. Despite a promising beginning, by the time Yeltsin left office on December 31, 1999, the military was a disaster, far worse than under Gorbachev. And as far as the generals and admirals were concerned, Yeltsin was the primary person responsible.

VLADIMIR PUTIN, 2000–PRESENT

Vladimir Putin had an advantage in dealing with the high command when he became president. The generals had been impressed by the way he ran the Second Chechen War while he was still prime minister. Yeltsin had put him in charge, but after ensuring that all segments were working (more or less) together, Putin left operational control in the hands of the military. He did not try to micromanage the war the way Yeltsin and his colleagues had, and he showed his support for the Army by flying to Chechnya in an Air Force jet. The chain of command was intact and if mistakes were made (and they were), it was the result of the generals' ineptitude, not civilian interference.

To the generals, Putin was a different kind of leader. He understood the military, because it was not so different from his own background in the intelligence community.[1] He was also convinced that stability was critical, not only for the military, but for the country as well. Generals and admirals had to be able to plan, even if it meant having fewer resources than they would have preferred. It was critical that they believed that the person in charge cared about them and was attempting to deal with their problems. Putin was also pragmatic and flexible. Most important, however, he was determined to get the military back on its feet. He would move slowly and cautiously, but he would keep pushing the process of reconstruction.

One of Putin's first tasks was how to handle the Sergeyev-Kvashnin dispute. He decided that the best approach was to avoid an open clash. He refused to make a quick decision and waited until the following year when he came out on Kvashnin's side. Putin believed Kvashnin's approach would achieve a better balance between nuclear and conventional weapons. From the generals' standpoint (unless they were from the Strategic Rocket Forces), Putin had taken a first step toward bringing order to a chaotic situation.

Then Putin decided to tackle another critical issue that Yeltsin had ignored, the question of the *kontraktniki,* an action that led to the Pskov experiment. He knew this meant taking on Kvashnin and other senior generals who wanted to keep their dreams of a mass army ready to fight the Cold War. Toward this end, he pushed the generals toward developing "permanent-readiness units" entirely composed of professionals. Getting money to pay these professionals as well as the officer corps was not easy, but Putin attacked the problem by incrementally increasing pay, although he admitted several times that much still remained to be done, since the raises hardly kept pace with inflation.

In pushing for a professional military Putin was also convinced that it would help eliminate chronic problems such as *dedovshchina.* He compromised with the generals by keeping conscription at one-year terms, but Ivanov and others believed that if NCOs were added (much to the chagrin of many generals) and if they lived in the barracks and trained and disciplined conscripts, then the problem would gradually disappear. There has even been talk of using chaplains to deal with personnel problems, an action pushed by some generals looking for a way to improve morale and discipline. Similarly, the change in the university educational system, whereby fewer than three dozen universities will be permitted to have ROTC programs, meant that the "paper lieutenants" would be replaced by individuals who knew they were going to serve for at least three years. Those who do not take ROTC will be required to serve for a year as conscripts, thereby expanding the recruit pool.

Putin also adopted a systematic approach to dealing with weapons. First, he worked to reform and modernize the military-industrial complex. Only with an effective weapons-producing program, one that provided weapons to be sold abroad, would the military begin to have the resources to develop and purchase weapons. At the same time, he made it clear to the generals that, like it or not, the weapons-modernization process would be a slow, very incremental process; weapons would not begin to come into the military's inventory in significant numbers until 2008 or more likely 2010. In the meantime, they would have to modernize weapons they had, even if it meant keeping some very old planes, tanks, and ships in operation for several more years. The high command might not like the delayed acquisition of weapons, but at least they knew they were coming, a significant improvement over Yeltsin.

One of Putin's most important actions was his decision to fire Kvashnin and to resubordinate the General Staff to the Ministry of Defense, while removing the General Staff from operational responsibilities. In the process, he took on the most formidable officer in the military—Kvashnin. While such an action no doubt upset many in the military, others found it reassuring. Putin was acting like a leader. From that point on, Defense Minister Sergei Ivanov—who was named a deputy prime minister in addition to his defense portfolio—would be in charge of the military instead of a chief of the General Staff who often ignored him. Kvashnin's successor, General Baluyevski, would be subordinate to Ivanov, and he and the General Staff were restricted to planning. If nothing else, that meant greater stability and predictability. Now the officers knew who was giving the orders; Putin had reestablished the chain of command.

While it could be said that the generals had hidden behind the lack of money for the past fifteen years, arguing that everything that was wrong about the military was the result of a shortage of financial resources, there was no question that money was a problem. Salaries were abysmal, housing was lacking, while crime, corruption, and suicides all were leading to a serious drop in combat readiness. Putin understood the fiscal aspect of the problem, and, thanks in part to the rising price of oil, he consistently increased the military budget. Some shortages remained; there was not enough money to pay for salaries, infrastructure, weapons, training, etc. The important point, however, was that in comparison with Yeltsin, Putin had begun to turn matters around.

Putin and Ivanov also came up with a number of structural modifications in an effort to rationalize military life. The idea of mortgage credits meant that, instead of constantly complaining that the military was underfunded, the armed forces now had a plan to enable junior officers to find housing. Granted, the money was insufficient, but at least the Ministry of Defense was trying to deal meaningfully and systematically with the problem. The same was true of the single purchasing agent. Instead of permitting fifty or more purchasing agents on behalf of the Ministry, Ivanov reduced this figure down to one.

Putin also took on the generals' refusal to come to grips with the post–Cold War world by modifying doctrine so the military would play a bigger role in the war against terrorism, especially in the aftermath of the slaughter of civilians at

Beslan. The details are still being worked out, but the military, together with the FSB and Interior Ministry, has begun exercises to make the doctrine operational. Furthermore, while there is no exit strategy for the war in Chechnya, the military is grateful to Putin for having placed a limit on its contribution, the 42nd Division with about 30,000 soldiers, all of whom are supposed to be professionals.

So where does that leave Putin vis-à-vis the generals? He has created a stable environment that the generals find easier to work in. He has also pushed them to modify their thinking, although there is still a significant segment that continues to believe that World War II is the model for future military operations. He also accepted responsibility for the successes, but more importantly for the failures of military reform, something that the generals appreciate.

Putin understands Russian political culture. As a result, he has not tried to force the military to permit initiative from below. He knows that Russia remains a subject culture, and he is well aware that Russian military culture is an even more extreme example of a subject culture. If generals do not want to delegate authority, so be it. NCOs and junior officers will never have the kind of autonomy and responsibility that their counterparts in the West enjoy. As far as he is concerned, Russia will never be a copy of the West and that includes its military culture as well.

Putin has also legitimated civilian involvement in military matters. He himself has been directly involved in discussing things like strategy and weapons, and his defense minister is a civilian—or at least not a professional soldier. Perhaps most important, Putin understands bureaucracies, and he knows that change is very difficult for them, especially for a closed organization like the Russian military. As a result, he adopted a gradualist approach and while he guided the military, he never disrespected the generals the way Yeltsin did. His message has been, "help is on the way," even if it may take longer to get there than many would prefer. As far as leadership is concerned, the generals and admirals are well aware who is in charge.

Does this mean that the military under Putin has turned the corner on military reform? Hardly. Much will depend on the continued high price of oil to pay for salaries, weapons, equipment, etc. Furthermore, he is assuming that the move to a professional army will solve horrendous problems inside the military such as *dedovshchina*. Maybe it will, maybe it won't. Then there is the question of Putin's successor in 2008. Who will he be and how devoted will he be to continuing the process Putin began? Putin's policies also assume that Russia will have a relatively benign external environment for the next five to ten years while the process of reform is carried out.

THE GENERALS, THE PRESIDENT, AND
LEADERSHIP

Despite the way they were treated first under Gorbachev and then under Yeltsin, Moscow's generals never seriously considered a military coup. They may have been unhappy with—and disdainful of—the president, but they acknowledged his role as commander-in-chief. Yazov was involved in the August 1991 coup against Gorbachev, but he was undermined by his colleagues in uniform. The generals protested the First Chechen War, but that meant that they went into retirement—not revolt. There was no sign that they seriously considered using military force against Yeltsin. Rodionov, Lebed, and Rokhlin all thought Yeltsin an amateur, and at least one of them would have loved to replace him, but with the exception of Rokhlin's half-hearted attempts, no one seriously tried to mobilize the military against the president. This meant that the Russian military remained outside of the political process, not because it was "controlled," but because its military culture and training over the past hundred years has impressed upon those in uniform that the country's leader wears civilian clothes.

At this point, the reader may feel I have been too hard on presidents such as Gorbachev and Yeltsin. After all, they faced tremendous problems in trying to oversee, in the first case, the revitalization of communism, and in the second, its destruction. The military was only one factor they had to consider, and certainly not the most important one for them. Indeed, from Gorbachev's position the Army was part of the problem, given its tremendous slice of the country's budget, and the formidable image that it projected abroad at a time when he was trying to convince the world that Moscow was not a threat on the international stage.

Similarly, one could argue that Yeltsin's goal was to destroy the remnants of communism. If he did not, he feared that it could creep back into power. The military was not important, as there was almost no likelihood of a war. If anything, the armed forces got in the way, demanding resources at a time when there were not any. Yeltsin thought the generals could not manage their own affairs. Every time he saw a general he had his hand out for more money. They should make do with what they had, according to Yeltsin.

My point is not that the president did not have the right to follow whatever policy he wanted. No Russian or Soviet generals (Yazov and Varennikov excepted) would question that premise. The problem was that the generals and admirals expected the president to be a leader. Had Gorbachev and Yeltsin paid attention to Russian military culture, and provided the generals with the stability and predictability they sought, the military might have avoided the hell that it went through, especially under Yeltsin. The generals would have attempted to hold on to the past, a large army backed up by massive reserves, but if Gorbachev had followed through with his push for a new strategy, or if Yeltsin had taken an interest in developing one instead of just keeping the generals on his side for political purposes, many of the problems during the 1990s could have been minimized, if not avoided.

The president of a transitional polity such as the USSR/Russia has a choice. He can either take the military seriously and exert leadership that provides the kind of stability and predictability that serve his own interests as well as that of the Army and society as a whole, or he can be impulsive, and unpredictable. Certainly, if Yeltsin had provided a stable environment, Putin would not have been faced with an Army struggling with problems of such magnitude as happened in 2001. On the other hand, despite the many problems facing the Army, from the generals' standpoint, Putin has shown leadership, even if they do not always agree with his decisions.

What kind of guidance should a president provide? What makes leadership meaningful? These questions are probably best answered by examples. Putin's decision to fire Sergeyev in order to stop the chaos in the military is an example of meaningful leadership, as was his decision to retire Kvashnin and resubordinate the General Staff to the Ministry of Defense. The same could be said for his insistence on a professional military, the new means for handling the housing situation, and the single purchase procedure. There are more examples, but the bottom line is that in contrast with the Gorbachev and Yeltsin years, now the generals and admirals know what policy is, and they have a degree of confidence that it will remain the same for the indefinite future. They can begin to plan.

Does this mean that the generals and admirals "like" Putin? I have no idea, and that is not relevant. Generals and admirals often do not like each other. They live in a very competitive environment and bureaucratic prisoners are seldom taken. This is especially true of the Russian military. They will fight hard for their bureaucratic interests. As in the United States, brown-shoe sailors will fight black-shoe sailors for their piece of the pie. Tankers will fight the infantry, which is likely to line up against the airborne, and the process goes on and on. My point is that senior military officers, especially in a country like Russia, have not shown an interest in getting involved in civilian politics. Rather, they want and expect direction. After failing to receive directions under Yeltsin and Gorbachev, the generals now have orders from Putin.

NOTES

CHAPTER ONE. INTRODUCTION

1. Richard E. Neustadt, *Presidential Power and the Modern Presidents* (New York: Free Press, 1990), p. 11.

2. For a discussion of the American process, see Dale Herspring, *The Pentagon and the Presidency: Civil-Military Relations from FDR to George W. Bush* (Lawrence: University Press of Kansas, 2005).

3. From a social science standpoint, I am arguing that presidential leadership is the independent variable and the high command's response is the dependent variable.

4. See Dale R. Herspring, "Nikolay Ogarkov and the Scientific-Technical Revolution in Soviet Military Affairs," *Comparative Strategy* 6, 1 (1987): 29–59; idem, *The Soviet High Command, 1967–1989* (Princeton, N.J.: Princeton University Press, 1990), pp. 166–214.

5. Samuel Huntington, *The Soldier and the State: The Theory and Politics of Civil-Military Relations* (Cambridge, Mass.: Harvard University Press, 1957). See also Dale Herspring, "Samuel Huntington and Communist Civil-Military Relations," *Armed Forces and Society* 25, 4 (Summer 1999): 557–577.

6. See Dale R. Herspring, *Russian Civil-Military Relations* (Bloomington: Indiana University Press, 1996), pp. 55–71.

7. The conversation took place in Moscow during a visit by an American diplomatic delegation.

8. See Dale R. Herspring, *Requiem for an Army: The Demise of the East German Military* (Boulder, Colo.: Rowman and Littlefield, 1998).

9. This distinction between internal and external enemies played a key role in the refusal of the East German military to become involved while the communist system collapsed in the German Democratic Republic. See Herspring, *Requiem for an Army*.

10. This section is based on numerous conversations with military officers, my own thirty-two years with the U.S. Navy, and a variety of academic studies. See, for example, A. J. Bacevich, "Tradition Abandoned: America's Military in a New Era," *National Interest* 58 (Summer 1997): 311; Edgar F. Puryear, *American Generalship: Character is Everything: the Art of Command* (Novato, Calif.: Presidio, 2002), pp. 1–43; Peter Maslowski, "Army Values and American Values," *Military Review* 70, 4 (April 1990): 10–23; Richard Betts, *Soldiers, Statesmen, and Cold War Crisis* (New York: Columbia University Press, 1977), pp. 157–158; Richard H. Kohn, "How Democracies Control the Military," *Journal of Democracy* 4, 8 (1997): 140; Thomas E. Ricks, "The Widening Gap between the Military and Society," *Atlantic Monthly* (July 1997): 66–77; "Cultural Demolition in the Military," *Washington Times* (November 20, 1998): 20; Peter Feaver, "The Gap: Soldiers, Civilians, and Their Mutual Misunderstandings," *National Interest* 61 (Fall 2000): 27–37; Gregory D. Foster, "Failed Expectations: The Crisis of Civil-Military Relations in America," *Brookings Review* 15 (Fall 1997): 46–48: and Eliot Cohen, *Supreme Command: Soldiers, Statesman, and Leadership in Wartime* (New York: Free Press, 2002). See also articles in Peter Feaver and Richard Kohn,

eds., *Soldiers and Civilians: The Civil-Military Gap and American National Security* (Cambridge, Mass.: MIT Press, 2001).

11. This section is based on numerous conversations with serving Soviet and Russian officers as well as numerous former Soviet and Russian servicemen, my own thirty-two year association with the Soviet and Russian militaries, as well as a variety of academic studies: Pavel K. Baev, "The Challenge of 'Small Wars' for the Russian Military," in *Russian Military Reform, 1992–2002,* ed. Anne C. Aldis and Roger N. McDermott (New York: Frank Cass, 2003), pp. 189–208; Aleksandr Golts, "The Social and Political Condition of the Russian Military," in *The Russian Military: Power and Policy,* ed. Steven E. Miller and Dmitri Trenin (Cambridge, Mass.: MIT Press, 2004), p. 80; Anatol Lieven, *Chechnya: Tombstone of Russian Power* (New Haven, Conn.: Yale University Press, 1998), citing General Vrobyev, p. 293; Christopher C. Locksley, "Concept, Algorithm, Indecision: Why Military Reform Has Failed in Russia Since 1992," *Slavic Military Studies* 14, 1 (March 2001): 1–26; Michael Orr, *Manpower Problems in the Russian Armed Forces* no. D62 (Camberley, Surrey: Conflict Studies Research Centre, Royal Military Academy Sandhurst, February 2002), p. 8; idem., "Reform and the Russian Ground Forces, 1992–2002," in Aldis and McDermott, *Russian Military Reform,* p. 136; Brian Taylor, "The Russian Military Outside Politics: A Historical Perspective," *PONARS Policy Memo,* no. 2 (October 1997); Robert V. Barylski, *The Soldier in Russian Politics* (New Brunswick, N.J.: Transaction, 1998), pp. 9–12, 57–58.

12. For example, one former Chinese general told me about a situation in which Soviet officers had demanded that he be court-martialed because he had deviated in a war game with the Soviets. He said that the fact that he had lowered the casualty rate from the expected 25 percent to 10 percent was not relevant in the minds of his Soviet colleagues.

13. During the visit of the *Ustino* to Norfolk, Virginia, in 1989 I witnessed an officer beating a sailor on a remote part of the ship, an action that would have resulted in a court martial with the possibility of prison time for an American officer.

14. To cite only one example: While visiting a U.S. warship, a Soviet admiral spoke with a third-class petty officer (E-4) who was standing next to a missile mount. Asked what he did, the young man replied, "I man and repair the missiles." The astounded Soviet admiral asked for a retranslation after which he replied, "We have two junior officers carrying out that function in the Soviet Navy."

15. Both conversations took place in Moscow while I was a foreign service officer.

16. Based on a conversation with Ambassador Paul Nitze in 1991.

17. Stephen White, *After Gorbachev* (New York: Cambridge University Press, 1993), p. 89.

18. See Herspring, *The Pentagon and the Presidency,* chap. 3.

19. William E. Odom, *The Collapse of the Soviet Military* (New Haven, Conn.: Yale University Press, 1998).

20. Dale R. Herspring, *The Soviet High Command, 1967–1989;* Mark Galeotti, *Gorbachev and His Revolution* (New York: St. Martin's Press, 1997); and Dale R. Herspring, *Russian Civil-Military Relations.*

21. Pavel Baev, *The Russian Army in a Time of Troubles* (London: Sage, 1996); Barylski, *The Soldier in Russian Politics;* John P. Moran, *From Garrison State to Nation–State* (Westport, Conn.: Praeger, 2002); Brian D. Taylor, *Politics and the Russian Army: Civil-Military*

Relations, 1689–2000 (New York: Cambridge University Press, 2003); David J. Betz, *Civil-Military Relations in Russia and Eastern Europe* (London: RoutledgeCurzon, 2004).

22. Yuri Fedorov and Bertil Nygren, eds., *Russian Military Reform and Russia's New Security Environment* (Stockholm: Swedish National Defense College, 2003); Anne C. Aldis and Roger N. McDermott, eds., *Russian Military Reform, 1992–2002* (London: Frank Cass, 2003); and Steven E. Miller and Dmitri Trenin, eds., *The Russian Military: Power and Policy* (Cambridge, Mass.: MIT Press, 2003).

23. Herspring, *The Pentagon and the Presidency.*

CHAPTER 2. GORBACHEV, THE COUP, AND THE MILITARY, MARCH 1985–DECEMBER 1991

1. Mark Galeotti, *Gorbachev and His Revolution* (New York: St. Martin's Press, 1997), p. 28.

2. In accordance with Soviet/Russian military usage, "the Army" refers to all of the services.

3. *Krasnaya zvezda* (April 24, 1985).

4. The enormity of the task facing Gorbachev was brought home to me by the late General Dmitry Volkogonov. In response to a question I posed, he answered, "You don't understand just how big the task facing us is. What is the heart of perestroika? It is initiative, creativity and a willingness to accept responsibility for one's actions. Fifty years ago a Russian would have been shot for showing any of those characteristics. Our task is to build a new Soviet man." Conversation during a visit to Volkogonov's institute in Moscow in 1989.

5. *Krasnaya zvezda* (April 25, 1985).

6. *Voyennyy vestnik* (Moscow), no. 2 (1986): 5.

7. *Krasnaya zvezda* (April 25, 1985).

8. Ibid.

9. *Krasnaya zvezda* (June 25, 1985).

10. *Krasnaya zvezda* (July 2, 1985).

11. *Izvestiya* (February 23, 1986); *Krasnaya zvezda* (September 1, 1985); *Krasnaya zvezda* (February 23, 1986).

12. *Pravda* (November 8, 1985).

13. *Krasnaya zvezda* (August, 9, 1985).

14. *Krasnaya zvezda* (February 23, 1986); *Pravda* (February 23, 1986).

15. Ibid.

16. *Krasnaya zvezda* (November 15, 1986).

17. *Pravda* (January 28, 1987).

18. "Oktyabr i Leninskoe uchenie o zashchite revolyutsii," *Kommunist,* no. 3 (February 1987): 85–96. This annual article, published in *Kommunist,* usually on Army or Navy Day, was normally authored by the minister or first deputy minister of defense. The selection of a man such as Lizichev for this honor appears to be primarily a result of his support for perestroika.

19. S. Sokolov, "Watching Over the Peace and Security of the Homeland," *Pravda* (February 23, 1987) and S. F. Akhromeyev, "The Glory and Pride of the Soviet People," *Sovietskaya Rossiya* (February 1, 1987) as translated by Foreign Broadcast Information Service, *Soviet Union* [hereinafter, FBIS:SOV] (February 27, 1987): V1–4.

20. *Izvestiya* (February 23, 1987); *Krasnaya zvezda* (February 23, 1987); *Kommunist Vooruzhennykh Sil*, no. 5 (March 1987): 9–17; *Krasnaya zvezda* (February 5, 1987); *Krasnaya zvezda* (March 21, 1987); and A. Koldunov, "Tak," Moscow Television Service (April 12, 1987) in FBIS: SOV (April 16, 1987): V2–4.

21. *Krasnaya zvezda* (March 18, 1987).

22. *Krasnaya zvezda* (March 30, 1987).

23. Nikolai Ogarkov, "Voennaya nauka i zashchita sotsialisticheskogo otechestva," *Kommunist*, no. 7 (1978): 112.

24. S. Akhromeyev, "Prevoskhodstvo sovetskoy voennoy nauki i sovetskogo voennogo iskusstva—odin iz vazheyzhikh faktorov pobedy v velikoy otechestvennoy voyne," *Kommunist*, no. 3 (February 3, 1985): 62.

25. Galeotti, *Gorbachev and His Revolution*, p. 62.

26. "The Political Report of the Central Committee of the CPSU to the 27th Congress of the Communist Party of the Soviet Union. Report of General Secretary of the CC CPSU Comrade M. S. Gorbacheva," in *XXVII S'yezd Kommunisticheskoy Partii Sovetskogo Soyuza: Stenograicheskiy Otchet* (Moscow: Politizdat, 1986), vol. 1, pp. 24, 98.

27. *Krasnaya zvezda* (October 28, 1982).

28. "CPSU Program New Edition Adopted by the 27th CPSU Congress," *Pravda* (March 7, 1986) in FBIS: SOV (March 10, 1986): O12.

29. "Gorbachev Says Military Budget Faces Cutbacks, Soviet Military Fought Cuts," *Washington Post* (December 9, 1988).

30. Coit D. Blacker, *Hostage to Revolution: Gorbachev and Soviet Security Policy, 1985–1991* (New York: Council on Foreign Relations Press, 1993), p. 58.

31. Brian D. Taylor, *Politics and the Russian Army: Civil-Military Relations, 1689–2000* (New York: Cambridge University Press, 2003), p. 216.

32. Richard Sakwa, *Gorbachev and His Reforms, 1985–1990* (New York: Prentice-Hall, 1990), p. 335.

33. Ibid.

34. S. Akhromeyev, "Na strazhe mira i sotsializma," *Krasnaya zvezda* (February 22, 1985).

35. Blacker, *Hostage to Revolution*, p. 150.

36. John P. Moran, *From Garrison State to Nation–State* (Westport, Conn.: Praeger, 2002), p. 116.

37. M. S. Gorbachev, "Politicheskii doklad Tsentralnogo Komiteta KPSS XXVII S'ezdi Kommunisticheskoi Partii Sovetskogo Soiuza," in *XXVII S'ezd Kommunisticheski Partii Sovietskogo Soiuza: Stenograficheskii Otchet*, vol. 1 (Moscow, 1986), p. 8.

38. "O voennoi doktrine gosudarstv-chastnikov Varshaveskogo Dogovora," *Krasnaya zvezda* (May 30, 1989).

39. Dmitry T. Yazov, *Na strazhe sotsializma i mira* (Moscow: Voennoe izdatelstvo, 1987), p. 31.

40. S. Akhromeyev, "Velikaia podeda," *Krasnaya zvezda* (May 9, 1987); "The Doctrine of Preventing War, Defending Peace, and Socialism," *Problemy mira i sotsializma*, no. 12 (December 1987) in FBIS: SOV (January 4, 1988).

41. Yazov, *Na strazhe sotsializma i mira*, p. 28.

42. S. Akhromeyev, "The Glory and Pride of the Soviet People," *Sovietskaya Rossiya* (February 21, 1987) in FBIS:SOV (February 27, 1987): 18.

43. "Oboronnaya moshch—kakoi ei byt?" *Mirovaya ekonomika i mezhunarodnye otnosheniya,* no. 1 (1990): 110.

44. Raymond L. Garthoff, "New Thinking and Soviet Military Doctrine," in *Soviet Military Doctrine from Lenin to Gorbachev, 1915–1991,* ed. Willard C. Frank, Jr. and Philip S. Gillette (Westport, Conn.: Greenwood Press, 1992), p. 204.

45. Blacker, *Hostage to Revolution,* p. 84.

46. Dale Herspring, *The Soviet High Command, 1967–1989: Personalities and Politics* (Princeton, N.J.: Princeton University Press, 1990), p. 269.

47. Blacker, *Hostage to Revolution,* p. 76.

48. Dusko Doder, *Gorbachev: Heretic in the Kremlin* (New York: Viking, 1990), p. 108.

49. The following biographical material is from my personal files: *Voyenno-entsiklopeicheskiy slovar* (Moscow: Voyenizdat, 1986), p. 844; *Krasnaya zvezda* (April 13, 1985); and Alexander Yanov, "Why Yazov," *Radio Liberty Research Report,* no. RL 212/7 (June 1, 1987).

50. *Krasnaya zvezda* (April 2, 1987); *Krasnaya zvezda* (November 23, 1989).

51. *Krasnaya zvezda* (January 16, 1987).

52. Robert V. Barylski, *The Soldier in Russian Politics: Duty, Dictatorship, and Democracy under Gorbachev and Yeltsin* (New Brunswick, N.J.: Transaction, 1998), p. 43.

53. While Gorbachev was sincere in his effort to improve, his action would have unintended consequences. The officers responded in good bureaucratic fashion. Rather than damage their careers, efforts were made to avoid reporting disciplinary violations—after all, if none occurred (or were reported), officers could hardly be blamed for them. As a consequence, many of the disciplinary problems continued, the only difference was that they went unreported.

54. Zoltan Barany, "Politics and the Russian Armed Forces," in *Russian Politics: Challenges of Democratization,* ed. Zoltan Barany and Robert G. Moser (New York: Cambridge University Press, 2001), p. 177.

55. Barylski, *The Soldier in Russian Politics,* p. 41.

56. Mikhail Gorbachev, *Memoirs* (New York: Doubleday, 1996), p. 233.

57. Dale Herspring, "The Soviet Military and Change," in *Soviet Military Doctrine from Lenin to Gorbachev,* ed. Frank and Gillette, p. 218.

58. Gorbachev, *Memoirs,* p. 233.

59. Garthoff, "New Thinking and Soviet Military Doctrine, p. 203.

60. *Krasnaya zvezda* (June 3, 1990).

61. The following is based on Dale Herspring, *Russian Civil-Military Relations* (Bloomington: Indiana University Press, 1996), p. 107.

62. Michael Orr, "Reform and the Russian Ground Forces, 1992–2002," in *Russian Military Reform, 1992–2002,* ed. Anne C. Aldis and Roger N. McDermott (London: Frank Cass, 2003), p. 125.

63. William E. Odom, *The Collapse of the Soviet Military* (New Haven, Conn.: Yale University Press, 1998), p. 291.

64. Mark Rhodes, "Political Attitudes in Russia," *RFE/RL Research Report* (January 15, 1990): 42.

65. Barylski, *The Soldier in Russian Politics,* p. 81.

66. As cited in Moran, *From Garrison State to Nation-State,* p. 152.

67. C. J. Dick, "The Crisis in the Soviet Military," *Jane's Intelligence Review* (February 1992): 73–74.

68. Odom, *The Collapse of the Soviet Military*, p. 287. *Starik* means "old man," another word for *ded*. The Russian Army has a very "rich" vocabulary to describe soldiers and the positions they occupy in the Army.

69. Alexander Alexiev, *Inside the Soviet Army in Afghanistan* (Santa Monica, Calf.: RAND Corporation, 1988), p. 40.

70. Ibid., p. 38.

71. Odom, *The Collapse of the Soviet Military*, p. 293. Another source reported that between 23 and 27 percent of those who died on active duty, died as a result of suicide. C. J. Dick, "The Crisis in the Soviet Military," p. 72.

72. Odom, *The Collapse of the Soviet Military*, p. 278.

73. Ibid.

74. "Military Reform: Generals and Radicals," *Komsomolskaya pravda* (November 13, 1990) in FBIS: SOV (November 16, 1990): 90.

75. C. J. Dick, "The Crisis in the Soviet Military," p. 74.

76. "The Army and Restructuring," *Sovietskaya Rossiya* (January 14, 1989) in FBIS: SOV (January 18, 1989).

77. Blacker, *Hostage to Revolution*, p. 165.

78. "Kontseptsia voennoy reformy," *Voennaya mysl* (Special Issue 1990): 3–23.

79. "Armiya, Kokoy ey byt?" *Krasnaya zvezda* (February 12, 1989).

80. Odom, *The Collapse of the Soviet Military*, p. 295.

81. Ibid.

82. Ibid., p. 302.

83. Ibid., p. 289.

84. Ibid., p. 302.

85. I have discussed this issue with a number of senior Soviet officers, some of whom claimed that it was their most difficult task, namely trying to set up a relationship with a farm that provided enough food, but still did not take away from training.

86. S. Lavrentev, "Tainy n-skovo dvora," *Kommunist vooruzennykh sil*, no. 19 (October 1989): 45–48.

87. Rensselaer W. Lee, "The Organized Crime Morass in the Former Soviet Union," *Demokratizatsiya* 2, no. 3 (1994): 396.

88. Odom, *The Collapse of the Soviet Military*, p. 249.

89. Alexiev, *Inside the Soviet Army in Afghanistan*, p. 53

90. Ibid.

91. Odom, *The Collapse of the Soviet Military*, p. 302.

92. Lee, "The Organized Crime Morass in the former Soviet Union."

93. A. Kokoshin and V. Larionov, "The Battle of Kursk in Light of Today's Defensive Doctrine," *Mirovaia ekonomikai mezhdunarodnye otnosheniia*, no. 8 (August 1987): 32–33. This was the typical way to discuss military issues in the Soviet military—by placing them in a historical context, most notably World War II.

94. Ibid.

95. "Vooruzhennye sily," *Novoe vremya*, no. 8 (February 1988): 12–13.

96. V. N. Lobov, "K voprosu vnezapnosti i neozhidannosti," *Voennaya mysl*, no. 3 (1988): 3–8.

97. V. N. Lobov, "Trategiya Pobedy," *Voenno-istorisheskiy zhurnal*, no. 5 (1988): 6.

98. V. Achalov, "A Professional's View on the Prospects and Problems of Military Reform in the USSR, *IAN Military Bulletin,* nos. 4–5 (February/March 1991) in FBIS: SU (May 23, 1991): 10.

99. Orr, "Reform and the Russian Ground Forces, 1992–2002," in *Russian Military Reform, 1992–2002,* ed. Aldis and McDermott, p. 125.

100. International Institute of Strategic Studies, *The Military Balance, 1986–1987* (London: IISS, 1986), p. 36.

101. International Institute of Strategic Studies, *The Military Balance, 1991–1992* (London: IISS, 1992), p. 36.

102. "Pust armiya budet armiey," *Pravda* (November 22, 1991).

103. "Dialogue, Ask Questions," *Komsomolskaya pravda* (February 11, 1990), in FBIS: SOV (February 21, 1990): 118.

104. "Zadachi u nas odin," *Krasnaya zvezda* (February 10, 1990).

105. Blacker, *Hostage to Revolution,* p. 169.

106. Ibid.

107. Ibid., pp. 170–171.

108. William J. Crowe, *The Line of Fire* (New York: Simon and Schuster, 1993), p. 278n.

109. Odom, *The Collapse of the Soviet Military,* p. 254.

110. Taylor, *Politics and the Russian Army,* p. 223.

111. See General Alexander Lebed, *My Life and My Country* (Washington, D.C.: Regency, 1997), pp. 221–238.

112. Barylski, *The Soldier in Russian Politics,* p. 84.

113. Phillip A. Petersen and Joshua B. Spero, "Military Reform and the Struggle to Redefine Security in the post-USSR," in *The Soviet Military and the Future,* ed. Stephen J. Blank and Jacob W. Kipp (Westport, Conn.: Greenwood Press, 1992), p. 16.

CHAPTER THREE. YELTSIN AND THE CREATION OF THE RUSSIAN MILITARY, SEPTEMBER 1991– DECEMBER 1994

1. The following compilation is based on: Lilia Shevtsova, *Yeltsin's Russia: Myths and Reality* (Washington, D.C.: Carnegie Endowment for International Peace, 2003); Michael McFaul, *Russia's Unfinished Revolution: Political Change from Gorbachev to Putin* (Ithaca, N.Y.: Cornell University Press, 2001); Leon Aron, *Yeltsin: A Revolutionary Life* (New York: Norton, 2000) and my own research. I am totally responsible for this characterization. Not all of these writers will agree with all of these characteristics.

2. Robert V. Barylski, *The Soldier in Russian Politics: Duty, Dictatorship, and Democracy Under Gorbachev and Yeltsin* (New Brunswick, N.J.: Transaction, 1998), p. 127.

3. Ibid., p. 88.

4. Ibid.

5. David J. Betz, *Civil-Military Relations in Russia and Eastern Europe* (London: Routledge-Curzon, 2004), p. 48.

6. Boris Yeltsin, *The Struggle for Russia* (New York: Random House, 1994), p. 54.

7. The following is based on ibid. and William E. Odom, *The Collapse of the Soviet Military* (New Haven, Conn.: Yale University Press, 1998).

8. Barylski, *The Soldier in Russian Politics,* p. 88.

9. McFaul, *Russia's Unfinished Revolution,* p. 115.

10. Ibid.

11. I met many Soviet and Russian officers during the late 1980s and early 1990s and asked questions on political issues only to be told (almost unanimously): "Ja nie znau, eta politicshki vopros" (I don't know, that is a political question).

12. Odom, *The Collapse of the Soviet Military,* p. 313.

13. As quoted in Barylski, *The Soldier in Russian Politics,* p. 103.

14. Odom, *The Collapse of the Soviet Military,* p. 316.

15. Barylski, *The Soldier in Russian Politics,* p. 112.

16. Ibid., p. 140.

17. Dale Herspring, *The Soviet High Command: Personalities and Politics* (Princeton, N.J.: Princeton University Press, 1990). Lopatin was a major because Soviet Naval Aviation officers carried army, rather than navy ranks.

18. Yevgeny Shaposhnikov, *Vybor* (Moscow: Nezavisimoe Izdatelstvo PIK, 1995), p. 128.

19. Ibid., p. 137.

20. As cited in Barylski, *The Soldier in Russian Politics,* p. 153.

21. I spoke with a number of Naval Infantry officers in the Crimea during a ship visit in 1989. Many of them saw the writing on the wall and told me that if push came to shove, they would become Ukrainian citizens to protect their apartments, which they would otherwise lose.

22. As cited in Barylski, *The Soldier in Russian Politics,* p. 158.

23. Odom, *The Collapse of the Soviet Military,* p. 215.

24. Barylski, *The Soldier in Russian Politics,* p. 135.

25. Shaposhnikov, *Vybor,* p. 97.

26. Ibid., pp. 99–101. I had two discussions with line officers about political officers that illustrate the problem. In 1989, while discussing the role of political officers with the commander of the North Sea's Soviet submarine fleet, the admiral commented, "They are useless, they cannot even stand watch. They just take up space on a submarine and waste the sailors' time with their silly lectures." In 2005, while discussing the question with a former Army colonel who had been a regimental commander on three occasions; he had a more mixed view. "They could be very useful. Helped with discipline, training, etc. On the other hand, they could be a pain in the ass. I had one who didn't like what I told him to do. Thirty minutes later I got a phone call from the political section at division headquarters. 'Colonel, I suggest you rethink your order or next time the party commission may have to investigate your behavior.'"

27. This was reported in O. Valdykin, "Iz Moskvy: Kommissiya zavershaet rabotu," *Krasnaya zvezda* (November 20, 1991).

28. Barylski, *The Soldier in Russian Politics,* p. 186.

29. "Vsearmeiskoe ofitserkoe sobranie: Armiya dolzhna byt edinoi," *Krasnaya zvezda* (January 18, 1992).

30. "Minister's Position," *Rossiyskiye vesti* (January 4, 1993) in FBIS: SOV (January 6, 1993).

31. "Russian Army Close to Chaos," *Dagens Nyheter* (September 12, 1992) in FBIS: SOV (September 16, 1992).

32. As quoted in Shevtsova, *Yeltsin's Russia*, p. 49.

33. Barylski, *The Soldier in Russian Politics*, p. 229. Italics in original.

34. Shevtsova, *Yeltsin's Russia*, p. 42.

35. Ibid., p. 59.

36. "Grachev Comments on Army Situation," Moscow Russian Television Network (February 28, 1993) as translated by Foreign Broadcast Information Service, *Central Eurasia* [hereafter FBIS: CEU] (March 1, 1993).

37. "Pavel Grachev garant stabilnosti," *Rossiyskiye vesti* (March 6, 1993).

38. Shevtsova, *Yeltsin's Russia*, p. 74.

39. Stephen Foye, "Russia's Fragmented Army Drawn into the Political Fray," *RFE/RL Research Report* 2, 15 (April 9, 1993): 6.

40. Barylski, *The Soldier in Russian Politics*, p. 248.

41. "General Armii Pavel Grachev: U armii zadacha odna—zashchita otechestva," *Krasnaya zvezda* (September 23, 1993).

42. "Obrashchenie Prezidenta Rossiiskoi Federatsii—Glavnokomanduyushchego Vooruzhennymi Silami Rossii," *Krasnaya zvezda* (September 24, 1993).

43. Barylski, *The Soldier in Russian Politics*, p. 257.

44. Yeltsin, *The Struggle for Russia*, p. 272.

45. Ibid., p. 277.

46. Ibid., p. 278.

47. Ibid.

48. Brian D. Taylor, *Politics and the Russian Army: Civil-Military Relations, 1689–2000* (New York: Cambridge University Press, 2003), p. 284.

49. "The Army Is Not a Policeman," *Nezavisimaya gazeta* (October 29, 1993) in FBIS: CEU (November 2, 1993).

50. Barylski, *The Soldier in Russian Politics*, p. 275.

51. Zoltan Barany, "Politics and the Russian Armed Forces," in *Russian Politics: Challenges of Democratization,* ed. Zoltan Barany and Robert G. Moser (New York: Cambridge University Press, 2001), p. 182.

52. Pavel K. Baev, *The Russian Army in a Time of Troubles* (London: Piro, 1996), p. 67.

53. Barylski, *The Soldier in Russian Politics*, p. 287.

54. Vitaly Shlykov, "The War in Chechnya: Implications for Military Reform and Creation of Mobile Forces" (conference paper, Naval Postgraduate School, Monterey, Calif., November 7–8, 1995), p. 6.

55. Ibid., pp. 4–5

56. Ibid.

57. *Nezavisimaya gazeta* (October 29, 1993) in FBIS: SOV (November 2, 1993).

58. Ibid., p. 5.

59. Pavel Felgenhauer, "Russian Military Reform: Ten Yeas of Failure," Russian Defense Policy Towards the Year 2000, Proceedings of a conference held at the Naval Postgraduate School on May 26 and 27, 1997, p. 8.

60. *Segodnya* (November 15, 1994).

61. Felgenhauer, "Russian Military Reform," p. 13.

62. Charles Dick, "The Russian Army—Present Plight and Future Prospects," *Jane's Intelligence Review Yearbook, 1994–1995*, p. 44.

63. One of the most difficult problems facing an analyst is to get accurate figures for the military budget. Since the Russian armed forces were created, the numbers have varied depending on the source utilized. The purpose of the figures used in this book is to provide the reader with an approximation: with an idea of the direction in which the budget was heading and how precipitous the increase or decrease was. For most of the Yeltsin period, I have relied upon "Russian Military Budget," Global Security.org as cited in Steven E. Miller, "Moscow's Military Power: Russia's Search for Security in an Age of Transition," in *The Russian Military: Power and Policy,* ed. Steven E. Miller and Dmitri Trenin (Cambridge, Mass: MIT Press, 2004), pp. 1–42.

64. "The Sword of Crisis Over the Military Budget," *Oriyentir,* no. 2 (February 1999) in *Military Affairs* (February 1, 1998).

65. "Armiya vypolnaet zvoi zadachi, nesmotrya na vse slozhnosti i problemy," *Krasnaya zvezda* (March 17, 1994).

66. "Officers! Russian Federation of Ministry of Defense Information Publishes Data on Armed Forces' Officer Corps," *Rossiiskaya gazeta* (August 26, 1995), in FBIS: CEU (August 31, 1995).

67. "Leytanty XXI veka," *Krasnaya zvezda* (July 27, 1994).

68. "The Crisis in the Soviet Union," *Jane's Intelligence Review* (February 1992): 73.

69. Dick, "The Russian Army," p. 42.

70. Ibid.

71. "Lyudi v pogonakh: kogda Vooruzhennye Sily RF sokrashchayitsya shislennost silo-gykh struktur rastet, *Krasnaya zvezda* (August 2,1994).

72. Ibid.

73. Christopher C. Locksley, "Concept, Algorithm, Indecision: Why Military Reform has Failed in Russia since 1992," *Journal of Slavic Military Studies* 14, 1 (March, 2001): 11.

74. "Armiya budet takoy, kakim budet ee ofitserskiy korpus," *Krasnaya zvezda* (May 17, 1994).

75. Stephen Foye, "Rebuilding the Russian Military: Some Problems and Prospects," *RFE/RL Research Report* (November 6, 1992): 53; "Minfin rygaetsya tropedirovat zakonaproekt o statuse voennosluzashchikh," *Krasnaya zvezda* (September 3, 1992).

76. "General Grachev ob armii i ob soldate," *Krasnaya zvezda* (February 5, 1993).

77. "Komplektovat Vooruzhennye Sily po ostanotenomu printsipu nelezya," *Krasnaya zvezda* (September 21, 1994); Dick, "The Russian Army," p. 41.

78. "Radio Rossii Interviews Grachev on Military Issues," Moscow Radio Rossii (February 23, 1993) in FBIS: CEU (February 24, 1993).

79. "Grachev Comments on First Year of Armed Forces," *Krasnaya zvezda* (May 7, 1993) in FBIS: CEU (May 10, 1993).

80. Robert W. Duggleby, "The Disintegration of the Russian Armed Forces," *Journal of Slavic Military Studies* 11, 2 (June 1998): 11.

81. Rensselaer W. Lee, "The Organized Crime Morass in the Former Soviet Union," *Demokratizatsiya* 2, 3 (1994): 396.

82. "Predsezdovskie khlopoty vlastey," *Nezavisimaya gazeta* (November 25, 1992).

83. "Pavel Grachev: "Armii segodnya trudno, kak i vssmu narodu," *Krasnaya zvezda* (February 23, 1993).

84. "Letter to the Editor," *Argumenty i Fakty,* no. 40 (October 1992): 8.

85. "Posle ubiytsva u raketnogo kompleksksa," *Izvestiya* (May 14, 1994).

86. "Explosion 'Equivalent of Nuclear Bomb'," Vladivostok Radio (May 16, 1994) in FBIS: CEU (May 16, 1994).

87. Dick, "The Russian Army," p. 43.

88. Ibid., p. 44.

89. "Minister's Position," *Rossiyskiye vesti* (January 4, 1993) in FBIS: CEU (January 6, 1993).

90. "The Defense Minister Has It in for Everyone," *Novaya yezhednevaya gazeta* (December 9, 1994) in FBIS: CEU (December 12, 1994).

91. "'Admiral' Navy Broke But Ready," *RFE/RL Daily Report* (November 17, 1994).

92. Barylski, *The Soldier in Russian Politics,* p. 287.

93. "Defense Ministry on Reform Efforts, Budget," *RFE/RL Daily Report* (August 22, 1994).

94. "Minister's Position," *Rossiyskiye vesti* (January 4, 1993) in FBIS: CEU (January 6, 1993).

95. "Grim Picture of Russian Missile Forces," *RFE/RL Daily Report* (November 3, 1994).

96. Duggleby, *The Disintegration of the Russian Armed Forces,* p. 14.

97. "Russia's Ground Forces in Trouble," *RFE/RL Daily Report* (November 17, 1994).

98. Dick, "The Russian Army," p. 43.

99. Ibid., p. 44.

100. Aron, *Yeltsin,* p. 644.

CHAPTER FOUR. CHECHNYA, MILITARY DISINTEGRATION, AND YELTSIN, NOVEMBER 1994–JUNE 1996

1. "Grachev Tells Duma, 'I am Clean Before the Army'," Moscow Mayak Radio Network (November 18, 1994) as translated by Foreign Broadcast Information Service, *Central Eurasia* [hereafter FBIS: CEU] (November 21, 1994).

2. Taken from Steven E. Miller, "Moscow's Military Power: Russia's Search for Security in an Age of Transition," in *The Russian Military: Power and Policy,* ed. Steven E. Miller and Dmitri Trenin (Cambridge, Mass.: MIT Press, 2004), p. 11.

3. Pavel Baev, *The Russian Army in a Time of Troubles* (London: Sage, 1996), p. 55.

4. Quoted in ibid., p. 71.

5. I heard this sentiment expressed often by Russians at this time.

6. Interior Ministry troops are separate from those under the Defense Ministry. They are under the command of the Minister of the Interior.

7. Anatol Lieven, *Chechnya: Tombstone of Russian Power* (New Haven, Conn.: Yale University Press, 1998), p. 64.

8. Robert V. Barylski, *The Soldier in Russian Politics: Duty, Dictatorship, and Democracy Under Gorbachev and Yeltsin* (New Brunswick, N.J.: Transaction, 1998), p. 305.

9. Roy Allison, "Russia, Regional Conflict, and the Use of Military Power," in *The Russian Military,* ed. Steven E. Miller and Dmitri Trenin (Cambridge, Mass.: MIT Press, 2004), p. 124.

10. I can remember talking about the issue of casualty rate with senior (colonel) level officers who fought in Chechnya and was surprised to discover that they seemed to find it

difficult to understand the problem. The idea was to take an objective, and it made little difference if that meant 20 percent or 50 percent casualties.

11. C. W. Blandy, *Chechnya: Two Federal Interventions: An Interim Comparison and Assessment*, no. P23 (Surrey: Conflict Studies Research Centre, Royal Military Academy Sandhurst, January 2000): p. 13.

12. Timothy Thomas, "The Battle of Grozny: Deadly Classroom for Urban Conflict," *Parameters* (1999): 2.

13. General M. A. Gareev, "Applying Zhukov's Command Heritage to Military Training and Reform in Today's World," *Journal of Slavic Military Studies* 12, 4 (December 1999): 84.

14. Pavel Felgenhauer, "Russian Military Reform: Ten Years of Failure," in *Russian Defense Policy Towards the Year 2000*, ed. Elizabeth Skinner and Mikhail Tsypkin (Monterey: Naval Postgraduate School, 1992), p. 42.

15. Tim Thomas, "Soldiers Sent to Battle After 8 Days Training," *Moscow News* (April 17–23, 1997).

16. See Olga Oliker, *Russia's Chechen Wars 1994–2000* (Santa Monica, Calif.: Rand, 2001), pp. 9–10.

17. Quoted in Blandy, *Chechnya*, p. 15.

18. Baev, *The Russian Army in a Time of Troubles*, p. 64.

19. Timothy Thomas, "The Russian Military and the December 1995 Duma Elections: Dissatisfaction Continues to Grow in the Armed Forces," *Journal of Slavic Military Studies* 9, 3 (September 1996): 529.

20. Oliker, *Russia's Chechen Wars*, p. 35.

21. *Moscow Times* (April 8, 1996).

22. Sven Simonsen, "Going His Own Way: A Profile of General Aleksandr Lebed," *Journal of Slavic Military Studies* 8, 3 (1995): 545.

23. Quoted in Barylski, *The Russian Soldier in Politics*, p. 315. Emphasis in original.

24. "General Kondratyev on Differences with Grachev," Itar-Tass (January 20, 1995) in FBIS: CEU (January 23, 1995).

25. Lieven, *Chechnya*, p. 106.

26. Ibid., p. 105.

27. Felgenhauer, p. 46.

28. Felgenhauer, p. 42.

29. Lieven, *Chechnya*, p. 103.

30. Oliker, *Russia's Chechen Wars*, p. 18.

31. Lieven, *Chechnya*, p. 109.

32. Timothy L. Thomas, "The Caucasus Conflict and Russian Security: The Russian Armed Forces Confront Chechnya III: The Battle for Grozny, 1–26 January 1995," *Journal of Slavic Military Studies* 10, 1 (March 1997): 52.

33. Cited in Gregory J. Celestan, *Wounded Bear: The Ongoing Russian Military Operation in Chechnya* (Fort Leavenworth, KS: Foreign Military Studies Office, August 1996), p. 4.

34. Based on a number of reports from U.S. military personnel.

35. As quoted in Lieven, *Chechnya*, p. 47.

36. Oliker, *Russia's Chechen War*, p. 31.

37. Celestan, *Wounded Bear*, p. 10.

38. Ibid., p. 7.

39. As quoted in Lieven, *Chechnya*, p. 111.

40. Celestan, *Wounded Bear,* p. 11.

41. Michael Orr, "Reform and the Russian Ground Forces, 1992–2002," in *Russian Military Reform, 1992–2002,* ed. Anne Aldis and Roger N. McDermott (London: Frank Cass, 2003), p. 130.

42. Lilia Shevtsova, *Yeltsin's Russia: Myths and Reality* (Washington, D.C.: Carnegie Endowment for International Peace, 1999), p. 119.

43. Vitaly Shlykov, "The War in Chechnya: Implications for Military Reform and Creation of Mobile Forces" (conference paper, Naval Postgraduate School, Monterey, Calif., November 7–8, 1995), pp. 7–8.

44. Ibid.

45. Ibid., p. 8.

46. Ibid., p. 9.

47. Shevtsova, *Yeltsin's Russia,* p. 167.

48. Military academies in Russia are on a level with American War Colleges. American military and naval academies correspond more closely to Russian officer schools.

49. Shlykov, "The War in Chechnya," p. 13.

50. Miller, "Moscow's Military Power," in *The Russian Military,* ed. Miller and Trenin, p. 11.

51. "Army Faces Disruption in Food Supply," Interfax (August 27, 1996) in FBIS: SOV (August 28, 1996).

52. Thomas, "The Russian Military," p. 525.

53. Jacob W. Kipp, and Timothy L. Thomas, "The Russian Military Election and the 1995 Parliamentary Elections: A Primer," Foreign Military Studies Office (October 5, 1995): 2.

54. "Kto i kak geolosuyet v Gsudeme," *Krasnaya zvezda* (March 3, 1995).

55. Robert W. Duggleby, "The Disintegration of the Russian Armed Forces," *Journal of Slavic Military Studies* 11, 2 (June 1998): 7.

56. Cited in Michael McFaul, *Russia's Unfinished Revolution: Political Change from Gorbachev to Putin* (Ithaca, N.Y.: Cornell University Press, 2001), p. 290.

57. Ibid., p. 293.

58. Barylski, *The Soldier in Russian Politics,* pp. 369–370.

59. Cited in ibid., p. 370.

60. Ibid., p. 416.

61. Shevtsova, *Yeltsin's Russia,* p. 172.

62. Cited in David J. Betz, *Civil-Military Relations in Russia and Eastern Europe* (London: RoutledgeCurzon, 2004), p. 56.

63. Pavel Felgenhauer, "Russian Military Failure: Ten Years of Failure" (conference paper, Naval Postgraduate School, Monterey, Calif., March 26–27, 1997), p. 8.

64. Cited in Vitaly V. Shlykov, "Does Russia Need a General Staff?" *European Security* 10, 4 (Winter 2001): 64.

65. Makhmut Gareev, *If War Comes Tomorrow? The Contours of Future Armed Conflict* (London: Frank Cass, 1998), p. 143.

66. "Federalnyy zakon 'Ob Oboronie'," at http://www.mil.ru/articles/article3863.shtml

67. C. J. Dick, "The Russian Army—Present Plight and Future Prospects," *Jane's Intelligence Review Yearbook,* 1994–1995, p. 41.

68. Miller, "Moscow's Military Power," in *The Russian Military,* ed. Miller and Trenin, p. 11.

69. Duggleby, "The Disintegration of the Russian Armed Forces," p. 5.

70. Betz, *Civil-Military Relations in Russia and Eastern Europe*, p. 54.

71. "Pavel Grachev, Emphasis on Force in Chechnya Should Be Retained," *Nezavisimoye voyennoye obozreniye* (November 3, 1995) in FBIS: CEU (November 20, 1995).

72. "Yevgeniy Podkolzin: 'I am Proud of the Airborne Troops,'" *Zavtra* (December 1995) in JPRS *Russian Military Affairs* (February 7, 1996).

73. Duggleby, "The Disintegration of the Russian Armed Forces," p. 5.

74. Deborah Yarsike Ball, "The Unreliability of the Russian Officer Corps: Reluctant Domestic Warriors," in *Director's Series on Proliferation,* ed. Kathleen Bailey and M. Elaine Price, November 17, 1995, University of California Radiation Laboratory, Livermore, Calif., Report UCRL-LR-114070–9, p. 19.

75. "Grachev on Effects of Defense Budget Underfunding," Itar-Tass (July 11, 1994) in FBIS: CEU (July 12, 1994).

76. Cited in Betz, *Civil-Military Relations in Russia and Eastern Europe*, p. 56.

77. Michael J. Orr, *Manpower Problems of the Russian Armed Forces,* no. D62 (Surrey: Conflict Studies Research Centre, Royal Military Academy Sandhurst, February, 2002), p. 2.

78. Lester W. Grau and Timothy L. Thomas, "The Russian Military and the December 1995 Duma Elections: Dissatisfaction Continues to Grow in the Armed Forces," *Journal of Slavic Military Studies* 9, 3 (September 1996): 514.

79. Christopher C. Locksley, "Concept, Algorithm, Indecision: Why Military Reform has Failed in Russia Since 1992," *Journal of Slavic Military Studies* 14, 1 (March 2001): 10.

80. Orr, *Manpower Problems of the Russian Armed Forces,* p. 4.

81. Michael J. Orr, *The Russian Armed Forces as a Factor in Regional Stability* (Surrey: Conflict Studies Research Centre, Royal Military Academy Sandhurst, June 1998), p. 8

82. Cited in Baev, *The Russian Army in a Time of Troubles,* p. 77.

83. Duggleby, "The Disintegration of the Russian Armed Forces," p. 8.

84. *Rabochaya tribuna* (March 23, 1996) in FBIS: SOV (April 3, 1996).

85. Duggleby, "The Disintegration of the Russian Armed Forces," p. 7.

86. Cited in Orr, *Manpower Problems of the Russian Armed Forces,* p. 11.

87. Dick, "The Russian Army," p. 42.

88. "Conversation without Middlemen," Moscow Television (September 14, 1995) in FBIS: CEU (September 18, 1995).

89. "Chinovnichya volokita tormozit povyshenie denezhnogo soderzhaniya voennosluzhashchikh," *Krasnaya zvezda* (September 12, 1995).

90. Dick, "The Russian Army," p. 43.

91. Betz, *Civil-Military Relations in Russia and Eastern Europe*, p. 52.

92. Graham Turbiville, "Mafia in Uniform: The 'Criminalization' of the Russian Armed Forces," Foreign Military Studies Office, July 1995, p. 34.

93. Ibid., p. 25.

94. Ibid., pp. 24, 25.

95. Lieven, *Chechnya,* p. 121.

96. Aleksandr Golts, *Armii Rossii: 11 Poteriannykh let* (Moscow: Zakharov, 2004), p. 172.

97. "Grim Picture of Russian Missile Forces," *RFE/RL Daily Report* (November 3, 1994).

98. "The Defense Minister Has it in For Everyone," *Novaya yezhednevaya gazeta* (December 9, 1994) in FBIS: CEU (December 12, 1994).

99. "Yeltsin Aide Favors Cossack Military Service," Interfax (September 8, 1995) in FBIS: CEU (September 9, 1995).

100. "Russia's Red Army Has Lost its Roar," *Christian Science Monitor* (June 2, 1997).

101. "Russia: Damage and Casualty Effect of Advancement Weapons," *Technika i vooruzhenniye* (February 2, 1998) in FBIS: CEU (March 27, 1998).

102. Lieven, *Chechnya,* p. 278.

103. "Conversations without Middlemen," Moscow TV (September 14, 1995).

CHAPTER FIVE. YELTSIN AND THE MILITARY, JULY 1996-DECEMBER 1999

1. Cited in Michael J. Orr, *Rodionov and Reform,* no. C92 (Surrey: Conflict Studies Research Centre, Royal Military Academy Sandhurst, January 1997), p. 1.

2. Ibid., p. 3.

3. Cited in ibid., p. 4.

4. Aleksandr Golts, *Armiya rossii: 11 poteryannykh let* (Moscow: Zakharov, 2004), p. 34.

5. Quotes cited in Orr, *Rodionov and Reform,* p. 3.

6. Gustaf Brunius, "Organizational Evolution within the Russian Federation Armed Forces," in *Russian Military Reform and Russia's New Security Environment,* ed. Yuri Fedorov and Bertil Nygren (Stockholm: National Defense College, 2003), p. 70.

7. Golts, *Armiya rossii,* p. 41.

8. "Nada zdelat vse vozmozhnoe, shtoby armiya bystree vyshla iz rizisa," *Krasnaya zvezda* (October 2, 1996).

9. John P. Moran, *From Garrison State to Nation-State* (Westport, Conn.: Praeger, 2002), p. 94.

10. "Rodionov Thinks Professional Army by 2005 Impossible," *Nezavisimoye voyennoye obozreniye* in FBIS: SOV (April 12, 1997).

11. Golts, *Armii rossii,* p. 44.

12. Moran, *From Garrison State to Nation-State,* p. 94.

13. Ibid., p. 95

14. Lilia Shevtsova, *Putin's Russia* (Washington, D.C.: Carnegie Endowment for International Peace, 2003), p. 198.

15. Ibid.

16. Robert V. Barylski, *The Soldier in Russian Politics: Duty, Dictatorship, and Democracy Under Gorbachev and Yeltsin* (New Brunswick, N.J.: Transaction, 1998), p. 420.

17. Boris Yeltsin, *Midnight Diaries* (New York: Public Affairs, 2000), p. 4.

18. Barylski, *The Soldier in Russian Politics,* p. 420.

19. Cited in David J. Betz, *Civil-Military Relations in Russia and Eastern Europe* (London: RoutledgeCurzon, 2004), p. 61. Emphasis in original.

20. Michael J. Orr, *The Russian Armed Forces as a Factor in Regional Stability* (Surrey: Conflict Studies Research Centre, Royal Military Academy Sandhurst, June 1998), p. 5.

21. Cited in Orr, *Rodionov and Reform,* p. 8.

22. Ibid., p. 433.

23. "Vernem lyudam v pogonakh dostoinstvo i uvazhenie," *Krasnaya zvezda* (August 7, 1996).

24. Steven E. Miller, "Moscow's Military Power: Russia's Search for Security in an Age of Transition," in *The Russian Military: Power and Policy,* ed. Steven E. Miller and Dmitri Trenin (Cambridge, Mass.: MIT Press, 2004), p. 11.

25. As quoted in Betz, *Civil-Military Relations in Russia and Eastern Europe,* p. 57.

26. Barylski, *The Soldier in Russian Politics,* p. 347.

27. "Glavnoe-Znat Armiiu. A Parlamenskii Opyt Pridet," *Krasnaya zvezda* (February 2, 1996).

28. Barylski, *The Soldier in Russian Politics,* p. 478.

29. *Voennaya reforma v Rossii: materially konferentsii provedennoi v ISK RAN v 9 Dekabra 1996 g* (Moscow: Rossiiskaya Nauk, 1997), p. 50.

30. As cited in Brian D. Taylor, *Politics and the Russian Army: Civil-Military Relations, 1689–2000* (New York: Cambridge University Press, 2003), p. 310.

31. Moran, *From Garrison State to Nation-State,* p. 173.

32. Golts, *Armii Rossii,* p. 155.

33. According to one source, Yeltsin signed an order permitting Kvashnin to have direct access to the president, bypassing the defense minister. "President Shows Sergeyev His Place: Dyarchy in the Russian Army?" *Moskovsky komsomolets* (July 22, 1999) as translated by World News Connection [hereafter WNC] (July 22, 1999).

34. Moran, *From Garrison State to Nation-State,* p. 59.

35. Cited in Orr, *The Russian Armed Forces as a Factor in Regional Stability,* p. 5.

36. Frank Umbach, "Nuclear versus Conventional Forces: Implications for Russia's Future Military Reform," in *Russian Military Reform, 1992–2000,* ed. Anne C. Aldis and Roger N. McDermott (London: Frank Cass, 2003), p. 78.

37. Michael Orr, "Reform and the Russian Ground Forces, 1992–2002," in *Russian Military Reform,* ed. Aldis and McDermott, p. 131.

38. Golts, *Armii Rossii,* p. 44.

39. Brunius, "Organizational Evolution within the Russian Federation Armed Forces," in *Russian Military Reform and Russia's New Security Environment,* ed. Fedorov and Nygren, p. 73.

40. Ibid., p. 60.

41. Walter Parchomenko, "The State of Russia's Armed Forces and Military Reform," *Parameters* (Winter 1999–2000): 101.

42. Pavel K. Baev, "The Trajectory of the Russian Military: Downsizing, Degeneration, and Defeat," in *The Russian Military: Power and Policy,* ed. Miller and Trenin, p. 54.

43. Mikhail Tsypkin, "The Russian Military, Politics, and Security Policy in the 1980s," in *The Russian Armed Forces at the Time of the Millennium,* ed. Michael Cruthers (Carlisle Barracks, Pa.: U.S. Army War College, 2000), p. 39.

44. Barylski, *The Soldier in Russian Politics,* p. 481.

45. "Kontseptsiya stroitelstva vooruzhennykh sil utverzhdena: S press-konferentsii ministra oborony RF general armii I. D. Sergeyeva," *Krasnaya zvezda* (August 9, 1997).

46. Igor Sergeyev, "Reform the Armed Forces by the 21st Century," *Military New Bulletin* 6, 12 (December 1997): 1–3.

47. Baev, "The Trajectory of the Russian Military," in *The Russian Military: Power and Policy,* ed. Miller and Trenin, p. 54.

48. "Position: Military Reform: Words and Deeds," *Nezavisimoye voyennoye obozreniye* (October 24–30, 1997) in WNC (December 15, 1997).

49. Brunius, "Organizational Evolution within the Russian Federation Armed Forces," in *Russian Military Reform and Russia's New Security Environment,* ed. Fedorov and Nygren, pp. 76–77.

50. Ibid., p. 78.

51. Lilia Shevtsova, *Yeltsin's Russia: Myths and Reality* (Washington, D.C.: Carnegie Endowment for International Peace, 1999), p. 247.

52. Ibid., p. 252.

53. "Promah Andreiya Kokoshina," *Itogi,* no. 36 (1998).

54. Michael J. Orr, *The Deepest Crisis: The Problems of the Russian Army Today* (Surrey: Conflict Studies Research Centre, Royal Military Academy Sandhurst, October 4, 1996), p. 1.

55. "The Sword of Crisis Over the Military Budget," *Krasnaya zvezda* (January 30, 1999) in WNC (February 1, 1999).

56. Alexei Arbatov, "The Transformation of Russian Military Doctrine: Lessons Learned from Kosovo and Chechnya," *Marshall Center Papers,* no. 2 (July 20, 2000): 8.

57. Victor Esin, "The Military Reform in the Russian Federation: Problems, Decisions and Prospects," in *Russian Military Reform and Russia's New Security Environment,* ed. Fedorov and Nygren, p. 107.

58. Taylor, *Politics and the Russian Army,* p. 308.

59. "Russian Armed Forces Equipment at 100%," Itar-Tass (September 28, 1999).

60. Taylor, *Politics and the Russian Army,* p. 308.

61. Parchomenko, "The State of Russia's Armed Forces and Military Reform," p. 104.

62. Richard Holbrooke, *To End a War* (New York: Random House, 1998), pp. 203, 206, 209, 212–13, 214.

63. CNN, "Sources: Top NATO Commanders Clashed over Russian's Actions in Kosovo," CNN.com (August 2, 1999).

64. Cameron Ross, *Russian Politics Under Putin* (Manchester, UK: Manchester University Press, 2004), p. 260.

65. Dmitri V. Trenin and Aleksei V. Malashenko, *Russia's Restless Frontier: The Chechnya Factor in Post-Soviet Russia* (Washington, D.C.: Carnegie Endowment for International Peace, 2004), p. 29.

66. Paul Murphy, *The Wolves of Islam* (Washington, D.C.: Brassey's, 2004), p. 91.

67. Trenin and Malashenko, *Russia's Restless Frontier,* p. 34.

68. Cited in Murphy, *The Wolves of Islam,* p. 99.

69. Mathew Evangelista, *The Chechen Wars: Will Russia Go the Way of the Soviet Union?* (Washington, D.C.: Brookings Institution Press, 2002), p. 63. Blandy uses the term "up to 2,000." C. W. Blandy, *Dagestan: The Storm Part I—The "Invasion" of Avaristan,* P30, Conflict Studies Research Centre, March, 2000, p. 40.

70. Murphy, *The Wolves of Islam,* p. 100.

71. Ibid., p. 65.

72. C. W. Blandy, *Chechnya: Two Federal Interventions. An Interim Comparison and Assessment,* no. P29 (Surrey: Conflict Studies Research Centre, Royal Military Academy Sandhurst, January 2000), p. 39.

73. Murphy, *The Wolves of Islam,* p. 101; Blandy, *Dagestan: The Storm,* p. 43. Blandy suggests that the decision to use fuel-air explosives may have been taken by acting Prime Minister Vladimir Putin on August 22 in a meeting with Sergeyev, Kvashnin, Vladimir Rushailo, the Interior Minister, and Nikolai Patrushev, director of the FSB, pp. 43–44.

74. Blandy, *Dagestan: The Storm*, p. 41.

75. Evangelista, *The Chechen Wars*, p. 65.

76. Figures are from Murphy, *The Wolves of Islam*, p. 104.

77. Ibid., p. 106.

78. Shevtsova, *Putin's Russia*, p. 39.

79. Olga Oliker, *Russia's Chechen Wars, 1994–2000* (Santa Monica, Calif.: Rand, 2001), p. 33.

80. Blandy, *Chechnya: Two Federal Interventions*, p. 42.

81. C. W. Blandy, "Moscow's Failure to Comprehend," in *The Second Chechen War*, ed. Anne Aldis, Strategic and Combat Studies Institute Occasional Paper, no. 40 (September 2000): 17.

82. In conversations with senior Russian officers in 2001, I asked several ground force, airborne, and naval infantry officers who had just come from Chechnya about the idea of "winning the hearts and minds" of the local populace, and they all seemed to have a problem understanding the concept. It was simply not something that concerned them. They saw their job as smashing the enemy, and collateral damage (for example) was not a primary concern to them.

83. The comment was actually made in March 2000, but he made no attempt to avoid responsibility for it from the time that Yeltsin gave him the assignment.

84. Shevtsova, *Putin's Russia*, p. 39.

85. "Putin and the Chechen War: Together Forever," *Moscow Times* (February 11, 2004).

86. M. A. Smith, "The Second Chechen War: The All-Russian Context," in *The Second Chechen War*, ed. Aldis, p. 8. Emphasis in original.

87. Ibid.

88. Ibid.

89. Ibid., p. 9.

90. Blandy, "Moscow's Failure to Comprehend," p. 14. Emphasis in original. "Invasion" refers to the invasion of Dagestan by Basayev and Khattab.

91. Taylor, *Politics and the Russian Army*, p. 314. There is also a report that one of the key generals warned that if the civilians interfered in Chechnya II, as they had in the first war, "There will be a powerful exodus of officers of various ranks, including generals, from the armed forces," because the officer corps could not survive another "slap in the face." See "Generals Tell Politicians: Hands Off," *Moscow News* (November 5, 1999). In reality there was no cause for concern, because Putin let the generals run the conflict.

92. Pavel Baev, "Putin's War in Chechnya: Who Steers the Course?" *PONARS Policy Memo*, no. 345 (November 2004): 2.

93. Smith, *The Second Chechen War*, p. 6.

94. See Robert Garwood, "The Second Russo-Chechen Conflict (1999 to date): 'A Modern Military Operation'," *Journal of Slavic Military Studies* 15, 3 (September 2002): 69.

95. Ibid., p. 71.

96. Andrew Meier, *The Heart of a Conflict: Chechnya* (New York: Norton, 2005), p. 48.

97. "Crimes of War: Chechnya, The World Looks Away," *Moscow Times* (April 18, 2003).

98. N. Vorobyev and N. F. Kuznetzov, "Oborona po printsipu ochagovykh deystviy," *Voyennaya mysl* no. 3 (May/June 2001): 14.

99. Meier, *The Heart of a Conflict*, does an excellent job of tracing the impact of such weapons and Moscow's policy of total destruction in Chechnya. C. W. Blandy, *Chechnya:*

Dynamics of War, Brutality and Stress, no. P35 (Surrey: Conflict Studies Research Centre, Royal Military Academy Sandhurst, July 2001) also documents a number of war crimes committed by Russian forces against the Chechen civilian population.

100. Parchomenko, "The State of Russia's Armed Forces," p. 3n10.

101. Orr, *The Russian Armed Forces as a Factor in Regional Stability,* p. 6.

102. Tsypkin, "The Russian Military, Politics, and Security Policy in the 1980s," in *The Russian Armed Forces at the Time of the Millennium,* ed. Cruthers, p. 28.

103. "Armed Forces Crime Figures for 1998 Announced," Interfax (December 1, 1999).

104. "Russia Continues to Lose Officers," *Monitor* (October 13, 1999).

105. "Russian Air Force Chief Interviewed," Moscow NTV (June 22, 1998) in WNC (June 25, 1998).

106. Cited in David J. Betz and Valeriy G. Volkov, "A New Day for the Russian Army? Reforming the Armed Forces under Yeltsin and Putin," in *Russian Military Reform,* ed. Aldis and McDermott, p. 51.

107. "The Army is Shooting its Own Men," *Izvestiya* (June 6, 1997).

108. "Russia Armed Forces Battle Housing Problem," *Russia Journal* (April 5, 1999): 2.

109. Roger N. McDermott, "Putin's Military Priorities: The Modernisation of the Armed Forces," in *Russian Military Reform,* ed. Aldis and McDermott, p. 266.

110. Stephen L. Webber, "Public Attitudes toward the Armed Forces in Russia: Do They Count? in *The Russian Military into the Twenty-First Century,* ed. Stephen J. Cimbala (London: Frank Cass, 2001), p. 162.

111. "Moscow Military Urges Deserters to Return," *Monitor* (May 14, 1998).

112. "Doctors Find New Draftees Less Fit for Duty," *Russian Journal* (March 8, 1999): 3.

113. "The Russian Army, Reeling from the War in Chechnya and Facing Brutality in its Ranks, Has Found a New Enemy—Itself." *Transactions* (November 1998).

114. Orr, *Manpower Problems of the Russian Armed Forces,* p. 4.

115. Parchomenko, "The State of Russia's Armed Forces," p. 3.

116. "Russia's Army Faces Battle Within its Ranks," *Christian Science Monitor* (February 1, 1999).

117. Ibid.

118. "Crime Increases in Russia's Armed Forces, *Russia Journal* (March 15, 1999).

119. V. A. Zolotareva, V. V. Marushchenko, S. S. Antyushina, *Vo Imya Rosii. Rossiyskoe gosudarstvo, armiya i voinskoe vospitanie* (Moscow: Izdatelstvo, Rus-RKB, 1999), p. 214.

120. "The Army is Shooting its Own Men," *Izvestiya* (June 6, 1997).

121. "Defense Ministry to Submit Program on Contract Service by Autumn," Novosti (July 15, 1997).

122. "Army Struggles with Contract Military Service," *Monitor* (October 15, 1997).

123. Betz, *Civil-Military Relations in Russia and Eastern Europe,* p. 53.

124. "Generals, Admirals Convicted of Corruption," *RFE/RL Daily Report* (July 6, 1999).

125. "Yeltsin Order Probe of Security for Nukes," *Washington Times* (October 21, 1998).

126. "Armed Forces Crime Figures to 1998 Announced," Interfax (December 1, 1999).

127. "Russia Fired 20 Nuke Soldiers on Mental Concerns," Reuters (October 11, 1999).

128. "State Duma 'Alarmed' Over Army Crime," Itar-Tass (October 21, 1999).

129. Lieven, *Chechnya,* p. 279.

130. Stephen Blank, "Valuing the Human Factor: The Reform of Russian Military Manpower," *Journal of Slavic Military Studies* 12, 1 (March 1999): 83.

131. "Defense Chief Describes Army's Woes," *Monitor* (April 9, 1999).

132. "Russia Tries to Save Military," AP (July 2, 1999).

133. Parchomenko, "The State of Russia's Armed Forces," p. 3.

134. "Ilyukhin, Russia's National Security Threatened," Interfax (September 17, 1998).

135. "Russian Army Woes Outlined," *Monitor* (December 14, 1998).

136. "Russian Arms Exports Reach Record High," Agence France-Presse (July 22, 1999).

137. Oliker, *Russia's Chechen Wars, 1994–2000,* p. 59.

138. There is a saying that is common among militaries around the world, "Praise in public, criticize in private." One can only wonder why Yeltsin decided he had to be so public and humiliate these two men.

139. Shevtsova, *Putin's Russia,* pp. 62–63.

CHAPTER SIX. PUTIN, THE GENERALS, AND STABILIZING THE MILITARY, JANUARY 2000– JANUARY 2006

1. Unless otherwise noted, the following characterization of Putin is based on: Dale Herspring and Jacob Kipp, "Searching for the Elusive Mr. Putin," *Problems of Post-Communism* 48, 5 (September/October 2001): 3–17; and "Conclusion," in *Putin's Russia: Past Imperfect, Future Uncertain,* ed. Dale R. Herspring (Boulder, Colo.: Rowman and Littlefield, 2005), pp. 293–300.

2. Richard Sakwa, *Putin; Russia's Choice* (London: Routledge, 2004).

3. As Putin put it in his Millennium Address, "The key to the resuscitation and progress of the country has to be found in state power." Vladimir Putin, "Russia at the Turn of the Millennium," Government of the Russian Federation, http://www.government.gov.ru/english/statVP_egl_1.html.

4. "Survey of Military Reform in the Russian Federation," *Yadernyy kontrol* (April 19, 2002) as translated by World News Connection [hereafter WNC] (September 6, 2002).

5. Frank Umbach, *Future Military Reform: Russia's Nuclear and Conventional Forces,* no. D65 (Surrey: Conflict Studies Research Centre, Royal Military Academy Sandhurst, August 2002), p. 12.

6. Aleksandr Golts, *Armii Rossii: 11 Pteryannykh let* (Moscow: Zakharov, 2004), p. 79.

7. Umbach, *Future Military Reform,* p. 12.

8. S. J. Main, "Russia's Military Doctrine," Conflict Studies Research Centre Occasional Brief no. 77 (April 2000), p. 5.

9. The text of the doctrine was published in *Nezavisimaya gazeta* (April 22, 2000).

10. Charles Dick, "Russia's New Doctrine Takes Dark World View," *Jane's Intelligence Review* (January 2000): 14. Dick's comment was directed at the draft document released in 1999, but it holds for the final document as well. A similar comment was contained in Brian Taylor's article, "Superpower Rogueness," *Moscow News* (October 26–November 1, 1999).

11. Pavel K. Baev, "The Challenge of 'Small Wars' for the Russian Military," in *Russian Military Reform, 1992–2002,* ed. Anne C. Aldis and Roger N. McDermott (London: Frank Cass, 2003), p. 192.

12. Nikolai Sokov, "'Denuclearization' of Russia's Defense Policy?" Center for Nonproliferation Studies Report, Monterey Institute of International Studies (July 17, 2000); Phillip

C. Bleek, "Russia Ready to Reduce to 1,500 Warheads, Addressing Dispute Over Strategic Forces' Fate," *Arms Control Today* (September 2000).

13. "Hope Glimmers for Reform," *Moscow Times* (March 29, 2001) via Johnson's Russia List (March 29, 2001).

14. "Development Strategy of the Armed Forces Defined," *Military News Bulletin*, no. 8 (August 2000). See also "Decisions on the Reform of the State's Military Organisation Have Been Adopted," in which Putin's is quoted as saying, "It is absolutely wrong to maintain a bulky and often ineffective military organisation in our conditions." *Military News Bulletin*, no. 11 (November 2000).

15. Steven J. Main, *The Strategic Rocket Forces, 1991–2002*, no. D66 (Surrey: Conflict Studies Research Centre, Royal Military Academy Sandhurst, July 9, 2003), p. 26.

16. Ibid.

17. Golts, *Armii Rossii*, p. 80. There was a report that Putin had intended to introduce a plan that would "delineate the responsibilities of the Ministry of Defense and the General Staff similar to the United States. This reform would be capped by the appointment of a civilian as Minister of Defense. The General Staff, under the new system, would report directly to the President." Nikolai Sokov, "The Fate of Nuclear Weapons: An Anticlimax on August 11," Center for Nonproliferation Studies Reports, Monterey Institute of International Studies (August 14, 2000). But for whatever reason, Putin decided not to make any structural changes.

18. "The Kursk Investigation: Issues and Ramifications," *RFE/RL Daily Report* (February 25, 2002).

19. Cited in ibid., p. 84.

20. "Vystuplenie Prezidenta Rossiyskoi Federatsii V. V. Putina na sborakh rukovodyashchego sostava Vorruzhennykh Sil Rossiyskoy Federatsii, 20 noyabrya 2000 goda," http://president.kremlin.ru/events/102.html.

21. "Russia: Survey of Military Reform in the Russian Federation," *Yadernyy kontrol* (April 19, 2002) in WNC (September 6, 2002).

22. V. V. Putin, "Strategic Deterrence and the Prevention of Aggression," *Military News Bulletin*, no. 12 (December 2000).

23. "Decisions on the reform of the state's military organization have been adopted," *Military News Bulletin*, no. 11 (November 2000).

24. Main, *The Strategic Rocket Forces, 1991–2002*, p. 29.

25. "Russia: Analysts Assess Kremlin Reshuffle," in Johnson's Russia List (March 29, 2001).

26. Ibid.

27. Ibid.

28. Ibid.

29. Patrick E. Tyler, "High Level Shake-up, Putin Replaces Russia's Defense, Interior, and Nuclear Energy Chiefs," *New York Times* (March 29, 2001).

30. Vladimir Mukhin, "Reshuffle Bring Putin People to the Top," *Russia Journal* (May 4, 2001).

31. See Roger N. McDermott, *The Recreation of Russia's Ground Forces High Command: Prepared for Future War?* no. A103 (Surrey: Conflict Studies Research Centre, Royal Military Academy Sandhurst, March 2002), p. 2.

32. "Assessing Putin's Meeting with the Military Command," *Monitor* (October 29, 2001).

33. "Survey of Military Reform in the Russian Federation," *Yadernyy kontrol* (April 19, 2002) as translated by World News Connection [hereafter WNC] (September 6, 2002).

34. "More than Half of Russians Unfit to Serve in the Army," Agence France-Presse (November 29, 2001) via Johnson's Russia List (December 1, 2001).

35. Ibid.

36. "What is the Price of a Professional?" *Itogi* (January 22, 2002) via Johnson's Russia List (January 28, 2002).

37. "Major Clash Shaping Up Between Rightist Politicians and Military Chiefs on Military Reform," *Obshchaya gazeta* (December 13, 2001) in WNC (December 17, 2001).

38. "General Staff Stripped of Power Over the Army," *Izvestiya* (June 10, 2004) in WNC (June 16, 2004).

39. "General Staff Should be the Brain of the Army," RIA-Novosti (February 8, 2004) via Johnson's Russia List (February 9, 2004). See also Steven J. Main, *Couch for the MoD or the CGS? The Russian Ministry of Defence and the General Staff, 2001–2004* (Surrey: Conflict Studies Research Centre, Royal Military Academy Sandhurst, April 2004).

40. "Federalnyi zakon 'Ob oborone'," April 24, 1996 in http://www.mil.ru/articles/articles3863.shtml.

41. "As Defense Minister Says General Staff to Focus on Future Wars," *RFE/RL Daily Report* (July 20, 2004). Golts called Baluyevsky "one of the few Russian generals who really does possess the necessary abilities to organize strategic planning." Steven J. Main, "'And the occupier of the couch is . . .': The Removal of General Anatoliy Kvashnin and the Appointment of Russia's New Chief of the General Staff (CGS), Colonel General Yury Nikolaevich Baluyevsky (June/July 2004)," *Journal of Slavic Military Studies* 18, 1 (2005): 11.

42. "Kvashnin Won't be Missed," *Moscow Times* (July 20, 2004) via Johnson's Russia List (July 21, 2004).

43. "General Staff Relieved of Superfluous Functions, While Defense Minister is Handed All the Reins of Control Over the Army," *Rossiiskaya gazeta* (June 15, 2004) in WNC (June 17, 2004).

44. "Problems, Including Low Pay, in Converting 76th Airborne Division to Unit of Contract Soldiers," *Rossiiskaya gazeta* (August 16, 2002) via Johnson's Russia List (August 21, 2002).

45. Roger McDermott, "Putin's Military Priorities: The Modernisation of the Armed Forces," in *Russian Military Reform,* ed. Fedorov and Nygren, p. 270.

46. "Leaking, Lobbying, Looting," *Moscow Times* (July 18, 2002) via Johnson's Russia List (July 18, 2002).

47. "Russia's Army Still Mired in Conscript Crisis," *Russia Journal* (April 24–30, 2000) via Johnson's Russia List (April 27, 2000).

48. "Scandal Brews over Military Reform, Pskov Contract Service Experiment," *Moskovskiye novosti* (October 8, 2002) in WNC (October 10, 2002).

49. Rod Thornton, "Military Organizations and Change: The Professionalization of the 76th," *Journal of Slavic Military Studies* 17, 3 (July/September 2004): 464.

50. "Kvashnin Attacks Airborne Forces," *RFE/RL Daily Report* (December 11, 2002).

51. Thornton, "Military Organizations and Change," pp. 463–464.

52. "The Military Reform Card," *Moscow Times* (May 22, 2003).

53. "Military Reforms: The First Steps," *Mir novostei* (July 18, 2002) via Johnson's Russia List (July 18, 2002).

54. "Litovkin: 'Political Games' Doom Contract Service Experiment in 76th Division," *Vremya* (October 8, 2002) in WNC (October 24, 2002).

55. "Russian Defense Minister To Address Government on Military Reform," Itar-Tass (November 20, 2002) in WNC (November 21, 2002).

56. "MOD Ivanov Visits 76th Airborne Division, Satisfied with Experiment," *Trud* (December 4, 2003) in WNC (December 31, 2003).

57. "First Deputy Defense Minister Aleksandr Belousov: 'In Order to Make it Worth People's While to Serve, We Should Not Be Afraid to Spend'," *Izvestiya* (September 22, 2005) in WNC (September 23, 2005).

58. Ibid.

59. "Soldiers' Pay Seen as 'Main Stumbling Block' to Contract Manning of Russian Army," *Rossiiskaya gazeta* (August 25, 2004) in WNC (August 31, 2004).

60. "Defense Minister Ivanov Claims Russian 2005 Budget Jeopardizes Military Reform," *Nezavisimaya gazeta* (August 24, 2004) in WNC (August 31, 2004).

61. "Chief of Russia's General Staff Speaks About Current Challenges," *Krasnaya zvezda* (November 6, 2004) via Johnson's Russia List (November 13, 2004). See also "Army Optimization Inspires No Optimism: The Quantity of Equipment in the Fighting Forces That Is Being Sold Off and Stolen Is Equal to Industry's Annual Arms Deliveries," *Nezavisimoye voyennoye obozreniye* (February 18, 2006) in WNC (February 19, 2006), which is also critical of the quality of contract soldiers, especially those in the 76th Airborne Division and the Pacific Fleet's diesel submarine fleet.

62. First Deputy Defense Minister General Alexander Belousov.

63. "Putin Says Technical Strengthening of Rapid Reaction Units Priority Task," Agenstvo voyennykh novostey (February 28, 2005); "Chief of Russia's General Staff Speaks About Current Challenges," *Krasnaya zvezda* (November 6, 2004) via Johnson's Russia List (November 13, 2004).

64. "Russia's TV Bid to Recruit Troops," BBC (January 9, 2005) via Johnson's Russia List (January 11, 2005).

65. "Russian Army Details Contract Servicemen's Pay in Chechnya," Itar-Tass (February 28, 2005) in WNC (March 1, 2005).

66. "Russia To Man 40 Units, Formations with Contract Soldiers in 2005," Itar-Tass (February 12, 2005); "Russian Military to Finish Building Housing for Chechnya-Based Units in 2005," Agenstvo voyennykh novostey (March 28, 2005) in WNC(March 28, 2005).

67. First Deputy Minister Alexander Belousov.

68. "All Volunteer Force Program Funding Expected to Increase by 15%," Agenstvo voyennykh novostey (September 9, 2005) in WNC (September 10, 2005).

69. "Russian Airborne Division Misses Contract Manning Deadline," Agenstvo voyennykh novostey (January 13, 2006) in WNC (January 14, 2006).

70. A source on the Duma Defense Committee argued in November 2005 that Russia could afford to spend up to 5.5 percent of its gross domestic product for defense security. "Duma Committee Says Russia Can Afford Spending 5.5% of GDP for Defense," Agenstvo voyennykh novostey (November 9, 2005), in WNC (November 10, 2005).

71. "Ivanov's Budget," *Rossiyskiye vesti* (September 8, 2005) in WNC (September 12, 2005).

72. "Russian General Says 2006 Budget Not to Improve Military Combat Potential," Agenstvo voyennykh novostey (December 7, 2005) in WNC (December 8, 2005).

73. Vladimir Mukhin, "Reshuffle Brings Putin People to the Top," *Russian Journal* (May 4, 2001).

74. Ibid.

75. "Duma Defense Committee Head Says Military Reform Not Yet Under Way," *RFE/RL Daily Report* (March 22, 2002).

76. "State OKs $2.5 billion Arms Budget," *Moscow Times* (January 18, 2002) via Johnson's Russia List (January 18, 2002).

77. "Klebanov Stresses Need for 'Modernization' of Old Army Hardware," *Rossiiskaya gazeta* (August 8, 2002) in WNC (August 9, 2002).

78. "Russia's Ground Troops Not to Get New Weapons Soon," Itar-Tass (December 26, 2001) in WNC (December 29, 2001).

79. "Russia's Military Aviation Said in Crisis," Interfax (September 18, 2002), via Johnson's Russia List (September 19, 2002).

80. "Russia Military Reform, A Priority on Paper, Continues to Confound Kremlin," *RFE/RL Daily Report* (February 11, 2002) via Johnson's Russia List (February 11, 2002).

81. "Russian Air Force to Receive 20 Modernized Planes in 2003," Itar-Tass (January 16, 2003).

82. "Russian Army Received 15 New Helicopter Gunships in 2003," Itar-Tass (August 27, 2003), in WNC (August 28, 2003).

83. "Plan to Double Military Procurement in 2004 Not to be Fulfilled," *Trud* (August 19, 2003) in WNC (September 6, 2003).

84. "Russian Air Force Command Worried by Aging of Aircraft," Itar-Tass (March 26, 2003) in WNC (March 27, 2003).

85. "80% of Russia's Defense Industry is Obsolete," Rosbalt (August 18, 2003) via Johnson's Russia List (August 20, 2003).

86. "Russian Army to Acquire 14 T-90S Tanks in 2004," Itar-Tass (July 6, 2004) in WNC (July 10, 2004).

87. "Defense Minister Says Russian Army to get First T-90 Tanks in 2005," RIA-Novosti (November 30, 2004) in WNC (December 1, 2004).

88. "Russia Without an Army," *Vedomosti* (November 18, 2004) via Johnson's Russia List (November 18, 2004).

89. "Defense Spending Is Growing, Armed Deliveries Are Sliding," *Nezavisimoye voyennoye obozreniye* (August 31, 2005) in WNC (September 2, 2005). Another source maintained that the 2006 procurement budget had been increased to 241 billion rubles, but the author considered that to be inadequate as well. "Army Optimization Inspires No Optimism: The Quantity of Equipment in the Fighting Forces That is Being Sold Off and Stolen is Equal to Industry's Annual Arms Deliveries," *Nezavisimoye voyennoye obozreniye* (February 18, 2006) in WNC (February 19, 2006).

90. "Russian Army to Get New Strike Helicopter from 2006," Itar-Tass (October 11, 2004). According to the Ground Forces Commander, "The volume of hardware supply has increased, and we have started receiving armaments of new types." See "Commander Says Land Forces Getting More New Hardware Lately," Agenstvo Voyennykh Novostey (November 2, 2005) in WNC (November 3, 2005).

91. "Russian General Says 2006 Budget Not to Improve Military Combat Potential," Agenstvo voyennykh novostey (December 7, 2005) in WNC (December 8, 2005).

92. "We Need at Least One Million Military Personnel," *Izvestiya* (February 22, 2005) via Johnson's Russia List (February 22, 2005).

93. "Demands for Military Reform," RIA-Novosti (July 12, 2005) via Johnson's Russia List (July 12, 2005).

94. Critics of Putin's efforts to modernize and equip the military have argued that he has consistently failed to provide enough funds for the armed forces because of the rate of inflation. See, "Armed Forces Modernization Plans Suffer Fiasco," *Nezavisimoye voyennoye obozreniye* (October 28, 2005) in WNC (October 29, 2005); "Achilles Heel of Defense, Regime's Inability to Carry Out Military Reform is Pushing Generals Into Ranks of Opposition," *Nezavisimaya gazeta* (October 26, 2005) in WNC (October 27, 2005).

95. "Is the Army Unhappy with Putin?" *RFE/RL Daily Report* (August 17, 2001).

96. "Russian Government Proposals to Remove Servicemen's Privileges Criticized," *Vremya MN* (May 31, 2003) in WNC (July 1, 2003).

97. "Army, Pay, Same Old Story," *Moscow Times* (March 21, 2002) via Johnson's Russia List (March 22, 2002); "Kvashnin: Military in Critical Condition," Associated Press (May 30, 2002) via Johnson's Russia List (May 30, 2002).

98. "Majority of Russian army officers live in poverty: official," Agence France-Presse (February 27, 2003) via Johnson's Russia List (February 28, 2003).

99. "Russia to Raise Military Salaries by 50–120 Percent," Interfax (August 12, 2004).

100. "Russia Without an Army," *Vedomosti* (November 18, 2004); "Defense Ministry Civilian Personnel's Wage Grievances Discussed," *Izvestiya* (December 14, 2004) in WNC (December 15, 2004).

101. "Roundtable Pushes Legislative Changes to Improve Service in Russian Army," *Trud* (June 24, 2003) in WNC (June 28, 2003).

102. "Russian General: Housing Situation for Servicemen in Moscow 'Catastrophic'," Itar-Tass (February 14, 2002) in WNC (February 15, 2005).

103. "House Issue Remains Among 'most serious' Problems for Military," Itar-Tass (May 31, 2002) in WNC (June 3, 2002).

104. "Russian Army Suffers from Mass Exodus of Officers," *RFE/RL Daily Report* (February 14, 2002).

105. "Declining Financial Well-Being, Training of Military Officers Alleged," *Nezavisimoye voyennoye obozreniye* (December 24, 2004) in WNC (January 1, 2005).

106. "Some 85 percent of Armed Forces Officers Negatively Assess Benefits Law," Itar-Tass (January 24, 2005) in WNC (January 25, 2005).

107. "No One to Defend the Defenders of the Fatherland: Angry Men in Uniform Have Taken to the Streets," *Nezavisimoye voyennoye obozreniye* (March 1, 2005) in WNC (March 2, 2005).

108. "An Expert Notes that Army Represents the Poorest Strata of Society," *RFE/RL Daily Report* (March 3, 2005).

109. "Russian Lawmaker Says Military Bonuses to Help Officer's Families Out of Poverty," Agenstvo voyennykh novostey (March 22, 2005) in WNC (March 28, 2005).

110. "Russia to Spend R770 Million on September Pay Raises," Agenstvo voyennykh novostey (June 20, 2005) in WNC (June 21, 2005).

111. "Russians Wounded in Military Service to Get Additional Monthly Payment," Itar-Tass (July 27, 2005) in WNC (July 28, 2005).

112. "Russian Servicemen Wages to Grow 15% from 1 January 2006," Agenstvo Voyennykh Novostey (September 12, 2005) in WNC (September 13, 2005); Vladimir Putin, "Stenograficheskiy ochet o soveshchanii rukovodyashchego sostava Vooruzhennykh (November 9, 2005) at http://president.kremlin.ru.

113. "Russian Defense Minister Welcomes New Housing Program for the Military," Itar-Tass (August 8, 2002) in WNC (August 9, 2002).

114. "Establishment of House Mortgage System in Russian Armed Forces Enters Final Stage," Agenstvo voyennykh novostey (April 21, 2005) in WNC (April 22, 2005).

115. "Ivanov Solves Apartment Problem: Defense Ministry Doubles Budget with Mortgages," Nezavisimaya gazeta (June 1, 2005) in WNC (June 2, 2005).

116. "Government Plans for Provision of Homeless Soldiers with Housing Not Working," Nezavisimoye voyennoye obozreniye (February 14, 2005) in WNC (February 15, 2005).

117. "Putin Says Government Must Stop Cheating Military with Housing Certificates," Itar-Tass (November 28, 2005) in WNC (November 29, 2005).

118. "Putin Instructs Government to Allocate Funds for Housing to Servicemen," Itar-Tass (December 5, 2005) in WNC (December 6, 2005).

119. "Hazing, Suicide, and Poverty Await Moscow and St. Petersburg Personnel in the Armed Forces," Nezavisimaya gazeta (March 10, 2005) in WNC (March 11, 2005).

120. "Russian Defense Minister Concerned by Number of Officers Leaving Army," Agenstvo voyennykh novostey (November 2, 2005) in WNC (November 3, 2005).

121. "Officers from Strategic Missile Forces Charged with Various Crimes," Interfax (December 20, 2000) in WNC (December 20, 2000).

122. "Kosovo: Top Russian Military Unhappy with Servicemen," Interfax (January 3, 2000).

123. "Commander of Russia's Leningrad Naval Base to be Prosecuted for Corruption," RIA (August 3, 2001) in WNC (August 6, 2001); "Army Crime on the Rise in Russia's Northwest," Itar-Tass (January 13, 2003) in WNC (January 14, 2003).

124. Michael Orr, "Reform and the Russian Ground Forces, 1992–2002," in Russian Military Reform, 1992–2002, ed. Aldis and McDermott, p. 137.

125. "Former Defense Minister CEO Gets Five Years," Monitor (July 25, 2003).

126. "Illegal Caviar Seized on Military Plane: Armed Forces are Involved in Poaching Rackets," Izvestiya (December 26, 2003) in WNC (December 31, 2003).

127. "Criminal Action Begins in Russia Conscripts Probe," Reuters (January 19, 2004) via Johnson's Russia List (January 19, 2004).

128. "More Than 2,000 Officers Convicted In Russia in 2005," Interfax (February 1, 2006) in WNC (February 2, 2005).

129. "Russian Soldiers Recruited on Streets," Moscow Times (December 26, 2000).

130. "Poll Reveals 11 Percent of Russian Soldiers with Alcoholism," Interfax (December 6, 2001) in WNC (December 7, 2001).

131. Paul Jenkins, "Red Army Blues," World Today (September 5, 2001).

132. "As Desertions Continue, Russia's Military Drafts Men with Mental Illnesses and Criminal Records," Associated Press (October 6, 2002).

133. Aleksandr Golts, "The Social and Political Condition of the Russian Military," in The Russian Military, ed. Miller and Trenin, p. 76.

134. "Russian Chief Prosecutor on Bullying, Draft Problems, Bribes, Specific Cases," Rossiiskaya gazeta (June 10, 2003) in WNC (June 13, 2003).

135. "Military Call-Up Expected to Decline Because of Low Birth-Rates," Itar-Tass (October 4, 2002) in WNC (October 7, 2002).

136. "Russian Army Fears Record-Low Draft," *RFE/RL Daily Report* (October 1, 2004).

137. "Russian Defense Minister to Cover Cost of Bullying Victim's Treatment," Itar-Tass (January 27, 2006) in WNC (January 28, 2006).

138. "Concealing Crimes in Russia to Carry Tougher Penalty," Itar-Tass (January 31, 2006) in WNC (February 1, 2006).

139. "Military Training in Schools Made Obligatory," Interfax (July 13, 2005) in WNC (July 14, 2005).

140. "Russian Defense Minister Says Military Departments in Universities 'Ineffective,'" Itar-Tass (February 2, 2005).

141. This process will begin in the spring of 2007, when the armed forces are scheduled to switch to a one and one-half year term of service. "Defense Minister: Russian Army to Switch to 1.5 Year Service Term in 2007," Agenstvo voyennykh novostey (March 22, 2006) in WNC (March 23, 2006).

142. There was a report suggesting that the military "will resume training" personnel-guidance officers. Their role is unclear. If they do the same thing that educational officers have done in the past, they will not make a significant difference. If, however, they are active down at the unit level, they could play an important role. "Russia Resumes Training Army Personnel Guidance Officers," Itar-Tass (November 2, 2005) in WNC (November 3, 2005). For a discussion of the Ombudsman, see "Russian Defense Ministry Backs Idea of Human Rights Ombudsman," Agenstvo Voyennykh Novostey (November 2, 2005) in WNC (November 3, 2005).

143. V. V. Savel'ev, *Kak vyzhit v neustavnoy armii* (Rostov-on-Don: Feliks, 2003), pp. 212–214.

144. "Armed Forces to Drop Institution of Priests," Itar-Tass (November 25, 2003) in WNC (November 27, 2003).

145. "Defense Minister Thanks Patriarch for Spiritual Support of Army," *RFE/RL Daily Report* (January 6, 2005); "Russian Prosecutor Dismayed at Rising Theft Among Army Officers," Itar-Tass (May 24, 2005) in WNC (May 25, 2005); and "Russian Defense Ministry Stepping up Work to Cooperate with Different Religions," RIA (June 10, 2005) in WNC (June 11, 2005).

146. "Chaplain Service in Russian Army Suggested," Itar-Tass (February 6, 2006) in WNC (February 7, 2006).

147. "Return to the Guardhouse: Rights of Advocates and Military Leaders are Ready to Strengthen Discipline in the Troops by Punitive Methods," *Nezavisimaya gazeta* (July 8, 2005) in WNC (July 8, 2005).

148. "Russian Cabinet Proposes Re-introduction of Disciplinary Cells in Army," Interfax (September 21, 2005) in WNC (September 22, 2005).

149. Yuri Zarakhovich "Russia Joins Coalition," *Time Online edition* at http://www.time.com (September 23, 2001).

150. "Putin Vows To Aid Taliban Foes, Clarifies Position on Air Bases," *Washington Post* (September 25, 2001).

151. "Russia Says U.S. May Use Facilities in Tajikistan," *Washington Post* (September 26, 2001).

152. "The Russian Military Gets a New Objective," *Novaya gazeta* (November 2, 2002) via Johnson's Russia List (November 4, 2002).

153. Ibid.

154. "Defense Minister Says Russia is at War," *Monitor* (November 6, 2002).

155. "Russia's Putin Says Armed Forces Should Focus on Opposing Terrorism," Itar-Tass (November 26, 2002) in WNC (November 27, 2002).

156. Ibid.

157. Ibid.

158. "Putin Says Armed Forces' Main Task to Fight Terrorism," Itar-Tass (November 26, 2002) in WNC (November 27, 2002).

159. "General Staff Orders Troops to be Ready for Terrorist Attacks," *Monitor* (December 11, 2002).

160. "Russian Army Readjusting to Meet New Challenges," RIA-Novosti (December 2, 2002) via Johnson's Russia List (December 4, 2002).

161. "Ivanov on Terrorist Threat," *RFE/RL Daily Report* (January 20, 2003).

162. See for example, "Vystuplenie Sergeya Ivanova na soveshchanii v Ministerstve oborony RF" (October 2, 20003) at http://www.mil.ru/articles/article3667.shtml.

163. The question of whether Putin was lying in wait for such an opportunity to gain control over the appointment of governors or whether he sincerely believed that such an action was critical in the fight against terrorism continues to be debated. Regardless of what his motive was, the Kremlin is now in a better position to control internal security at the local level.

164. "Using Every Means Available," *Izvestiya* (September 9, 2004) in WNC (September 14, 2004).

165. "Ivanov's Defense Manifesto," *Moscow Times* (October 9, 2003) via Johnson's Russia List (October 9, 2003).

166. "Poll Shows 84 Percent of Russians Support Stricter Counterterrorism Laws," Interfax (September 23, 2004) in WNC (September 25, 2004).

167. "Russian Regiment Stages Drill to Fight 'Gunmen' in the Far East," Interfax (September 23, 2005) in WNC (September 24, 2005).

168. "The General Staff Reveals a Secret Plan of Reforms that Can Make the Finance Ministry a Civilian Department," *Nezavisimaya gazeta* (February 2, 2006) in WNC (February 3, 2006). For a critical analysis of this plan, see "The General Staff Cutbacks Have Taken Charge of Military Reform," *Nezavisimoye voyennoye obozreniye* (March 22, 2006) in WNC (March 23, 2006).

169. Stephen Blank, "Rumors Suggest Major Russian Military Reorganization Imminent," *Eurasia Daily Monitor* (February 8, 2006).

170. Ibid.

171. "Russian Defense Minister Says No Enemy for Army in Chechnya," Itar-Tass (March 1, 2005) in WNC (March 2, 2005).

172. "Russian Defense Ministry Reports 150 Deaths in Chechnya in 2004," Itar-Tass (March 15, 2005) in WNC (March 16, 2005).

173. Ibid.

174. John D. Dunlop, "Putin's Upbeat Message on Chechnya Contradicted by Realities on the Ground," *Chechnya Weekly* (June 1, 2005).

175. "Russian Air Force Command Worried by Aging of Aircraft," Itar-Tass (March 26, 2003) in WNC (March 29, 2003).

176. "Russian General Says Troops' Training Inadequate to Deal with Modern Threat," Agenstvo Voyennykh Novostey (October 15, 2004) in WNC (October 19, 2004).

177. "Russian Land Forces Said Partially Ready for New Term of Instruction," Agenstvo Voyennykh Novostey (December 1, 2004) in WNC (December 2, 2004).

178. "Defense Official Says Increased Training Budget Will Benefit Armed Forces," Itar-Tass (January 30, 2005) in WNC (January 31, 2005).

179. "Russian Reservists Taking Part in Military Exercises in Siberia," Agenstvo voyen-nykh novostey (June 20, 2005) in WNC (June 21, 2005)

180. "Declining Financial Well-Being. Training of Military Officers Alleged," *Nezavisi-moye voyennoye obozreniye* (December 24, 2004) in WNC (January 1, 2005).

181. Ibid.

182. "Sergey Ivanov Tests His Doctrine—Armed Forces Train to Conduct One Major War and Two Local Wars Simultaneously," *Nezavisimaya gazeta* (August 21, 2005) in WNC (August 22, 2005).

183. "Russia Plans Over 60 Exercises in September for Armed Forces," Agenstvo Voyen-nykh Novostey (September 19, 2005) in WNC (September 20, 2005); "Colonels Will Soon Command Platoons," *Nezavisimoye voyennoye obozreniye* (September 28, 2005) in WNC (September 29, 2005).

184. "Russian Defense Ministry Drafts New Combat Training Concept," Agenstvo Voy-ennykh Novostey (November 7, 2005) in WNC (November 8, 2005).

CHAPTER SEVEN. CONCLUSION: PRESIDENTIAL LEADERSHIP AND THE RUSSIAN MILITARY

1. It is important to keep in mind that in the old KGB, officers and enlisted wore military-style uniforms, carried military ranks, and operated in a very similar command environment, even if working as spies.

INDEX